From Products to Services

From Products to Services

Insight and experience from companies which have embraced the service economy

Laurie Young

John Wiley & Sons, Ltd

Telephone (+44) 1243 779777

Email (for orders and customer service enquiries): cs-books@wiley.co.uk
Visit our Home Page on www.wiley.com

Other Wiley Editorial Offices

John Wiley & Sons Inc., 111 River Street, Hoboken, NJ 07030, USA

Jossey-Bass, 989 Market Street, San Francisco, CA 94103-1741, USA

Wiley-VCH Verlag GmbH, Boschstr. 12, D-69469 Weinheim, Germany

John Wiley & Sons Australia Ltd, 42 McDougall Street, Milton, Queensland 4064, Australia

John Wiley & Sons (Asia) Pte Ltd, 2 Clementi Loop #02-01, Jin Xing Distripark, Singapore 129809

John Wiley & Sons Canada Ltd, 6045 Freemont Blvd, Mississauga, ONT, L5R 4J3, Canada

Wiley also publishes its books in a variety of electronic formats. Some content that appears in print may not be available in electronic books.

Library of Congress Cataloging-in-Publication Data

Young, Laurie, 1955-
From products to services : insight and experience from companies which have embraced the service economy / Laurie Young.
p. cm.
Includes bibliographical references and index.
ISBN 978-0-470-02668-7 (cloth : alk. paper) 1. Service industries. 2. Customer services. 3. New products. I. Title.
HD9980.5.Y68 2008
658.8–dc22

2008002736

British Library Cataloguing in Publication Data

A catalogue record for this book is available from the British Library

ISBN 978-0-470-02668-7 (HB)

Typeset in 11/15pt Goudy by SNP Best-set Typesetter Ltd., Hong Kong

For Annie; my very own Bridget Jones.

Contents

Foreword

What do companies like IBM, HP, Unisys, GE, Ericsson, ABB, Michelin and Nokia have in common? Despite working in very different industries and being of very different size and culture, they have all had to consider an important strategic issue. They have had to reassess the importance of service to their business. With a product manufacturing heritage, most had seen service as a cost. For them it used to mean either the repair or support of equipment that had been sold to customers ('operational services') or advising them on how to use that equipment more effectively ('professional services').

Yet, following recent changes to the Western economies, there are very few sectors within them where service is not important to profit, customer relationships and growth. For instance, suppliers of domestic appliances and electronic entertainment products have learnt to increase product line profits through guarantees, extended warranty and maintenance. In retail, supermarkets now offer a range of services (such as insurance and legal help) in addition to consumer products. The car industry, on the other hand, having offered associated financial services for many years, has had to take the effect of 'after care' on repeat purchase much more seriously.

So, the senior managers of many manufacturing companies are now trying to create revenue and profit from service. Yet, this is a completely different type of business and involves massive change. It changes: operations, people management, finances, financial management, sales, brand strategy and marketing. In fact, there is very little which doesn't change when a product company seriously moves into the service industries.

Unfortunately, there is little help for management teams facing these important strategic decisions. There is no serious book, little research and few academic scholars who specialise in this specific area of change. So the issues they are facing must be tackled with little guidance from effective management theory or academics. However, the experience of companies in a range of different sectors shows there to be some clear steps involved. This book sets out to examine them and to find out what, from their experience, can be drawn into more generic lessons.

This is my third solo writing marathon but it has taken just as much planning, effort and endurance, especially for the very long last lap. I could not have finished it without the help of several people. My thanks go particularly to my editor Laura Mazur of Writers 4 Management. She has been encouraging and goading in equal measure at appropriate times. She teased out and refined the case studies and helped me with the very detailed task of pinning down references to published work. I also want to thank the Wiley team, Claire Plimmer and Jo Golesworthy; especially for their patience as deadlines came and went! Also Annette Musker for compiling the index.

A number of people provided case studies: IBM, Michelin, ThyssenKrupp Elevator, Fujitsu, Unisys, BT, Nokia, Ericsson, Avaya and Unilever. I am also grateful to economist Colin Fletcher and operations specialist Graham Clark, of Cranfield University, for reading some of the work before publication. David Munn, president and CEO of the Information Technology Services Marketing Association in Boston gave invaluable help and support on several case studies; while Thomas Lah, executive director of the Technology Professional Services Association gave access to detailed statistics of service industries in the high technology sectors of America. My thanks also to Dawn Southgate at Britain's Chartered Institute of Marketing and Tony Rogers for help with research; and Mark Young for script preparation.

Whenever I have been in a line job, running a part of a business, or advising a client, I have looked for access to insights, tools or techniques which would help round out decisions to reduce the risk of failure. In this work I have trawled published academic papers and worthy publications like the *McKinsey Quarterly* or *Harvard Business Review*. I have particularly tried to understand the experience of leading firms because, actually, business is very simple and there are very few who have not faced similar issues before. I have tried to tease out and present the best of all of those sources in this work and hope that their insight, freely acknowledged, will help the busy manager or business leader.

Laurie Young

1

Why product companies consider service business

Introduction and Overview

During the last thirty years, product companies from a wide range of industrial sectors throughout the Western economies have considered moving into service businesses. Some have rejected the idea after careful consideration, some have wandered into service markets without any real idea of what is involved and others have deliberately executed a carefully considered strategic manoeuvre. Included in this debate are some of the most famous names in the western world including: IBM, HP and Unisys in computing; Abbott Laboratories and GE Healthcare in medical diagnostics; ABB and GE in heavy engineering; Ericsson, Motorola and Nokia in telecommunications equipment. In fact, there are very few sectors where service is not important to profit, customer relationships and growth.

For instance, suppliers of domestic appliances and electronic entertainment products have learnt to increase product line profits through guarantees, extended warranty and maintenance. Supermarkets, like Tesco and Wal-Mart, now offer a range of services (such as insurance and 'money services') in addition to consumer products. While the car industry has had to take the effect of 'after-care' on repeat purchase much more seriously; some using different forms of service as a means to ensure future product sales.

What has pushed realistic business people in such widely different sectors to consider service? Does their experience contain

lessons or warnings for others? Is the trend likely to continue and affect other parts of the world?

There have been a number of forces prompting these changes. The first and most dramatic is a fundamental change in the employment patterns of Western economies. This has given rise to opportunities in service markets at home and abroad. Vast opportunities exist in several international service markets which tempt ambitious business people, whether from first world or developing economies.

For some, though, the drivers of change are much more immediate and domestic. The market for the core product offered by a number of companies has reached maturity. The resultant competition, costs and price pressure means that, for many, the service division (whose local service style is harder to copy) is the only business unit which makes reasonable profit. Others are driven by service offers made to their customers by competitors or by pressure from investors, puzzled by the lack of a response to competitors' service advances. For others, it is simply the belief, converted into hard headed policy, that service business is good business, which earns excellent margins while helping customer relationships and paving the way for repeat purchase. This first chapter explores these pressures and change stimuli in depth.

The rise of the service economies

One of the reasons that many firms have considered a move into service business is the rise in dominance of the service sectors of most developed economies and the apparent decline in manufacturing as a percentage of GDP. For instance, American manufacturing is, at the time of writing, reported to be 13% of GDP, a decline from 26% in 1970, whereas the service sector represents around 75% of economic activity, depending on definition. Any company with operations, headquarters or significant sales outlets in an economy undergoing such a dramatic change would be continually confronted with the relative attractiveness of service business and the relative unattractiveness of manufacturing or product distribution. Similar trends have affected companies in most of the developed economies.

The United Nations reports, for example, (see UN 2007) that the service sector grew from 65.4% of developed economies in 1990 to 73.5% in 2005.

So, over the past fifty years, the balance in many countries has shifted to the point where services account for almost three-quarters of their gross domestic product. This comprises a wide array of services, including financial, utility, professional and consumer services. Any supplier analysing its portfolio of businesses in these conditions is likely to have speculated more than once over the decades of economic transition that its manufacturing business may be a 'dead dog', or at best a 'cash cow', while its service businesses might be 'rising stars'. These broad economic statistics have driven several significant strategic reviews of this kind and prompted many senior management teams to invest in service. Some have remained in profitable manufacturing; some have found service businesses to be disappointing 'dogs', but many now report service revenues to be a large percentage of their business.

The effect of the service economy is most clearly seen in employment patterns. In the autumn of 2005 the *Economist* magazine published an analysis of the number of people employed in manufacturing as a percentage of the total workforce. It estimated that 10% of American workers were employed in manufacturing as opposed to 25% in 1970 (employment in services was 80%). The estimates for Britain (14% compared to 35% in 1970), France (15%) and Canada (14%) were similar; with other big economies, like Japan, at 18%. They found that the only big economy where more than a fifth of workers were in manufacturing was Germany (23%), which has a lot of innovative companies and a high content of capital goods that are not as easy to copy. Since a number of workers within manufacturing companies still occupy service roles (like marketing, design and facilities management) the actual employment in manufacturing roles among the developed economies could be much less.

Yet these reported trends and statistics can be misleading. The service economy is not, as it is often characterised, just the replacement of product manufacturing jobs with fast food outlets while real engineering moves to China or India. The situation is much more complex. For instance, much of the apparent decline in manufacturing, as a percentage of the developed economies, could actually be due to differences in price changes between product and service markets. In fact, some economists suggest that, at constant prices, the share of GDP taken by manufacturing in the US appears to be broadly unchanged since the 1980s. Moreover, real output of manufacturing has grown faster than GDP (at 4%) since the early 1990s and the country remains the world's biggest manufacturer. (At the time of writing, the world's third biggest manufacturer, China, still does not produce half of the mighty output of the USA.) The change in the percentage of manufacturing GDP is therefore much more likely to come from productivity improvement and price fluctuations than the wholesale flight to cheaper labour markets like India or China.

Over the long term, successful first world economies have replaced manufacturing workers with new technology to boost productivity and moved away from labour intensive products (like textiles) to high tech value added sectors (like pharmaceuticals and biotechnology). So the relatively high percentage of manufacturing jobs in, say, Italy is probably more a sign of economic weakness or protectionism. America led the world in productivity improvement during the last decade of the twentieth century and this, in turn, led to higher average incomes. In short, manufacturing is producing more while employing fewer people.

This seems to reflect more ancient patterns in economic development. The industrial revolution caused a dramatic change in the structure of economies and employment patterns. Due to long-term productivity gains, many of the developed economies now produce much more from their agricultural sectors while employing far fewer in them. For instance, 2% of Americans currently work in agriculture compared to 70% in 1820 but produce much more than their ancestors. A similar natural productivity evolution now seems to have occurred in manufacturing sectors. Yet this has led to economic prosperity and a rise in living standards.

So, while manufacturing has achieved unforeseen gains in productivity, employment in the service sector has boomed. Many workers and managers who have been 'downsized' from manufacturing have found new employment in the expanding service sectors of their economies. So, in fact, successful economies tend to be sophisticated at both manufacturing and services.

Growing service opportunities

In all the western economies there is now a wide range of flourishing new services. As people grow richer they want more education, better housing, improved healthcare, more restaurants, bars, car dealerships and shops which carry goods far beyond the mere basic amenities of life. Increasing prosperity unleashes a creative explosion in new service concepts, some of which become massive international chains.

Some of these arise from the growth and adaptation of established services due to social trends. In the last fifty years, for example, the rise of household ownership has been accompanied by growth in services such as legal conveyance, estate agencies/realtors, building, renovation and decoration (plus TV house makeovers shows). Some, on the other hand, are completely new services which would have been unheard of fifty years ago. An educated person returning from war in 1945 might not be surprised by today's fast food chains or modern opticians but psychoanalysts' practices, tanning salons, video rental stores and internet cafes would probably be a complete revelation. The range of new service businesses appears to be limited only by the power of human creativity.

Government policy has also created a swathe of newly competitive service businesses. In Europe, for instance, apart from progressive legislation to introduce competition to many service sectors like airlines and banking, privatisation has had a dramatic impact. It has created a number of large, profitable and successful service businesses which were once not fully recorded as part of economic activity. These include airlines, rail companies and utilities such as water, gas and telecoms. When they were funded by the public purse, all costs (both current and capital) were paid by the exchequer. However, investment was then artificially restricted by political policy rather than organisational or customer needs. Also, items which would normally increase in value (such as intangible assets like intellectual property, brand or customer loyalty) had no realisable value. As a result, many of the liberalised industries have grown in revenue, investment, profit and service provision since being freed from political constraints.

The market introduces into these organisations the relentless drive for process improvement, cost reduction and innovation natural to competitive organisations. Over the long term, privatised businesses have therefore sought productivity improvement in response to pressure from shareholders, customers, competitors and public commentators. They have served customers better, raised needed capital to invest in infrastructure, created employment and paid handsomely in corporate taxation. (In several cases the tax contribution far outweighs the profit earned when these businesses were publicly owned.)

This policy was pioneered by the 1980s' British government (under Prime Minister Margaret Thatcher) which initiated a major turn around of the economy using privatisation. Although several cultures are suspicious of it, the policy has been copied and adopted by many governments since. It is now, for instance, frequently a condition of lending from the World Bank and International Monetary Fund that developing nations create programmes to open their economies to competitive forces.

As a result, the line between public and private service is now a major issue of political policy and economic success. Generally there is a growing acceptance among administrators that, if an organisation can create sustainable, self-generated revenue, it should not by run by government. Now, with most possible privatisations completed in some developed economies (there are still some potential privatisations, such as postal services, in even the most liberalised economies) innovative 'public private partnerships', such as private finance initiatives (PFI), tend to be used. All contribute to a growth in the service sector.

Another group of businesses which have caused growth in service sector employment are those which were once an integral part of the support functions of major firms: those which have been 'outsourced'. In the past, most of the support infrastructure of major companies such as Hewlett-Packard, or IBM or ICI would have been owned and run by them. In the 1950s and 1960s, for example, many firms set up staff canteens or restaurants (often with separate facilities for directors and visitors) believing them to reflect the behaviour and policies of responsible, progressive employers. The chefs, waiters and equipment were all employed and owned by the firm as part of the cost of doing business.

In the early 1980s, for instance, British Telecom ran one of the largest catering chains in Britain, comparable to professional suppliers like the then Trust House Forte, but exclusively for its own staff. However, most of these and other services are now invariably outsourced to specialised providers whose business focuses in these areas. They have become competitive service businesses in their own right and the revenue is now recorded as part of the service economy.

This phenomenon distorts the view of both the service sector and manufacturing. If a computer manufacturer outsources its security, estates or cleaning staff to a private company, manufacturing appears to decline and service grow. There will be some overall productivity improvement because, not only will the outsourcing supplier be further down the 'experience curve' of its core service business, it will also be able to reap initial economies of scale by integrating with existing operations. Yet the effect on the total economy will not be as dramatic as appears from the overall statistics.

As economies change, then, the debate for thoughtful business people is not whether to evacuate the manufacturing sector due to its inevitable decline, but whether they can increase profit further through yet more productivity improvement or whether their business possesses the skills to generate profit by employing appropriate service people. It prompts a strategic dilemma which should be the subject of careful review and consideration.

Export opportunities for service businesses

Increasing international interdependence between countries and changes in the conditions of international trade have also had an important effect on the service economy. Huge, developing international service markets have tempted many firms to set up service businesses. Seeing growth in demand for a service on the world stage can cause them to make an initial move into their domestic service market, using this home base as a springboard to international trade. Increasingly, however, low cost suppliers enter international markets with ease and little local business base.

According to the United Nations conference on trade and development (UN, 2007), world trade in services grew 14 % in 2003, 19 % in 2004, 11% in 2005 and nearly 10 % in 2006 (up from $391,080 m in 1980 to $2,735,658 m in 2006). This followed a spell of annual growth at around 6 % per annum (in every year, except one, between 1990 and 2003). The United States was the lead service exporter during that period and commanded just over 15 % of world service trade in 2006. The results also show that services are one of the most important sectors for the European Union, contributing to around two thirds of GDP and employment. As a result, European countries together took nearly 50% of world service trade in 2006. However, international trade is also important to developing countries where several are gearing up to tackle international service opportunities. In 2006, they accounted for 24.5 % of world export in services (up from 22.6% in 2004).

Admittedly, the service sectors have produced healthy export business throughout the twentieth century and earlier. International trade in finance, tourism, transport, telecommunications, health and security has been successful for many years. In fact, some of the earliest international services were the banking houses of Europe, exporting financial services for several centuries, often to fund the wars and vanities of different kings or empires. Lloyd's of London, for example, has long earned 'invisible' exports from its world dominance of international shipping insurance and many Western banks have operated on a global scale for several generations. As a result, Wall Street and the City of London now draw in huge amounts of money to their respective countries.

Another long-standing service exporter is the professional services sector. It earns those countries where firms are based substantial revenues because of its global competitiveness. International networks like PricewaterhouseCoopers, Deloitte, Accenture, Clifford Chance and McKinsey employ many thousands of people and earn many billions of dollars each; and some are around a hundred years old. Their profits, although partly distributed to local partnerships, are often repatriated to host nations, boosting tax revenues.

At country level, international export success in services varies according to development of the economy, government policy and education of the population. India is a current, new, example of international service export success. In 2004 it had raised its share of world service trade to 1.3 % from 0.5 % in 1990, despite the huge growth in overall international service trade during that period. Moreover, the country then used its developing international competitiveness in IT skills to plan an incursion into the business process outsourcing market. One estimate put the number of Indian firms providing international, IT enabled, services, at over two hundred in 2004 (Javalgi *et al.*, 2004). As a result, its 'computer and information services' exports were 48.6 % of its total service exports in 2003, a growth of 28.5 % over the previous year.

India's growing provision of outsourced call centres also demonstrates how a nation can boost its own economy through international services. Call centres in India answered 10 billion telephone calls in 2005 supplying outsourced service for companies like Lloyds and HSBC. As a result, the country employed 700 000 call-centre workers, each earning nearly double the national average wage and, through their new-found wealth, having an impact on the country's economy and culture. China too, at the time of writing, is starting to rival India as an outsourcing hub for routine tasks like preparing tax returns and filing patents, where conversational English is less of a requirement.

Services are and have been, then, a healthy and viable means of earning export revenues. Now, though, a combination of forces is making the international conduct of service business even easier and more attractive, stimulating further growth. R.G. Javalgi and his colleagues suggest that they include:

- New technology like the internet and e-commerce. Cross border trade in a wide variety of services, such as professional advice and travel, can be delivered cost effectively through modern electronic highways.
- Increasing sophistication and the growth of middle classes in a number of developing nations. This creates demand for services in different parts of the world and socialises new concepts to a wide international community, paving the way for suppliers.
- Opening of trade through negotiations in forums like the GATT rounds which encourage focus on the competitiveness of specific service markets.
- Regional trading blocks like the European Union and North American Free Trade Area. These seek to bring down trade barriers between their members, stimulating international trade in services like air traffic or financial services and affecting demand by creating larger markets.
- Government legislation and support. Governments in countries like India, Singapore, Indonesia, Brazil and Mexico are, at the time of writing, actively promoting initiatives to encourage their service sector.
- Easier transport links, efficient international postal services and cheap flights. All make the cost of international service cheap and viable.

These growing international service opportunities are hard for businesses to ignore, prompting several to consider a move into service. Businesses in a number of sectors are therefore planning international market penetration, hoping to repeat in service markets the success of, say, the Japanese in consumer products during the 1980s and the 'tiger economies' in electrical components during the 1990s.

Service in developing countries

There appears to be a relationship between the size and vibrancy of the service sector of a nation's economy and its general wealth and economic development. Figure 1.1 compiled by Professor Adrian Palmer (Palmer, 2005), shows the relationship of GDP per capita to employment in the service sector of selected economies. It indicates that, as economies develop, service sector employment becomes more dominant. Since 1990, for instance, manufacturing's share of employment has fallen in Singapore, South Korea and Taiwan. Therefore, manufacturing companies there are likely to experience the same pressures and strategic decisions as those in the developed economies. They will need to consider how they respond to the service economy.

The Chinese economy is a good example. In December 2005 the Chinese government released official figures which showed its economy to be worth 16 trillion Yuan ($1.9 trillion) in 2004, 17% more than expected. Interestingly, 93% of the increase, $265 billion, was due to the service sector. As

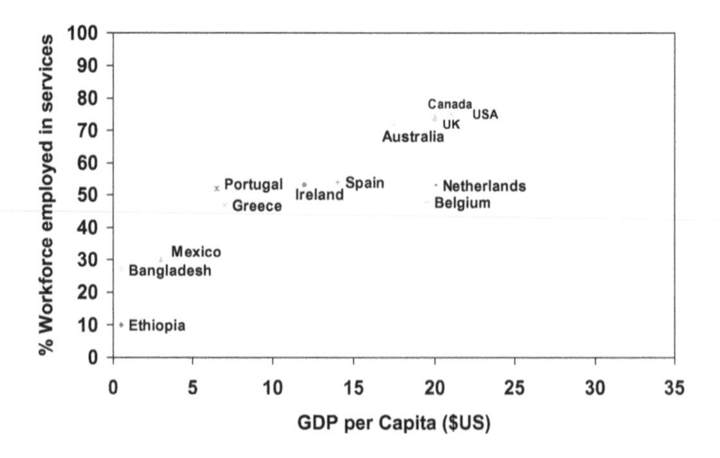

Figure 1.1 Relationship of GDP per head to service employment
Source: Palmer, 2005.

The Economist said, in reporting the figures: 'The world's factory, it turns out, has a sizeable canteen attached, not to mention an office block and shopping mall.'

In 2004 the service sector of the Chinese economy jumped 9 % to 41 % (compared with 46 % for manufacturing and 13 % for primary industries such as agriculture and mining) and to 45% in 2005. Some of this increase was due to the fact that the country's National Bureau of Statistics had started to track the service sector more closely after its previous emphasis on factories and manufacturing. It reported that the service growth came from three key sectors:

- Wholesale, retail and catering.
- Transport, storage, post and telecommunications.
- Real estate, architecture and building services.

Even then, the service sector might be understated because it is difficult to capture kerbside lending, tax-evading and cash deals in several sectors. One estimate puts that at another $ 300 billion.

The Chinese service sector is fast becoming as well rounded, varied and large as many developed economies. As living standards have improved, there has been a demand for the consumer services seen elsewhere. Its market for private education, for example, doubled to $ 9 billion and is second only to housing in terms of consumer spending, whereas the Chinese travel and tourism spend is expected to triple (up to $ 300 billion) by 2015. There has also been a surge in financial services, supporting the booming property market with loans and retail businesses with leasing deals.

Moreover, much of this is private economy activity. For instance, whilst postal services remain state controlled there are, at the time of writing, more than one million small trucking and removal companies. There is also a healthy market for professional services, ranging from accountants and lawyers to bankers, consultants and brand specialists. This is set to grow much further (*The Economist* estimates there to be one lawyer per 13 000 people compared with America's number of one per 300).

The issue for Chinese businesses, and exporters to them, is whether manufacturing will contract once the boom is over and whether there will be a switch to countries with still cheaper labour, such as Vietnam. Despite its emphasis on growth and manufacturing, the country has shed 15 million jobs in manufacturing since 1995 and is likely to shed more as market forces drive productivity improvement. If so, many might look to service for growth as they have in other, more developed economies.

Service differentiation in mature product markets

The maturing of industries is a natural development; an economic fact of life which occurs in both consumer and business markets. As a country gets richer, disposable income is spent on an increasing number of goods to make life easier or more enjoyable. This causes a boom in demand for a range of different products that can last a number of years. But households need only so many fridges, televisions, microwaves, computers and, even, mobile phones. Businesses, on the other hand, need only a finite number of laptops, printers, servers or offices.

A point is reached where the majority of people have bought their first version of the product. The number of sales in the market then falls (sometimes very fast and very dramatically) to replacement levels. It reaches the volume at which people are, largely, buying products to replace obsolete or broken items. Suppliers must then compete through product upgrades or differentiation (newer and more up-to-date versions of the product which are substantially different from competitors); or they must leave the market altogether. Some, though, have tried to differentiate through stylish new service offers (or enhanced quality of after care) which are harder to copy than commoditised products. Maturity of product markets therefore causes management teams to consider a move into service business.

The maturity of industries and markets occurs when there are multiple suppliers and multiple buyers, who, over time, learn about use and adaptation of a product concept from each other. An economic phenomenon, first observed in the 1950s, it is represented in the familiar diagram in Figure 1.2 which uses total industry sales and time as axes of the graph. The concept suggests that a market evolves through several key stages: introduction, growth, maturity and decline. Firms have different success criteria and cost challenges in these different phases of market development. In response, they should adopt different business strategies.

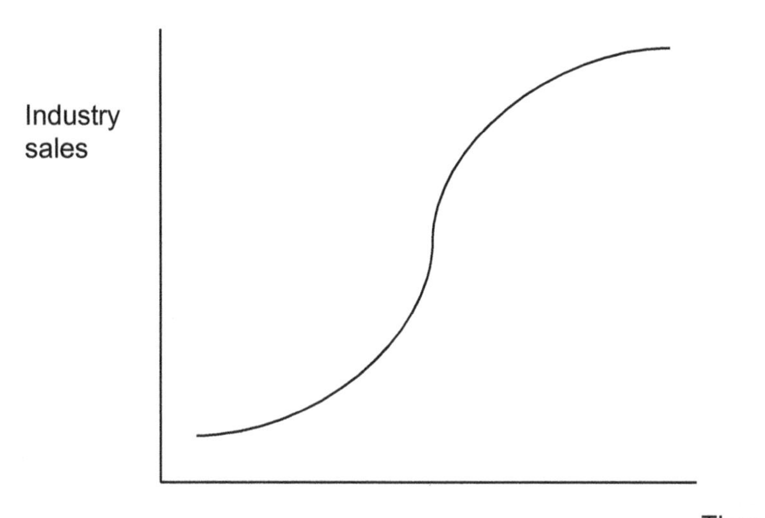

Figure 1.2 Industry maturity

The tell-tale signs of market maturity include:

- Informed and demanding buyers.
- Most buyers have made their original purchase, which means that suppliers have to concentrate on repeat business rather than new opportunities.
- Price pressure and slowing growth.
- Rationalisation and consolidation in the market.
- The rise of niche suppliers.
- New laws and regulations.
- The appearance of truly differentiated offers.

Despite the familiarity that most informed business people have with this concept and diagram, very few actually anticipate market maturity and some are incapable of facing up to it. Yet firms in these market conditions need to change their approach or they will be severely damaged. Leading businesses are particularly vulnerable. They will have succeeded in the growth phase of the market by meeting huge demand and will want to believe that the good times will continue or come back. But if they do not respond quickly to the changed conditions, their costs will remain static while their revenues drop dramatically.

Niche firms, on the other hand, are in a very strong position because they will have learnt to relate to a very clear group of buyers who they will know very well. As the whole market fragments, their appeal to one segment of customers allows them to dominate that part of the market and move into other corners. When these forces played out in the computer industry, the once-mighty IBM nearly went bankrupt while the upstart Microsoft cantered through to market dominance. In mobile phones, on the other hand, leading suppliers like Ericsson and Nokia suffered as markets in developed economies peaked, so they had to execute painful turnaround programmes.

In a mature market companies also find themselves dealing with changed, experienced or even different customers who force them to rethink their offer. In the earlier years of the medical diagnostics market, for instance, the customers for the analytical equipment produced by many companies had been mainly laboratory specialists, working on samples taken by front line practitioners from patients. If machines broke down, it wasn't a matter of life and death if they weren't repaired immediately. But over time this equipment began to move into intensive care units in hospitals. Patients were not only plugged directly into the machines but, even more worrying, the customer was now a demanding, intensive-care nurse who was intolerant of breakdowns. As importantly, they wanted the equipment to work with other instruments around the bed, even if manufactured by another company. So, suppliers were forced to move into service-based offers, using high quality equipment which could be integrated with other systems.

Market maturity affects the consideration of service in two major ways. Firstly, suppliers might offer the same benefits as the product through some form of innovative service experience. In the 'male grooming' market, for example, the manufacturers of razors have invested in different ways to produce razors which give a closer shave. They have differentiated their product by producing razors which have two, three or even four blades. There is now a wide a range of choice from electronic and battery razors to 'wet' razors and disposables. Each produces a new price point for the products but the price per shave is very low in most countries. Yet it took New York's Malka and Myriam Zaoui to create 'the art of shaving', a premium service focused on shaving. In addition to a range of innovative shaving products, the company offers a shave with a wet razor in its Manhattan based 'Barber spas'. Its 'Royal shave' combines master barber services with aromatherapy knowledge to produce a shave at a cost which is many times the price per shave of a man's own. It is sold as a unique and special service experience.

In the business to business market, on the other hand, the advent of 'system integration' services in the IT industry is an example of service being used to replace a mature product. During much of the early decades of the computer industry, the processing power of computers was bought through proprietary mainframe systems. These were unique to each supplier and bought to automate a specific task, like payroll or accounting. As time went by, the industry evolved to a point where suppliers had command of a 'footprint' in the computer departments of most major companies and managed a process of upgrades which ensured a steady income. However, new industry standards soon enabled these machines to communicate with each other, technology fell in price and, worst of all, customers started to demand that computing related much more to their business needs. In fact, the main buyers became business users and purchasing specialists as much as traditional IT employees.

So, rather than just supplying updated machines or software, leading suppliers began to offer an open minded review of all the customer's technology and how it suited developing business needs. A 'system's integration' service conducted an analysis of processing needs in a similar way to past computer purchases but it also undertook an audit of existing technology that the customer owned (whoever it was supplied by). By comparing all the hardware, software and service skills against the need, it was often better to buy a service which enhanced the infrastructure of existing technology than an upgrade of one product. In this fast maturing market, service, rather than machines, was used as a means to provide the processing power that customers had always been after.

Secondly, at this mature phase in the market, some firms try to use variations to industry standard after care or pre-sales support services in order to differentiate their product. This happened when, in 1994, the Korean car manufacturer, Daewoo, entered the mature British car market. It set out to use a new standard of service as its key entry strategy. The British new car market had peaked six years before, at 2.3 million new registrations and had fallen to 1.8 million by 1994. Daewoo was unknown to this brand loyal market but intended to gain one percent share after three years through a different approach. (This was ambitious bearing in mind that previous car launches, such as Hyundai, Kia and Proton had not exceeded 0.6% after three years.)

Its research showed that most new car buyers bought to get 'from A to B' rather than for any particularly sexy features. They wanted daily reliability and a relationship with a reliable supplier. Apart from a highly visible brand launch the company therefore aimed to keep complete control of customer contact, engineering the company experience around their buyers. It invested in a vast dialogue campaign aimed at publicly exploring what British people liked and disliked about new cars. It also operated only through owned outlets, placed in retail parks, which it stocked with service people trained to give accurate answers to questions and not 'pushy sales people'.

These 'service centres' contained a host of innovative packages including:

- interactive in store displays, so there was no need to be bothered by sales people.
- free collection and delivery for car servicing;
- free crèches;
- fixed, no haggle prices;
- extended test drives;
- three year warranty;
- 30 day money back guarantee;
- three years AA cover;
- free customer helpline.

The entire package was integrated with high profile marketing and achieved its entry objectives. It is a clear example of how manufacturers have been prompted to consider service business due to market maturity.

Changing customers, the 'I' society and the responsive, 'solutions' organisation

In the past fifty years a change in attitude among individuals in Western society, prompted largely by better educational standards, has caused many to challenge authority, to question professionals and to lobby for individual rights. Gaining momentum largely in the late 1960s and epitomised by the questioning 'baby boomer' generation, the 'I' society has had a profound effect on many areas of life, business included. Aided by protective consumer legislation, it has enabled customers to challenge the behaviour and attitudes of businesses. Business leaders have had to respond to a range of issues from product performance and after care to governance and environmental issues. Coupled with an expectation among employees that they will be treated as individuals and adults, the mighty industrial machines have been forced to be responsive to buyers. This has caused many to explore service responses such as improved after care or 'solutions' projects.

This mega trend was charted in detail by Sandra Vandermerwe in her book *From Tin Soldiers to Russian Dolls*, based on extensive long term research (Vandermerwe, 1993). She wrote:

> By the 1990s, trends which had begun, however loudly or even absurdly, with the counter-culture and anti-establishment fringes of the 1960s began to mellow into something much more profound. On the threshold of the third millennium, despite earlier fears that standardization would 'massify' the human race still further, the individual had triumphed to become more significant. Though technology and communications were now more preponderant, rather than being dwarfed by them, individuals would be the key driving force and agent for change in society.
>
> What did this mean for business? Well, if it was the individual that counted in society, then it was only a matter of time before this sentiment would be taken up by corporations. Indeed, there the notion began to take root on two fronts. First, the pulse within firms started moving from machines and their mega power to people and their mind power – what they carried in their heads. Second, individuals began to assert themselves more strongly as customers, and particularly as users. They were no longer willing to be part of the vague, so-called mass market somewhere down the distribution trail, accepting what business could produce more efficiently. Nor were they prepared to hide in their factories, plants and office blocks, satisfied with what had officially been bought for them.

Modern business leaders and managers have to spend so much time responding to the needs of their customers and attending to the motivation of their employees that it is easy to forget how impersonal, detached and mechanised big business had become. Until the mid-twentieth century, the Western attitude to business had been influenced by two powerful forces: mass production and scientific management (or 'Taylorism'). In all but a few backwaters, manufacturing had become synonymous with mass production and the human element of it reduced to the impersonal term 'labour'. Employees were 'costs of production', undertaking tasks that technology was not yet able to handle. The philosophy of scientific management, rooted as it was in the nineteenth century quest for reason and experimentation, broke their work into piecemeal routine, planned tasks. These could be measured, demonstrated and supervised. The pseudo science that resulted from this thinking, 'time and motion', was based on the unquestioned drive for efficiency, speed and mechanisation.

It was in the late 1960s and early 1970s that management thinkers were startled to find that human beings worked better and more productively when part of 'self-governing work groups'; or (as tested in pioneering organisational models at firms like Volvo) when they worked on complete tasks (like building one car) rather than soul-destroying repetitive tasks. Not only were people more productive, but industrial relations were less strained and profits improved. This led inexorably to today's concern to 'compete for talent', to find a 'good job fit' and to 'develop' the human beings employed by a firm so that they gain satisfaction through work that delivers company objectives.

Modern attitudes are most clearly seen in the professional services industry. Rather than the serried ranks of number crunchers, clerks or productivity analysts of the past, these huge businesses now regard their people as 'human capital'. They are, as the term suggests, a rich resource which will create wealth through their views, talents and skills. The professions compete seriously for the cream of the graduate crop, training and nurturing them to become 'lead advisors' to clients and partners of the future firm. Their instinctive drive to keep talent makes them move with the times, introducing state of the art human resources (HR) practices like diversity policy, flexible working contracts and work/life balance initiatives. They also keep up to date with the changing aspirations of the newest generation to reach work. Many are now, for example, trumpeting their environmental or social conscience credentials to attract the ('Generation Y') graduates of the early twenty-first century. Yet, the professions are only the bellwether of industry, as it learns to employ modern workers effectively.

Business has also had to respond to the demands of its buyers to be treated as human beings. This started, in many Western markets, by consumer groups lobbying government for regulation and law to curb abuse. Whereas many manufacturers of the early twentieth century took the view that their responsibility ended when the product was bought, few could by the close of the century. Industry learnt that product performance affected repurchase and, eventually, profit. They invested, sometimes after painful resistance, in warranty, guarantees, maintenance and after care.

But, in the last two decades, debate about the 'market of one' has caused practice in consumer businesses to change still further. There has been an increasing view that people want to be treated as individuals, to be offered choice based on an understanding of their needs and aspirations. As a result, many firms have revolutionised their marketing, trying to create a two-way dialogue with their customers which tries to understand their buying patterns, customise offers and encourage loyalty. They have invested huge sums in data warehouses and customer relationship management (CRM) systems to serve restless buyers better.

A similar change has occurred in business to business industries, driving suppliers to be more responsive. For example, the leading IT players have run 'user groups' for their large buyers for many years. They represent a huge investment by the firm in terms of time, event management and marketing materials. Often led by a committee of the customers themselves, they create a rich dialogue about investment directions, product development, performance and future trends. Many are rightly proud of these programmes and market them as an investment in service and responsiveness. What has been forgotten in history is that they began with frustration among key buyers at the lack of responsiveness of systems providers who had a large 'installed base'. Important customers, held captive by switching costs, began to meet up and lobby for response.

This unwillingness to be the victim of a remote industrial supplier is now best reflected in the demand for 'solutions'. Rather than buying the latest machine or piece of software, buyers in markets as different as communications, IT and copying expect a customised package which meets a specific need. The suppliers have had to go back to school to learn how to become a 'solutions supplier', deploying their people to create unique packages of product, software and services for their customers. This approach has damaged some, causing prices and margin to plummet. It has also prompted some appalling marketing and brought business language to new depths of awful jargon. Nevertheless, the move to 'solutions' is a reflection of the demand from modern business buyers for suppliers to be responsive.

Concepts like 'CRM', 'solutions marketing', customer loyalty and 'the market of one' may yet turn out to be short-term management fads. Yet all are a reflection of a major and profound change in Western society which has forced industry to treat the individual employee and buyer as a human being. While they might not apply in other cultures, they have caused many firms to assess the value of a service business or to consider a partial move into service programmes.

Price pressure, the collapse of product margins and the attraction of profitable service divisions

Many managers, in many markets, are familiar with the phenomenon of the profitable service division. In a car dealership, for example, the service section often has the highest margin over new or used sales groups. (Moreover, the attitude, behaviour and competence of the service people can influence the likelihood of the customer buying the make of car again.) While retailers of consumer electronics can make more from warranty and guarantees than the product itself. And, in technology companies, the service division can often be the most profitable or, at least, fills gaps in cash flow during seasonal fluctuations of sales. The fact that service has repeatedly made the difference between profit and loss in tight markets has caused many a company to consider a more ambitious move into service businesses.

Pure service companies like merchant banks, law firms and accountancy partnerships have astounding earnings. The lead firms have huge revenues and very healthy net margins (some well in excess of 30%) which make the owners very wealthy. They attract many new entrants into the advisory markets of the world every year. Yet, services associated with product companies can also appear cash rich and enticing to product companies fighting for every percentage of margin. In 2003, for instance, two McKinsey consultants (Bundschuh & Dezvane, 2003) reported that, in their experience, revenues from after care in a range of industries ('from elevators and freezers to security systems and transportation equipment') were 30% or more of total revenues and increasing. They also suggested that, in some industries, the service market is four or five times larger than the market for products.

Another study, which questioned three hundred and seventy product companies in twenty nine different countries (Alexander & Hordes, 2003), found that their service offers had 50% higher gross margin than their product lines, some as high as 60%.

Product companies often have service divisions associated with their business. Set up as cost centres to aid product sales, they might be involved in: training customers, complex project management, maintenance, upgrade management, financing or advice. Their aim is to help the company achieve product sales and their cost is carried by the firm. As a result, the company can be very flexible about how the support group's costs are absorbed. It may be that the costs are clearly calculated in a cost centre and have to be covered by revenue from support contracts. However, these costs can be discounted, or even disregarded, by sales people anxious to achieve product sales targets. Service directors in more than one industry and more than one company have complained that their service is 'given away free', even if the company must ultimately cover the cost by margin from product sales.

This becomes a difficulty if, in response to product price pressure or margin erosion, the company decides to turn its service arm into a profit centre. There is an immediate conflict of interest between service people wanting to maximise revenue from their support contracts and the product sales people. Frequently, there is a catching up exercise where the firm has to recover from unprofitable support contacts and agree a phased increase with individual customers. If the company is to survive this evolution it needs to understand costs, buying motivation and total cost of ownership in depth.

Real conflict can occur, though, if the firm frees its service arm to offer innovative support to the market in general. The unit may develop skills to support competitor equipment or may acquire consultants to advise buyers on the best use of equipment. The former can cause conflict if a sales person wants to sell a replacement to competitor equipment that the service division wants to support; especially as a long-term maintenance contract can be more rewarding than a short-term sale of a low margin product. The latter can cause fundamental schisms in the firm, leading to channel conflict and, in some cases, a change of management because it challenges the approach and offer to their customers. (A consultancy-led offer will often have a totally different content and outcome than a product-led sale.)

So the size, margin and opportunity of service businesses can be very attractive to firms suffering difficult product markets. The consequences of a move to a service profit centre are important and need to be managed carefully, and have led several firms into real difficulty. Nevertheless, the daily visibility of profitable service units has caused many to move more extensively into service businesses.

Michelin Europe develops service businesses

Michelin is the world's leading tyre company, with a 20.1 % share of the global market. With its headquarters in France, it operates in more than 170 countries, with seventy-five plants in nineteen countries producing 194 million tyres a year. It also publishes 19 million maps and guides and operates a number of digital services.

It was founded in 1889 by two brothers, André and Edouard Michelin, whose focus on excellence in innovation has led to numerous technological breakthroughs in mobility over the years. Sales in 2005 were €15.6 billion, with operating income of €1.4 billion. The replacement tyre market, in the passenger, car, light truck and the truck markets, represents some 70 % of sales in volume.

It is organised into a number of product lines:

- Passenger, car and light truck.
- Truck.
- Speciality product lines (aircraft, earthmover, agricultural, two-wheel and components).
- Travel publications.

The organisation also encompasses:

- Distribution networks: Euromaster in Europe and TCI in North America.
- Michelin Technology Centre, with three main sites in France, the US and Japan, plus a number of other testing or research facilities around the world.
- Eleven group services such as audit, communications, finance, etc.

Over the last few years Michelin has been experimenting with new, service-oriented offers to maintain its premium position and foster closer relationships with customers. This has stemmed from a growing awareness that tyre purchase is in danger of becoming commoditised, with more buyers giving price a higher priority than value and quality. The company is doing this under the banner of contributing to sustain-able mobility and innovation.

The early years

The seeds of this new approach were sown more than eighty years ago in both France and the UK. In France, the company's engineers would ask customers if they could perform regular technical assessments on the tyres to gauge their performance over time, as a basis for improvement.

Customers, however, weren't always keen to have Michelin engineers come along to dismantle their vehicles and take the tyres away to check them. After all, they owned them. So Michelin was smart enough to find a new solution: the company would own the tyres and the truck owners would pay per kilometre. Meanwhile, in the UK, the business was following a similar approach with buses, although for commercial rather than the technical reasons in France.

Over the years this approach to the business grew, although somewhat haphazardly. There was no overall vision or defined strategy. The service business developed on its own steam without any real focus, as more large fleet operators realised that outsourcing tyre management would not only leave them free to concentrate on their core business, but would also simplify all areas of tyre maintenance and purchase.

Building a new business model

By the end of the 1990s, however, senior management at Michelin, including Édouard Michelin, great-grandson of one of the founders, saw the potential for a compelling new business model and one which would help form closer and more valuable links to customers. They had been watching the progress of the experiments in the UK and France carefully and in 1999 the decision was taken to set up teams throughout Europe under the name Michelin Fleet Solutions (MFS) to target large fleet operators and formalise the concept. They were in place by 2000.

They were well aware that this would be a big shift in terms of how Michelin operated because it would be a radical departure from the traditional approach of being a seller of tyres. Charging customers per kilometre meant it would be in the company's interests for the tyres to last longer. The culture in this area of the business would have to shift from one of selling as many tyres as possible to one of producing services around tyres. This would include all aspects of maintenance and performance; and call for getting the most out of them for a longer period of time.

The success of this model would be based on the extent to which Michelin could bring added value to customers. That added value would come from areas such as decreasing fuel consumption by maintaining the correct pressures, specifying the most suitable tyres for the type of operation and lowering the number of breakdowns through high quality maintenance. It would also vastly simplify customers' administration and smooth out cash flow, since they would pay an agreed monthly amount throughout the contract (usually three years).

It was the right decision. The business has been growing substantially in the last few years, particularly as fleets have grown larger and are expanding across Europe. These fleet operators are keen to become more professional and run their businesses the same way wherever they are. Not only can MFS provide the same service across borders, it can also help with expansion by managing tyre maintenance across Europe. If a fleet operator is setting up in the Hungarian market, for example, it is very beneficial to have such a strong partner with such a good reputation as it builds its business. What Michelin has to determine in each case is whether a customer is truly European, with European-wide management and hence needs to be handled on a European basis; or whether a company is European in name only.

Getting systems and processes in place

MFS is part of the company's strategy to make it the leader in services as well as products for the truck tyre industry. However, getting this new business model to work has had to be managed carefully because new systems and procedures have had to be put in place, including working out the relationships with the third-party service providers who do the actual maintenance under Michelin's direction.

It has also called for talented administrators who can marry any conflicts between the company's traditional systems, which are geared to the straightforward selling of tyres, and those required under the MFS model. For example, almost a third of invoices sent to the company's central services now come from MFS. (This is hardly surprising, since every time a service provider works on a tyre under the contract, an invoice is generated.)

There was some discussion about making MFS a stand-alone subsidiary with its own systems to prevent confusion, but that suggestion was dismissed, based on the reasoning that having two separate Michelin offers in the market could damage the brand. Instead, MFS is now seen as a complementary business, with country managers able to choose the best option for customers.

Making a mark with marketing

It has also called for new thinking from the marketing specialists, who manage both external relations and the internal marketing necessary to achieve the changes in approach. There is a small central marketing team which works closely with the marketers in the various European countries to ensure consistency. There are regular meetings, with initiatives being tested in certain countries before the ideas are rolled out across borders. Each country receives a basic communications kit for any campaign but it can be tailored according to specific needs.

With MFS, the marketing professionals have to focus on designing propositions that create value not from the products themselves – which, after all, has been the company's historical strength for over 100 years – but from wrapping services around the core products. It demands a precise understanding of customer needs and the ability to identify segments to which specific offers can be addressed.

To take one instance: the company has been looking at the potential of building on one of the services it already offers to its MFS customers called Michelin Euro Assist. This is a European breakdown service which promises to arrive in two hours to help with any tyre-related breakdowns. So, for example, for fleets where delivery times are critical, the company could add value by not only offering to make sure that the trucks had the right tyres, but it could also carry out special examinations to prevent possible problems.

Getting the message across

One of the key objectives for Michelin's marketers is to persuade prospective customers of the value of what can be a complex concept. Some customers, for instance, can be reluctant to tie themselves into a long-term contract, so the added value they will receive in terms of higher productivity has to be made clear. They have to be persuaded of the benefits they will see in a new way of operating. This is more readily done in a country like the UK, where outsourcing of non-core business is a well-established concept. In other countries, the idea of not owning their own tyres sits uncomfortably with some truck operators. But acceptance of the model is moving slowly but steadily across the continent.

A powerful weapon in the MFS armoury is the growing database the company is building based on its increasing experience with tyre management. This is proving invaluable in creating benchmarks for customers so they know how they are doing and how they can manage their businesses better. For example, Michelin can help them analyse why one part of their operation is far more efficient than another or if their breakdown rate is different to the industry average.

Forming close relationships

Key account managers are in place to oversee the customer relationships in every aspect. They are carefully picked and not only have to know the basics about tyres but also have the ability to understand the different needs of individual customers. One of the biggest challenges they face is getting the contract right. Because the market is so new, there are few price comparisons to use in setting the amount to charge per kilometre. Moreover, the contract is only the beginning: 80% of the work is done after the contract is signed. However, one of the company's competitive advantages is its in-depth knowledge of tyre potential amassed over the years. This means that any calculations stem from a lot of know-how; a good barrier to entry against the growing number of competitors offering a similar service.

Keeping customers on the move

What has distinguished MFS from other areas of the business which are also experimenting with different types of payment methods (for example, the aircraft tyre business has a model where customers pay per touch-down) is its determination to be seen as actively helping clients to boost their productivity rather than just offering a different way to pay. Other parts of the company are now coming to MFS to learn and to understand what tools they might use.

This is the first big step Michelin has made in finding new ways to offer services to customers but it will not be the only approach the company adopts. There are lots of future opportunities to fulfil its aims of sustaining mobility, not least exploiting the potential of its travel service site ('Via Michelin') and its famous travel guides.

What has helped the company move in these new directions, along with the strength of its brand and its reputation for quality, is a culture where innovation and risk taking have been encouraged since the early days of tyre development. Michelin has long appreciated that to be an innovator in the market, there have to be allowances for the occasional failure.

Belief in the power of good service

Decision-making by managers is not always objective, rational or analytically determined. In a fast-moving and demanding job, decisions are frequently based on assumptions, emotions, accumulation of attitudes and acquired knowledge. People often resort to personal judgement or 'gut feel' rather than objective analysis. As a result, when major changes in management thinking, with associated publicity, have an effect on managers' views, they also affect their decisions and strategies. One management fad which had a profound effect on a generation of managers due to high profile publicity was the emphasis on quality of service and 'exceeding customer expectations' at the end of the twentieth century. It caused several firms to invest heavily in service programmes, some to their cost and detriment.

Although articles and debates about quality of service and 'customer care' have been in circulation for many decades, it really became a focus of management attention in the 1980s as a result of a number of significant forces:

(i) The then-steady decline in the competitive performance of much of Western manufacturing relative to certain Asian, particularly Japanese, companies.
(ii) Emphasis on after care and service in some sectors, particularly retail and computing.
(iii) The then-powerful quality movement and its emphasis on 'just in time' processes and the 'zero defects' policy of 'total quality management'.
(iv) The publicity gained by several writers and speakers, particularly Tom Peters, who in the book, *In Search of Excellence* (Peters & Waterman, 1982) modelled the dynamics of successful businesses, creating general principles out of case studies. His primary emphasis was on quality of service and customer care. He thought that much Western business had moved away from service to their buyers and had lost world leadership as a result.
(v) Certain well publicised, dramatic improvements in service which affected the share price of the firms involved. Two, for example, were in the European airline industry.

In 1983 the then-chairman of British Airways (now BA), Lord King, and his chief executive, Colin Marshall, created a radical improvement in the market position of the newly-privatised airline by engaging front line staff in a massive improvement prioritisation programme across the whole firm. Called 'putting people first', the programme engaged many thousands of staff in workshops where the importance of excellent service to passengers was stressed and barriers to such service were removed from the employees.

At the same time the new chief executive of the Scandinavian airline SAS, Jan Carlzon, introduced a similar programme under the banner 'moments of truth'. Carlzon introduced a company-wide programme to enhance all points where customers experienced the organisation. Again, it had a major impact on the company's market position.

(vi) The publication of a number of influential research reports. One which was frequently quoted was by TARP (Technical Assistance and Research Programmes) conducted in the United States and Canada, for the White House Office of Consumer Affairs. This research, which covered two hundred companies, showed that:
- The average business did not hear from 96% of its unhappy customers.
- For every complaint received, there were twenty-six other people with problems and six with serious problems.
- Most people did not think that it was worth complaining. Some did not know how and where to start. Some did not think it worth investing the time and effort in doing so. Some were sceptical of being dealt with effectively, because of considerable past experience of poor problem handling.
- People with problems who failed to complain were far less likely to repeat their orders (for the same product or service). They were also far more likely to stop completely their business with the supplier.
- People who complained and whose problems were handled well were much more likely to continue doing business.
- People with bad experiences were twice as likely to tell others about it as those with good experiences.
- The average service business lost 10–15% of its buyers each year through poor service.

This combination of factors attracted the attention of management and put a spotlight on quality of service principles. At the height of the associated publicity, a number of reputable academics, disturbed by the impact of exuberant presentations and exaggerated anecdotes, began to research the issue in depth. A series of studies into the business context of service quality strategies then established a number of reliable principles and techniques. They included: 'the service profit chain' (Heskett, Sasser & Schlesinger, 1997), 'the loyalty effect' (Reichheld, 2006) and 'the Gap model' (Berry & Parasuraman, 1991). They demonstrated the need for strategy, research, process and measurement in service programmes. At the time of writing, this accumulated work has stimulated emphasis on tackling the experience that buyers have of a company. Many are exploring, debating and constructing 'customer experience management' (CEM) programmes.

As a result of this accumulated experience, many business people have a belief that service should be 'good', that customer expectations should be exceeded and that buyers should be 'wowed'. Many will nod to platitudes (like: 'the average unhappy customer tells thirteen others' or 'it costs more to recruit new customers than to serve existing buyers') without knowing their source, validity or relevance to their particular business. Yet, if prompted to apply normal business rationale, they should probably ask what service style is appropriate to their company's market position; or if it would be more cost effective to manage customer expectations than exceed them and what the return would be on 'wowing' buyers. Whatever its merits, this heritage has caused many business leaders to press for service strategies and some have forged into service business based on little more than an intuitive belief that good service creates good profitable business.

Summary

Over the past fifty years a number of forces have combined to prompt product companies to consider entering service businesses. This might be little more than unforseen opportunity presented to a service cost centre or the chance to earn from the growing service economies at home and abroad. Some have been forced to differentiate with service in mature product markets while others have pressed ahead due to little more than belief in the power of good service as a business tool. These forces, combined with a demand from Western societies for greater respect for the individual, have forced industry to be more responsive and service orientated. They have produced massive new service businesses, CRM programmes plus the concepts of 'solutions' marketing and customer experience management.

2

Clarifying the strategic intent of the service business

Introduction and overview

While a number of the famous moves into service, such as those by IBM and GE, have been led by top management, a surprisingly large number have occurred in response to lobbying and pressure from middle management. Some, too, have happened as a result of an unstructured response to opportunistic service projects developing naturally in the market. As a result of both, a process of osmosis has driven many firms further and further into service markets until the momentum has tipped them fully into becoming service businesses.

This sort of evolution toward fundamental business change is more normal and healthy than is generally acknowledged. A number of successful service strategies, trumpeted at shareholder meetings or in the press, are actually post hoc rationalisation of middle management experimentation. But service businesses are different from product companies and, as a result, risky for a manufacturer to move into. At some stage the firm's leaders should step back and properly assess the strategic implications of the change. They should then decide whether to validate, invest in or withdraw from these fledgling businesses.

The leadership needs to ensure that strategy is developed which clarifies the role, purpose and targets of each service business. Unfortunately, modern attitudes to strategy and strategy

development can be dismissive, cursory or superficial. Recent history has tended to emphasise speedy business decision-making and a short-term perspective based on scant analysis. In fact, some corporations seem to be driven by PowerPoint and expediency rather than an objective or reflective perspective based on sound analysis or deep experience of customers in any given market. This is probably a reaction to the large, over-engineered corporate strategy projects of the past. Yet it is a dangerous undervaluation of strategy development and strategic management.

The corporate centres of larger firms and the leaders of smaller companies have a duty of care to reflect on a number of strategic issues that cannot be successfully addressed at business unit level. One of these is the 'strategic intent' of the service business: its business focus or 'mission'.

First, a word on the value of strategy

Good strategy is a framework of ideas, developed by the leadership of a company, which sets a course for the firm by creating a common purpose. It involves making decisions about direction, communicating those decisions and allocating the resources to make them possible. It contrasts to tactics, which are short-term, action-oriented and accomplish limited goals.

A company's corporate strategy should be known to all employees so that it becomes a touchstone for decisions throughout the organisation. In fact, all strategic devices and tools are aimed at achieving this common understanding of the firm's strategy. Properly communicated, members of the firm will use it as a reference point when making decisions. Without it, decisions throughout the organisation will be based on the judgement of local people with a local perspective and information which, while valid, may conflict with priorities developed from knowledge of the needs of the total firm. Chaos and poor results can then follow.

All companies, even when no strategy is explicitly developed or communicated, must take a direction. However, if that direction is a rudderless drift, or if it flies in the face of market realities, or if it is not communicated throughout the organisation, the health of the business is likely to be damaged. The leadership of a company has, therefore, a duty of care to create clear, market-conscious, achievable strategic direction.

Origins and evolution of strategy

Some business strategy techniques originated from the military, where they evolved over a long period of time to help improve decision-making, resource allocation and, above all, success. Military history has shown that victory in the heat of battle is more likely if there has been prior thought given to likely scenarios. As far back as 500 BC the Chinese general, Sun Tzu, said:

> In warfare first lay plans which will ensure victory and then lead your army to battle; if you will not begin with stratagem but rely on brute strength alone, victory will no longer be assured.

In other words, a little forethought, using methods that have been successful elsewhere, reduces risk and increases the likelihood of success. Stunning military successes as different as the Roman campaigns against ill-disciplined tribes, Napoleon's conquest of Europe and General Norman Schwarzkopf's 'Operation Desert Storm' in Kuwait, have demonstrated the power of strategy, experience and forethought.

Mankind has learnt, after thousands of years of bloody combat, that good strategy is more effective than rushing at the other side with sticks. So early business leaders, many experienced in warfare, speculated that strategy approaches would improve their resource management and competitive success. If good strategy was effective in military endeavour it was likely to be effective in business. Over time, many came to compare business with warfare and concluded that good business leadership is more than 'gut feel' or decisions made on the hoof. Business managers have therefore adopted and shaped many of the military's strategic techniques in order to improve their chances of success and, as a result, developed their own.

However, strategy as a management discipline appears to have been through several evolutionary phases. In the 1970s, for example, it was dominated by new analytical tools (such as the 'Boston matrix' or 'scenario planning'), focusing largely on the corporate strategy of large corporations such as the oil companies. By the 1980s strategy was often overseen by large, central, strategic planning functions in multinationals running complex models. This was reinforced by the apparent success of Japanese firms and their famed focus upon long-term planning. Some, for example, had fifty and twenty year investment planning cycles in addition to their annual operating plans.

By contrast, in the 1990s, the combination of recession, the collapse of the Asian model and a tougher competitive environment, combined with the perception that business must be more responsive to change, created much more of a feverish, short-term focus. This culminated in the excesses of the dot.com boom when the lack of a proper business model was no barrier to raising large amounts of capital. Since the burst of that market bubble, and the associated recession, strategy has remained short-term and need-driven. In fact, many of the specialised consultancies report that strategy projects have become a distress purchase, responding to hostile bids or the need for turn around. So the appetite for large, long-term strategic planning and analysis appears to have diminished in many business sectors. This suggests that strategy, in the sense of longer-term detailed strategic plans, is less valued.

Yet, whatever the size and shape of the company, leaders need to take time to think of the future health of their business and how they go to market. They need to focus on the strategic imperatives relevant at any one time and allocate resources appropriately to chart the next steps of the organisation. This should be done in a style and manner geared to the culture of the firm and the judgement of the leadership. It can be elaborate, planned and documented or intuitive and iterative. But it should be done.

The development of strategy can be 'procedural' (where a number of prescribed steps are followed to arrive at a particular point), 'functional' (where it is someone's job to draw up a well-presented and detailed strategic document), or 'extant' (consisting of a pattern of decisions by a dominant business leader which are largely intuitive and often understood only in retrospect). All have their strengths and weaknesses and none is an ideal approach. Whichever method is used, at some stage strategic thinking should be applied to any fledgling service business to validate, reject or invest in the new venture. Through this strategic review, the business focus or strategic intent of the service business, one of the most crucial aspects of strategic development, should be made clear. It will give direction and context to everything else.

The need for clarity of purpose in each service business

It is surprising how many product companies have wandered into offering competitive services without completing, at any level in their organisation, a proper evaluation of the costs, risks and competencies involved. Very often they are drawn into this by a debate among their middle management rather than through a specific initiative that has been assessed, managed and funded by top management.

In fact, some of these initiatives start as 'skunk' works, hidden from sceptical or resistant senior people until sufficient revenue has accumulated. As a result, service businesses within manufacturing companies are often confused about their purpose or strategic aims. They suffer tensions in their business unit and with other parts of their own firm which seem irresolvable. They might, for example, aim for growth in revenue but have the price of their skills discounted by a sales force intent on selling products. As a result, service units which were very profitable when supporting the company's products, can lose margin and erode profits when used as a springboard into more directly competitive service markets.

Moreover, most of the moves into service have been in industries where there has been a boom in service needs or where there have been large margins due to inefficiencies in the market. This has allowed novices to learn the dynamics of the new business and to survive internal conflict or profound mistakes. It has hidden or compensated for tensions, depressed margins and errors. A number of these markets have since tightened, however, and the suppliers now have to address fundamental strategic issues such as pricing, discount controls, channel conflict and market position. These all depend on the focus of the business.

As the McKinsey Quarterly said in the spring of 2006:

> As relative newcomers to the service economy, many product companies have yet to make money there. Until recently, brisk sales growth, buoyed by a rising tide of demand for services, kept trouble from view. But as the estimated $50 billion 'embedded' service sector becomes more competitive, too many companies find themselves grappling with strategic questions they should have resolved when first entering the market: are they offering embedded services for offensive or defensive purposes? Are they playing a skill- or a scale-based game? Confusion about fundamental issues of strategic intent and the source

> of competitive advantage now seriously hampers the profitable pricing and delivery of embedded services and the effective management and governance of product and service organizations alike (Auguste, Harmon & Pandit, 2006).

At some point, then, the firm needs to clarify the purpose of its service business or businesses if it is to make good profits and compete successfully. This might lead to the creation of several different service businesses with different strategic intents, or a spate of acquisitions or, at the other extreme, withdrawal from some markets. By clarifying the new service businesses' strategic intent, the leaders are more likely to be successful in their move from products to services.

This is much more than a few words in a bland statement. Strategic intent is the *raison d'être*, the overriding purpose of a business. It gives direction to the management team and all operational decisions, avoiding extraneous activities and unnecessary costs. As the famous strategy writers, Hamel and Prahalad said in their article which coined the phrase:

> Strategic intent is more than unfettered ambition. The concept also encompasses an active management process that includes focusing the organization's attention on the essence of winning; motivating people by communicating the value of the target, leaving room for individual and team contributions; sustaining enthusiasm by providing new operational definitions as circumstances change; and using intent consistently to guide resource allocations. Strategic intent captures the essence of winning (Hamel & Prahalad, 1989).

The benefits of clarifying the strategic intent of a service business were examined, and dramatised, in a report by two academics called 'Service companies: focus or falter' (Davidow & Uttal, 1989). They used several examples of service businesses (the most memorable being a Canadian hospital which specialised in hernia operations) to demonstrate the remarkable effect that strategic focus has on profit and service quality. They showed that it leads naturally to co-production of service with customers, investment in technology, the industrialisation of erratic service components, productivity improvement and to the setting of expectations with potential buyers. They said:

> . . . fuzzy or conflicting strategies make good customer service impossible. . . . Without a strategy, you can't develop a concept of service to rally em-

> ployees or catch conflicts between corporate strategy and customer service or come up with ways to measure service performance and perceived quality. In short, without a strategy you can't get to first base.

There appear to be a number of different types of business focus which product companies adopt when moving into service markets. They include:

1. Tied maintenance and after care.
2. Tied technical advisers.
3. 'Third party' maintenance.
4. Suppliers of scaleable services
5. The knowledge-based professional service supplier.
6. The hybrid offer.
7. Flight from service.

1. Tied maintenance and after care

A tied maintenance unit exists to repair faults exclusively with a firm's sold products. Whether directly employed by the company or sub-contracted to dedicated dealers, it is tied to one manufacturer and its range of products. Simple maintenance seems to be a straightforward, even boring, part of most product companies. Yet it is an important ingredient in customer satisfaction, has an impact on repurchase intent and has been the start of a complex profitable journey for many over the past two decades.

It is rare that a modern company does not have an arrangement to repair any faults that might arise with the products it sells. No matter how high the quality of engineering, the selection of components or the control of manufacturing processes, a number of products are likely to develop faults. The warranty and maintenance services provide buyers, whether consumers or businesses, with an emotional reassurance that any difficulties in product use will be resolved without fuss; and this reassurance helps sales.

In the early months of use, this is normally provided by a new product guarantee or warranty. Any failures are quickly addressed by a repair or, in many instances, by product replacement. Usually this warranty work is undertaken by the firm's maintenance resource. However, at some stage, the buyer has to contract specifically for maintenance support as the product ages. Often a variety of contracts are available offering different standards of response depending on the needs and wallet of the buyers.

There are, though, several conflicting aspects to this seemingly simple business process. Firstly, a number of suppliers try to sell 'extended warranty' at point of purchase. This can undermine the future sale of a maintenance contract, extending the warranty period; sometimes up to the life of the product. Pricing of extended warranty is therefore a careful calculation. Although it is easily sold at point of purchase, the attractive additional revenues need to cover long-term maintenance requirements. Its boost to the earnings of a product line must be compared to the cost of end-of-life products, borne by the maintenance unit.

A second tension arises because investment in excellent maintenance service can delay the moment when buyers think they need to replace an old product, affecting the revenue from new product sales. Good maintenance, routine equipment checks and modern approaches to preventative maintenance can extend product life and reduce new product sales. In fact, some customers hang onto old products in non-essential areas of their life or work.

The maintenance business needs to manage these customers carefully, progressively increasing maintenance costs as obsolescence approaches. They also need to signal carefully the time at which an obsolete product will no longer be supported. Failure to manage communication with them is likely to affect their propensity to buy again.

Another tension is the way in which the increasing stability of new technologies affects the buyers' willingness to invest in maintenance or extended warranty. People become less willing to buy cover as faults become infrequent in a product type. Few, for example, buy extended warranty with modern televisions while the falling price of personal computers for business makes maintenance almost uneconomic.

These tensions normally arise within a tied maintenance business and have to be managed. However, the move into competitive service often exacerbates them and adds more fundamental and traumatic pressures. For instance, in some sectors of the developed economies, maintenance contracts and warranties have become more profitable than the associated, commoditised, products they support. As a result, firms often look to their service businesses for revenue contribution when margins are under pressure. Service teams can then be encouraged to take on isolated projects for customers using, say, their problem solving or project management skills.

Unfortunately service managers, even at the highest levels, are often inexperienced in sales or effective negotiation. They tend to spend their career responding to problems and resolving issues. As a result, they make simple mistakes when freed to offer deals or paid services. They can, for example, load all the costs of a 'one off' service onto one customer so that it becomes uneconomic, depressing margins, because they don't spread the costs. It is then impossible to gain support for this potential service to be industrialised and made more commonly available across the business. (The recent trend to offer customised 'solutions' has exacerbated this tendency in a number of technology companies, causing real damage to margins by undermining discount controls.)

Moreover, by allowing the maintenance unit to offer new services, perhaps supporting equipment sold by different suppliers, conflict is caused with other business units while, at the same time confusing its funding status. Previously its costs would have been covered by product margins. Whether recorded as a specific maintenance cost centre or washed in the generic business margin, its aim was to support product sales. Now, however, it is allowed to grow revenue and its confused status can lead it to take uneconomic business or to undermine product sales.

At some point these tensions need to be resolved. One strategy adopted by many who move fully into service markets is to set up separate units to deal with new service business and to re-create a tied maintenance unit focused on assuring customers about their own product performance and affecting satisfaction. Its strategic purpose is then defensive, contributing to customer loyalty and guarding against defection to other suppliers.

2. Tied technical advisers

Many businesses hire technical specialists to advise and assist their customers. For many years, the computer industry has, for example, employed programmers to analyse their customers' needs and design systems for them. Called 'professional services', they have been employed to work exclusively on the products supplied by their employers, helping sales and becoming part of the total offer. Some companies also employ specialists with more soft skills such as experienced project managers to help buyers design, plan and implement complex technical projects. Others, car dealers for instance, employ specialist finance people to offer a range of finance and leasing options to help purchase. All are part of the cost of business funded by product margins.

Like tied maintenance units, these specialists are primarily employed to support product sales and, in addition to ensuring that the product performs to specification, their value lies in the affect they have on customer satisfaction. If the customer is so pleased with specification, delivery and implementation that they become a repeat buyer, then the team has proved their worth.

In a number of industries, these units have been encouraged to grow revenues by the sale of independent advice. Yet, as with tied maintenance divisions, conflict can occur if they are successful. Moreover, despite being intelligent and highly proficient people, they can lack the personality traits needed in a competent consultant. It is difficult to move a large workforce of this kind into competitive, independent consulting; technical excellence does not necessarily mean excellent consulting.

Many experienced providers have, therefore, limited them to the role of a product support group, once they have moved effectively into service markets by, for example, buying consultancies which offer truly independent advice.

3. 'Third party' maintenance

This type of business exists to gain competitive advantage from its technical repair skills by repairing a range of products. They vary from the consumer maintenance companies which support domestic goods to technical companies repairing the complex computer and communications equipment owned by businesses. Many of the functions of the business (from field engineering management and logistic supplies to call reception and diagnostic processes) are similar to the tied maintenance arm of manufacturers. However, the focus is on a range of products owned by one customer. They therefore need to be particularly good at managing an asset register of equipment owned by customers and at the process of extending their business competencies to take on new equipment.

Their benefit, though, is that the focus of their business is on the customer and the customer's installation rather than any particular supplier's equipment. In situations where there are installations of different types of manufacturer's equipment they can get to know the customer well and anticipate their needs. Their other strategic advantage is in the experience they gain from their repair work. Their tools, systems and processes tend to give them cost advantage over time. As a result, many can undercut manufacturers' maintenance units (even when supporting their own equipment), keeping prices low.

Many manufactures have been attracted into 'multi-vendor maintenance' because, as in the ThyssenKrupp Elevator experience, it allows them to grow revenue and dominate one customer with its service. The aspiration is to then replace competitor equipment over time as customers learn to trust the supplier through their service experience. In fact, many have found that service is taken seriously for the first time in their company when the firm wins its first large maintenance contract in a new account which is independent of its own products.

For many though, this form of service is merely a step towards a more effective service business. They move on to business process management, for example, or the remote support of complex installations. Few are able to build truly economic, stand alone, service businesses of this kind while handling the channel conflicts it causes inside their firm. Those attempting to stay the course should, at least, ring fence this type of business as a separate profit centre.

ThyssenKrupp Elevator grows service business

ThyssenKrupp Elevator is the third largest elevator company in the world. In 2004/05 it had sales of approximately €3.8 billion and over 34 000 employees in 800 locations around the world. It is part of ThyssenKrupp, one of the world's biggest industrial technology groups.

Singling out services

The company is divided into manufacturing, installation and services. On the manufacturing side, there are twenty-five factories around the world where all the different parts of an elevator are made and/or assembled. The finished products are then sold to the field operations, which oversee sales, installation and service.

Over the last few years ThyssenKrupp Elevator has been focusing on service as a source of growth and profits in its bid to become the second largest supplier in the market (it is already the second-most profitable company in the sector). The fact that it is third is quite an achievement because ThyssenKrupp Elevator was only set up thirty years ago, and is a relative youngster compared to competitors such as Otis and Schindler, both of which are well over 100 years old.

And it is the services business which is growing the most solidly. Services account for more than 50% of the business, employing more than two-thirds of employees and generating higher amounts of revenue. As the company's chairman of the executive board, Gary Elliott, wrote in the annual report, 'Our aim is to grow faster in the high-quality service business while meeting ever-increasing market requirements.'

A lot of this growth in services has come from long-term service contracts following installations. That is why a key target for the company is to win new installations, particularly the big, high-profile and image-building projects such as major airports, high rise buildings or high value residential projects. This usually gains the company long-term service and maintenance contracts which run for ten to fifteen years. However, making money from them is by no means guaranteed. This is why ThyssenKrupp Elevator has invested heavily in making its service organisation as efficient as possible by ensuring it has enough people in key markets around the world with the most modern tools available.

The global service strategy

The company has decided to take a more structured approach to growing services by setting in place a global service strategy. This has three main strands. The first is to offer customers a full maintenance contract, involving a monthly fee for oversight of everything involved with the elevator maintenance and availability guarantees (rather than having to negotiate some of the aspects separately). This is much more comprehensive than normal service contracts.

The second strand is to win more business in the renewal and enhancement market. This could involve, for example, updating older equipment to enable it to meet health and safety requirements or new legislation concerning access for the disabled. The third is to win more long-term contracts to service the installed base of other suppliers. This makes sense: ThyssenKrupp Elevator is the relative newcomer compared to companies such as Otis and Schindler, which have a much larger installed base because they have been around so much longer.

To that end, for the last fifteen years, the company has been establishing a network of technical centres of excellence in different parts of the world to focus on equipment support (including their competitors'), diagnostic tools, training and simulators. It means that both technical and sales people can have instant access to the most up-to-date information on any product from any company. This has become an increasing competitive advantage for ThyssenKrupp Elevator because most facility management companies are in charge of hundreds of buildings with hundreds of elevators from a wide range of suppliers. It calls for a lot of accurate market intelligence, since the company has to know when an installation's long-term contract is coming up for renewal or when elevators need modernisation.

In some markets it can be effective to start with service. In Australia, for example, the company began a pilot scheme at the end of the last century whereby it focused on offering to service other suppliers' equipment. This has worked very well, and the service recognition ThyssenKrupp now has is beginning to translate into winning more and more lucrative new installations. The same approach has worked in the US. ThyssenKrupp Elevator is, at the time of writing, the largest elevator manufacturer in the country and, in New York City, despite having a smaller installed base than the competition, it services the most elevators.

Getting closer to customers

Corporate marketing is located in the Düsseldorf head office, and oversees activities such as annual reports, global image campaigns and worldwide key accounts. The central team also ensures the corporate guidelines are adhered to around the world.

Deciding what customers to go after and how this is done is decentralised. That is important, since markets differ. For example, in Europe and the US the company often works through middlemen such as architects, general contractors, engineering firms and facility management companies. These groups are handled by key account managers and relationships are built up through a range of activities such as customer events and newsletters. In Asia, on the other hand, the end customer, or building owner, tends to choose the equipment personally. That calls for a different, more retail-oriented approach to marketing and sales.

The web plays an important role in customer relationships, with micro web sites set up for special products so that prospective customers can learn about the specifications. It is also used to increase trust and transparency with existing customers by giving them access to their accounts online so they can get a complete record of what ThyssenKrupp Elevator has been doing in terms of service and main-tenance on a daily basis. This helps overcome the fact that, once the installation is complete, customers might have little regular contact with the company except for the monthly invoice.

In addition, state-of-the-art remote monitoring tools enable the company to collect accurate statistics on equipment usage, such as how many people use the elevators and how much of the time they should be operating successfully. It can then guarantee customers that it will meet these targets and offer them a refund if they aren't met. This knowledge also means the company can offer a customised service package depending on the amount of maintenance predicted.

Finding additional sources of growth

Along with boosting revenues from services, the company has identified four other ways to grow. The first is through acquisitions (90 % of the acquisitions the company has made in the last few years have been service companies). The second is innovation, or developing compelling new products such as their 'TWIN' or 'TurboTrack' initiatives. Another source of growth is to cross sell from its range of products. This range is more extensive than most of the competitors because it includes escalators, moving walkways, passenger boarding bridges and accessibility products.

Finally, the company is analysing its entire value chain and its worldwide business to find best practice, set new benchmarks and validate new working methods to increase its efficiency and effectiveness in services. It is also working on a worldwide IT system to help transfer this knowledge across its business.

4. Suppliers of scalable independent services

These businesses are unrelated to any specific product range, are based on the supply of a service which handles volume transactions and have, at their core, a process or a technology. Some, like EDS, are dedicated businesses and others, like those in IBM or Accenture, exist as business units within broader companies. The supplier earns revenue by replicating the service and increasing the number of customers but improves profit by deploying process and technology improvements to reduce costs.

In fact, any inability to replicate causes these businesses to earn lower margins or fail altogether. They must 'industrialise' their offer, reducing costs over time. It therefore takes determination and experience for newcomers, particularly manufacturers, to succeed when moving into this type of service provision. A number have quietly lost a fortune while learning the dynamics of this type of business.

The supply of independent business services has been a growing phenomenon in the last two decades. Based on the principles of outsourcing, suppliers as varied as Michelin, Accenture, EDS, BT, Nokia, Capita and IBM have won contracts to run parts of their customers' business. Some call them 'managed services' and some 'business process management' but all are based on the proposition that the supplier can, due to specialisation, knowledge or business experience, run the business process better than the firm itself. Apart from huge service contracts in the IT industry, this relatively new attitude to the management of big business has created the multi-million dollar 'facilities management' industry. Business after business has chosen to contract specialists to run their security, estate management and catering services; in fact most processes that are not an essential part of their main business.

Outsourcing is based on a concept called the 'experience curve'. This demonstrates that any organisation will, through productivity improvements, reduce costs over time in the area of its prime competence, its business focus. As illustrated in Figure 2.1, a firm whose business is focussed on a particular function is likely to be further down the experience curve than a customer's in-house team. A computer company will be better at managing computing operations than the in-house IT division of, say, a bank; whereas a security company will be better at controlling access than, say, an airline and a cleaning company better at cost effective office refreshment than, say, an accountancy firm.

If the in-house operations are passed to the supplier, the client gains advantage of the supplier's 'experience' and the savings can be dramatic. For instance, when the UK government's audit office first reviewed (in 1990) public sector outsourcing deals initiated by the Thatcher government in the 1980s, gains of up to 20 % were found due to this phenomenon. This sparked the outsourcing trend in much of Europe and has, as a result, become a much quoted (and distorted) statistic.

Unfortunately, after the initial deal, further dramatic gains are unlikely. The continuing success of the contract then depends on a number of different factors. One is the ability of the supplier to win other contracts and,

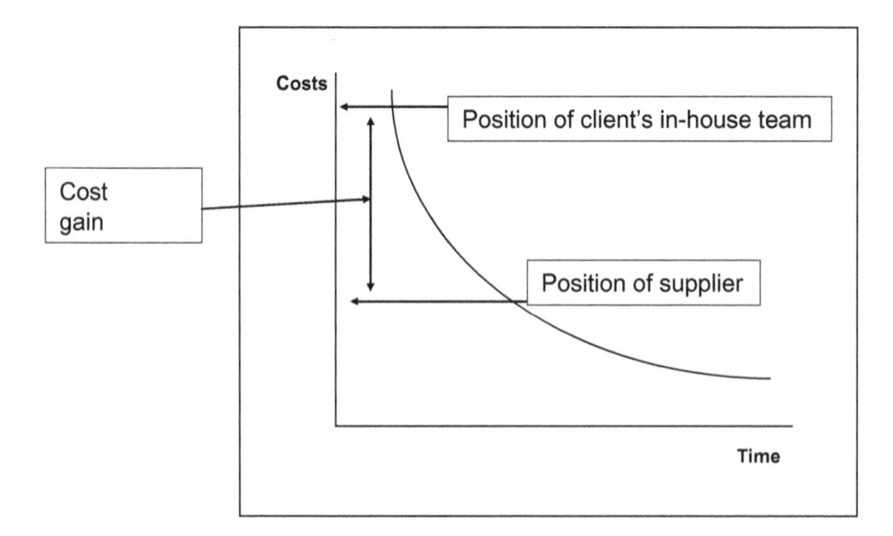

Figure 2.1 The experience curve as an explanation of outsourcing

through volume and economies of scale, continue to maintain a cost advantage for its customers. The second is the nature of the relationship between the two parties. The customer needs to have a senior manager responsible for managing the ongoing relationship with their 'outsourcer'. This person should not only monitor performance but also brief the contractor on the company's developing strategy so that plans can be adjusted if necessary.

The failure to do this has caused many relationships of this kind to break down. Yet, if that happens, the customer loses the supplier's experience and begins to build cost back into its business. For their part, suppliers of managed service therefore need contract managers who are trained in business strategy and understand their customers in depth if they are to maintain their business position.

5. The knowledge-based professional service supplier

A product company deciding to move into the provision of independent, competitive advice, perhaps through consultancy, enters the professional services industry and needs to understand against whom it is competing.

This sector of the world's economies is vast and varied. One estimate puts its revenues at $ 700 billion worldwide and another suggests that it employs up to one in five workers in the developed world. It encompasses a wide variety of businesses whose offer is based around specialist skill or knowledge. They range from executive search firms, recruitment agencies, education, training and coaching providers to consultancies in various specialities. Included are legal, accountancy, engineering, marketing and architectural practices. It comprises an array of medical practitioners such as doctors, dentists, opticians, pharmacists, osteopaths and physiotherapists. There are also a variety of retail professionals such as hairdressers, veterinarians and estate agents/realtors, which range from single shops to large chains.

The one thing they have in common is that their knowledge is the barrier to entry into their business and they make vast sums from this 'asymmetry of information'. The other is that their businesses are based on skill and people rather than scaleable processes. It is an entirely different service business to process management with very different margins and performance criteria.

The margins and earnings vary enormously but can be vast; outperforming the takings of all but the very elite directors of publicly listed companies. The top earners include: merchant bankers (whose million dollar bonuses can rival IPO takings or earn outs); partners in leading advisory firms (whose salary alone can be $1 million at the time of writing); individual gurus and fashionable stylists (whose brands make them into multi-millionaires). The professions include some of the world's most successful, enduring and profitable businesses. They have, through experience, common sense and brilliance, evolved a number of unique strategic approaches (like reputation management, 'demand pull' and 'thought leadership') which new entrants need to understand if they are to compete.

These approaches arise from the fact that the industry is dominated by a very different type of business ownership. Found primarily in the professions and entirely different to publicly-owned Plcs it is the partnership structure. The partners of a firm share its ownership, frequently having to earn their way into the business through outstanding long-term performance and capital investment. Yet they are also the elite leaders of the service. Not only do they own the business, sharing profit and loss, they lead client engagements, actively participating in the work.

They head up cells of business units (called 'practices') which, because they are run directly by an owner of the business, evolve and respond to market changes, even when the leadership of the firm makes fundamental errors of strategy or management. They are, perhaps, one of the business world's few self-righting organisational structures. These businesses range from two-person partnerships to the multiple networks of the better known firms with many thousands of partners.

The ownership structure of professional practices affects their approach to business, whether large or small. They work, for instance, through mutual consent and consensus. Top leaders are, often reluctantly, elected by their peers and frequently continue to practice while managing the firm. They have to carry their peers with them, even when there are two thousand partners working in many countries of the world. Aggressive or insensitive leadership is tolerated for only a short time, eventually causing a change, sometimes in an ugly leadership coup.

As a result, there is often surprisingly little direct decision-making. Whereas, in a corporate firm, individuals have clear accountability within a distinct area of responsibility, initiatives in a partnership are more often created by a wide consultation or 'buy in' process which creates a momentum for the idea. Providing no one strongly disagrees with the initiative, it will become, more or less, common practice within the firm.

They tend to use a 'situational approach' to strategy development. Leaders will identify and work upon immediate strategic imperatives, often as part of an annual budget round. This is less logical, less systematic and less well rounded than the 'procedural approach' which business schools emphasise. In fact, many routine issues can languish due to lack of attention. However, once the major strategic thrust is identified, the firm tends to tackle the most important issues as partners in each practice implement the actions agreed by consensus.

Project teams might be formed to implement different aspects of the strategy, often in addition to their normal jobs, and are disbanded when either the strategic intent is achieved or other priorities identified. Frequently, initiatives are started by partners in a practice and grow, in tune with a developing market, despite or in defiance of the firm's leadership. As a result, some professional service firms are entering their second century of successful, high margin business.

Manufacturers wanting to enter this type of business must have a clear idea of exactly how different it is. One dramatic example is the approach to revenue generation which is based on enhancing the natural reputation of the practice and is the complete opposite of product sales. Most first-rate professionals will say that 'all marketing starts with the work'. For a number of reasons clients talk about a professional service after it is finished. This creates a strong reputation (which may eventually turn into a brand) and this, in turn, draws in more work, as illustrated in Figure 2.2.

This 'demand-pull' is the complete opposite of 'product push' and has two very powerful benefits. First, it keeps the cost of sales low (because the firm does not have to go out and get work) and, second, keeps prices high (because practitioners can focus on diagnosing need and pricing becomes a consequence, not a focus, of discussion). Within the professions this makes the difference between an elite profitable practice and a grubby 'ambulance chaser'. As a result, all successful professionals focus their attention on it. They ensure that any strategy or business initiative is aimed at enhancing the firm's reputation or preserving it. Those that don't simply do not make good margins.

So newcomers must adopt this business dynamic. They must understand the competitive reputation of their firm in the new market through hard,

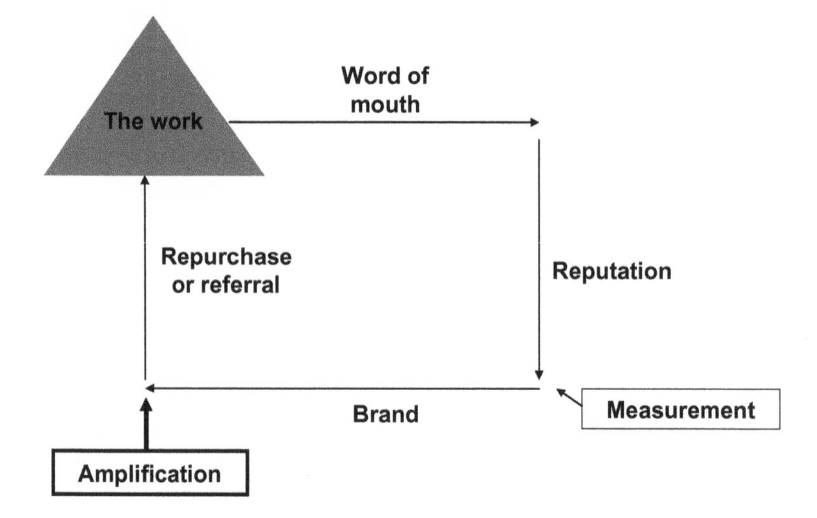

Figure 2.2 The role of reputation in creating demand pull for high end professional services

numeric analysis and then build programmes that enhance that reputation. Failure to do so has caused many product companies over the past two decades, particularly the large IT companies, to earn much lower margins than their peers in the advisory industry, often providing the same quality of service as leading consultancies at a much lower price. They have become the low margin ambulance chasers of the consultancy world, even if they have a blue-chip product brand.

Despite the flexibility and reputation of leading partnerships, Plcs do have competitive advantages to deploy against them. Partnerships, for example, are reluctant to use current profit to invest because there is pressure to distribute it among the owners. Plcs can, therefore gain an edge by using their capital budgets to improve productivity through technology, process and systems improvements. But their prime competitive weapon is their ability to employ top talent using share options. As shares are valued by the capital markets on different criteria than current performance, it means that senior people can be employed at lower current salary costs than partners in competing private practices. However, these potentially powerful competitive advantages are negated if the fledgling practice does not adopt the essentials of a professional services approach to market, such as reputation management.

6. The hybrid offer

A hybrid proposition is usually described as a combination of products and services. The example normally used is fast food services where low margin products are sold through an efficient service delivery system. In fact, the products could not be enjoyed without the service proposition. However, it also exists in complex business markets. Many business-to-business suppliers that have moved from products to services, have launched, for example, system integration projects.

As discussed in Chapter 1, these meet the customer's need by examining the installation of existing equipment and using technical service skills to upgrade it, deploying any new equipment or software as part of the project, even if it belongs to other suppliers. Many firms have taken this further, adopting a sales strategy which focuses on customised 'solutions' projects. These knit together products, services and skills to meet unique needs. They should create value for both the customer and the supplier which is beyond the price of each of the components.

Another type of hybrid exists, however: the service hybrid. This is a combination of scalable service processes and professional skills. The financial adviser in a car dealership has to be skilled in financial management and act as a professional service adviser. However, they rely on clear, scaleable processes to design and deliver their different financial products. Similarly, some technical support services are provided by sophisticated, world-class technical advisers while being based on advanced streamlined processes.

The success of a hybrid relies on the division of front and back office processes, together with a clear idea of the 'perceived transaction time'. Profit for an airline, a fast food chain, a software distributor and an international network support centre relies on the continual improvement of robust processes. The operations of the service must be as streamlined, effective and efficient as any manufacturing plant. Yet the 'front office' needs to cope with the erratic arrival of customers and the need to engage with them. Failure to spend appropriate time with them will damage future revenue growth.

7. Flight from service

A manufacturing firm can take the view that a move into service markets is not appropriate, is too risky or too expensive; several have. One of Japan's leading international product companies, for example, conducted an assessment of the developing service market in Europe as part of its 'twenty year' planning cycle. They formed an experienced team, supported by specialist external consultants, and embarked on an extensive research project. They interviewed customers, competitors and industry specialists before writing a detailed business plan.

However, after this thorough research, the company decided against the move because, primarily, its financial systems could not handle the very different measures needed to manage a service business. Similarly, one of America's leading mobile phone manufacturers set up a high-level project team to assess the service opportunity when several of its competitors first announced significant service investment. It too decided against any serious investment because other product opportunities, such as '3G', represented better return at the time.

If a product company decides not to move into service, the resulting strategy is frequently to focus on high quality, least-cost manufacturing. If the consideration of service has been caused by margin collapse, the company needs to streamline and reduce costs to thrive. It can lead to the outsourcing of functions, movement to cheap labour markets and the sale of businesses.

Although this is a manufacturing strategy, there are still service strategies for the efficient manufacturer to consider. For instance, it must decide whether service is to be supplied by the firm or contracted to others. This may involve outsourcing as much service as possible, perhaps retreating from direct customer contact by using service agents. It must develop a service (as opposed to 'services') strategy.

Unilever experiments with services

In the late 1990s traditional product-based companies were under assault from investors enamoured with the then-seemingly unstoppable advance of the dot.com companies. In this frenzied business environment, share prices in companies such as consumer goods specialist Unilever were slumping – in some cases by as much as 40%.

Yet, there was more to this than the love affair with the 'new economy' technology companies. The market for branded goods was becoming increasingly competitive and cut-throat, as retailers tightened their grips on the supply chain and put downward pressure on margins. A company like Unilever had to find new ways to generate growth and connect consumers with its brands.

It had been laying the groundwork for this for several years. In 1998 it had set up 'Project Foresight', staffed with young managers who were charged with researching potentially lucrative trends that the company could exploit. One of their findings was that consumers would increasingly favour services over products, with cleaning products, for instance, only a means to an end. As a result, Unilever decided to experiment with extending its business beyond manufacturing and into services.

The result was the launch of a pilot project called 'Myhome' in March 2000; a premium cleaning service aimed at the cash-rich/time-poor consumers in an affluent part of London. With an initial investment estimated at about £5 million (including funds for the acquisition of two other home cleaning services), this was not only seen as a way to raise the profile of Unilever cleaning brands, but also to tap into the UK cleaning services market. (That market was then estimated to be worth well over £1 billion and growing strongly.) The business would also give the company first-hand research that would feed back into new product development.

So, Myhome was clearly an experiment from which the company hoped to learn and, perhaps, build a scaleable service business. (It was one of a series of 'pilots' that Unilever was testing at the time, such as Lynx barbershops and Ch'a tea bars.) However it didn't take the company long to realise the skills demanded by this sort of market were very different from its traditional business model.

After all, Unilever has been a product manufacturing company since William Hesketh Lever began to make soap in 1885. It lacked even the service maintenance skills of product firms in other sectors. So, although the front-end marketing and branding of Myhome were excellent, Unilever eventually took the view that it did not have the right competencies to run a service business compared to its manufacturing and marketing activity.

Within eighteen months of the trial, and well before its original deadline of March 2003, it decided to sell the business to a home and fabric cleaning service, Chores, which covered southeast England. This coincided with the end of the dot/com boom, which meant that the pressure on the share prices of traditional companies lessened considerably.

Chores has since expanded the Myhome residential cleaning brand through a network of franchises, backed by a well-established support system from the parent company. Unilever, meanwhile, has returned to focusing on its core skills in brand development, although it has retained a small stake in Myhome to continue to benefit from customer insight.

As the chief executive of Unilever's Myhome Services, David Ball, said at the time of the sale, 'Our stake in Chores means that we will continue to maintain a link with the business and will be able to build on our knowledge of the service sector.'

Service or services: clarifying the service concept

A critical step in deciding the strategic focus of a service business is to clarify the 'service concept' the business is to offer to its buyers. This has been defined as:

> . . . a shared understanding of the nature of the service provided and received, which should encapsulate information about: the organising idea, the service experience, the service outcome, the service operation, the value of the service (Johnston & Clark, 2005).

Although there might be variation in the service for different groups of customers or different levels of contract, the business needs to decide where its competence lies and which form of service maximises those skills to ensure healthy margins. It might focus on high-end, customised professional services or more process-based advisory work; or volume-driven process services; or pure after care. Each of these business types has its own dynamics and success criteria.

The diagram in Figure 2.3 shows, for example, the extent of different service businesses. Professional services range from high-end customised services, at the top left of the diagram (such as some types of strategy consultancy and merchant banking), to the volume retail services of opticians and estate agents in the 'professional service shop'. Volume-based services,

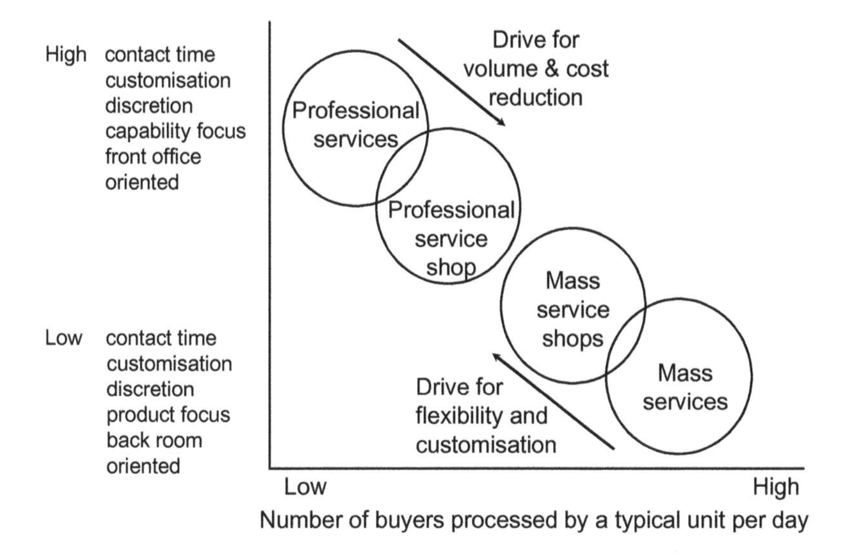

Figure 2.3 The service industry (Source: Johnston & Clark, 2001)

on the other hand, occupy the bottom right hand of the diagram. Many of these are trying to customise their offer a little through data warehousing and customer relationship management systems in order to give their buyers a more individual offer and to improve perceptions of service. They are trying to become 'mass service shops'. The margins, approach to market, degree of engagement with buyers and personnel used, vary enormously between these vastly different offers. Suppliers must be clear of their business model if they are to maximise profit and survive over the long term.

The evolution of concepts offered by the professional services industry demonstrates why it is important for firms to be clear about their position. Professional service concepts evolve through a commoditisation process which affects the nature of the offer. For instance, McKinsey partners usually undertake complex projects to solve unique client problems, working at the extreme upper left of the diagram. However, if their practice meets a problem several times, the type of engagement will be given a name and a new concept is born in the industry. Other suppliers will then take up the offer, creating processes and tools to handle it. It moves down the 'industrialisation' line, picking up volume but losing margin. Eventually the approach becomes commonplace, is captured in software tools, is trained in professional academies and undertaken by clients themselves. It becomes, over years, a professional service commodity.

Offers as diverse as: double entry book keeping, portfolio planning and process reengineering have followed this course; and it is seen throughout the professions today. For instance, several leading firms are currently concerned about the commoditisation of some legal services because expert internal buyers want to cut out, modify or replace parts of the service.

The strategic significance of this to new entrants (particularly product companies entering service markets), is the fact that different offers suit different firms at different stages in their commoditisation journey. A high-end strategy firm like McKinsey might specialise in unique customised approaches and pioneering new concepts, whereas one of the IT-based management consultancies, such as Accenture, might be better suited to more volume, process-based offers. One of the 'big four' accountancy firms, like Deloitte, on the other hand, might legitimise new concepts with the weight of their brand. For all these firms, though, offers which are so commonplace that they can be completely automated are unlikely to yield good margins. Each service business, particularly new entrants, needs a clear view of the concepts which are appropriate to their competence if they are to thrive.

BT finds its 'service concept'

BT is now one of Europe's leading telecommunications companies. Its principal activities include local, national and international telecommunications services, including high value internet services and complex business IT offers. The group's revenues were £18.6 billion in 2005. In the UK, it serves over 20 million business and residential customers with a wide range of communications services including voice, data, internet, multimedia and a range of 'managed and packaged communications solutions'. It also provides network services, as a wholesaler, to other licensed operators.

On the face of it, a service organisation like BT doesn't belong in a book on the transition from products to services. But its experience over the last twenty years is a good illustration of the need to be clear about the service concept of a business. Although its early experience of liberalisation and privatisation has made it one of the global pioneers in competitive telecommunications, it took the company a while to find the most effective direction.

Public sector restrictions

As recently as 1984, British Telecom (as it was then known) was a government department, with all that entailed. For example, prior to privatisation, there was no effective capital appraisal and all money was provided by the Treasury. This meant that, like many of the then government institutions, it was always a low priority for funding. Under a right-wing government issues like defence, police and security were higher priorities. Under a socialist government, on the other hand, issues like health and social benefits came to the fore. (A lot of other government-run businesses like the post office and the utilities also came last in the allocation of government money.)

As a result, by the mid 1980s the majority of BT's infrastructure was under-funded and out of date. For example, throughout its network it was still using the 'Strowger' electro-mechanical exchange for telephone switching (invented by a US undertaker in the 1880s) and much of this equipment was in a poor state of repair or in scarce supply. The British public had to apply to this government body for a telephone, which came in either black or cream. It was hard-wired into the network and, called 'customer equipment', was owned by the government (as were the wires and cables in the 'backbone' network). There was also a three-month waiting list for a new phone while repairs could take over a week and were often poorly done.

In addition, the organisation reflected its history as an engineering-led government department. For instance, while BT had the biggest fleet of vans in Europe after the then-Soviet army, there were few qualified accountants, no appreciable profit and no marketing department to speak of. Also, customers were served in strict order of request. This meant that a low earning residential customer was given exactly the same priority as a high earning business user.

In the run-up to privatisation in 1984, the company embarked on a massive project aimed at separating customer equipment from the backbone network by introducing a socket at the entry into the customer's premises. This, coupled with new legislation, enabled the country to create a competitive market in the supply of telecommunications equipment ranging from single telephones to large scale private switches (bought by companies to handle their internal telephone calls).

Surviving in a new competitive era

Upon privatisation BT, alongside new competitive entrants, started selling communication equipment. The race was on to capture as much of the market as possible before every major buyer had replaced their government rented apparatus with new technology. The company set up an extensive sales and marketing organisation which spent all of its time focusing on selling equipment. This market was vibrant from the time of privatisation to about 1990 and still exists now, although more as a replacement market. As it peaked, however, the company began to wonder what it would earn revenue from. It began to explore the sale of computers and IT equipment because 'clearly the telecommunications market is mature'.

However, there were even bigger and more dramatic changes to come. The British Telecommunications Act of 1984 had included a provision to introduce network competition. This was the first instance of this anywhere in the world and few believed it was viable. While it might now seem strange, most industry experts thought that competitive network telecommunications was an unrealistic aim and unworkable. Telecommunications businesses were thought to be 'natural monopolies' that would not benefit from competition. This proved to be wrong.

After an initial set-up period, two other network competitors began operating in the UK. As they established their networks, BT began to realise that huge network revenues, which had been taken for granted, were now at risk. Managers at the time were heard to say that if they lost the 'dialled revenue' from some of their major customers they may as well have given the equipment away because it affected profits so dramatically. In other words, they had been so focused on revenue from equipment sales that they had neglected the revenue from calls.

Marketing human relationships instead of technological products

Ridiculous as it now sounds, it was only about four years after privatisation that the company accepted that it was in the market of communications (rather than just the sale of telephone handsets) and its service concept was about enabling human communications. The director of advertising at the time, Adrian Hosford (now director of corporate responsibility), oversaw this dramatic change in emphasis. It included the creation of a series of memorable advertisements, some of which have now become part of British culture. Much of the public, for instance, will still recall those with actress Maureen Lipmann starring as 'Beattie' and her 'ologies'. These began to make the process of communication human and had a measurable effect on the amount of telephone calls made in Britain; and therefore increased network revenue for BT.

However, the most dramatic examples were the series of advertisements starring actor Bob Hoskins. These were designed by Hosford's team to exploit a piece of research which showed that men in families were then the 'gatekeepers' of the family's communications by phone, limiting the amount they talked and the amount of time the rest of the family spent on the phone. The campaign included advertisements which showed the positive and negative way a middle-aged man might talk to his elderly mother, and the positive effect of using the phone as part of the full repertoire of human communications in all contexts.

As time went by, competition increased, packages of calls which were unlimited by time were introduced and, of course, the staggering impact of mobile phones on personal communications. All this changed the context of BT's business but not its service concept.

The company continues to use this approach in many of its core programmes: for example, in its Millennium project – Future Talk, which included the Talk Zone at the Millennium Dome and an extensive education programme in schools. Now the theme is used in BT's national advertising and corporate social responsibility projects. If it had simply limited itself to providing products, the business would have been badly damaged, perhaps irreparably. Instead, its business is flourishing. The BT service concept is still about enabling human communication.

Strategy for after care service, the 'service concept' for tied business units

If the primary focus of the service unit is on product support and after care, an explicit service strategy should be developed which emphasises its importance to customers' repurchase intent and sales. It should be based on research and should address several issues.

The first is the style and ambience of service, which should reflect the positioning of the firm (See Chapter 4, pages 115–118). For example, the service style of IBM should be substantially different to those of Unisys or HP and that of Ericsson different to Nokia and Motorola.

The second issue is strategic impact. There are moments in the evolution of a market when quality of service is strategically significant and can enable a supplier to gain real competitive advantage. By creating a new standard of service for the market, the suppliers can improve their profit and share price dramatically. There are several examples of this, such as the two airlines (BA and SAS) quoted in Chapter 1. In their markets, at the time of those programmes, general service standards were very poor. Frequent flyers would move from airline to airline as their dissatisfaction grew and would circle back to their original supplier after time. Interestingly, both the leaders of the two initiatives were new to the industry and brought with them expectations and standards from other businesses. By creating new service standards, they surprised their buyers and retained them.

Another example is the famous British retail store Marks and Spencer. In the mid-twentieth century, a time when consumer spending power in Britain was just beginning to increase, they met one of the emotional needs of their buyers (fear of product failure and dislike of product returns) with a money-back guarantee. This meant that consumers were happy to buy and felt a warmth and loyalty to the company which underpinned their profits for many years to come. IBM met a similar emotional need with business buyers in the early computer market by offering leasing deals. This made it easy and low risk for buyers to invest in the new technology, enabling IBM to become global market leader for many decades.

However, all of these companies (BA, SAS, M&S and IBM) have been through real business difficulty at moments since their famous quality initiatives. This suggests that the immense gains from their exploitation of the strategic significance of their service were dissipated by later management teams who failed to institutionalise service improvements; even if they have since recovered.

A current example of strategically significant service gains are those suppliers creating new service offers using self-service technology. Those companies (like airlines introducing self-service check in or supermarkets introducing self-service bar coding) who do this, capture a new position in the market. They provide better quality for the frequent user at less cost and dominate segments of experienced buyers.

The third issue is the adjustment of the features of the core service in order to meet changed buyer values. (See 'Features analysis and the core service', Chapter 5, pages 151–159.) The firm should know those values which are important to customers and how they match its competencies. It should also know customers' views of competitor services; their strengths or weaknesses. These should be integrated into a view of how the human, technical and process components of the service need to be changed over time.

The service strategy also ought to address: resources, measurement and service recovery policy. So, the final format should include:

Format of a service support strategy

- Strategic context, the role of after care and service quality in business success.
- Summary of relevant buyer research and market insights (including views of service attributes contrasted to competitor services).
- Service style.
- Improvement or change programmes.
- Marketing communications on service issues.
- Resources.
- Measurement.
- Service recovery policy and practice.

Methods of determining the strategic focus of service businesses

There are several concepts and tools which have been developed by strategy specialists to help leaders, whether in charge of one service business or responsible for a large business with multiple service units. Each can be found in a good corporate strategy book and applied relatively easily. They are also, probably, interchangeable. Of overriding importance, though, is the achievement of clarity. Whether leaders use the 'experience curve', or a 'mission statement' or a 'statement of strategic intent', there comes a time when the developing business needs clarity to thrive. It is more important to create a sense of mission than, for example, to create a neatly composed, bland 'mission statement'.

Hamel and Prahalad (1989) themselves observed several common components in their researches. Good strategic focus:

- captures the essence of winning;
- is stable over time;
- creates a sense of urgency;
- develops competitor focus at every level through widespread use of competitive intelligence;
- provides employees with the skills needed to work effectively;
- gives the organisation time to digest one challenge before launching another;
- establishes clear milestones and review mechanisms.

Probably the most useful and well worked conceptual tool is the 'experience curve' referred to earlier in this chapter. This concept, pioneered by the Boston Consulting Group during the early 1960s, suggests that, in the area of its prime focus, the unit costs of a firm fall with experience of operating in an industry and with cumulative volume of production. The consultancy invested in substantial research in many different industries (including service industries) and used 'the scientific method' to validate the concept. Although appearing deceptively simple, and intuitively right, the concept is used to set cost targets, based on a projection of the curve for each business.

Costs decline due to a combination of economies of scale, the learning curve of the company, process improvement and the substitution of technology for people. This, in turn, gives competitive advantage because new competitors face higher costs if not entering with a major innovative advantage. Some have argued that the advantage is so great that established leaders should gain further advantage through price-cutting.

So a manufacturer moving into a service market should identify the prime operations of the proposed business and centre management's attention on gaining productivity in that area. This will consolidate its position in the market. Targets for future cost gains can be set by projecting the developing experience curve. The leaders should also be clear about the 'experience' and cost base of established competitors and how the new business will gain a foothold against their existing advantages.

Other concepts which could be used include:

- 'Business mission': creating one simple statement of what the business is about.
- 'Business vision': used best in an environment where change is needed, this creates a scenario of where the business is headed in order to engage all in the change process.
- The 'core competence': similar to the thinking behind the experience curve, this causes the business to concentrate on the one major function in which it excels. It is particularly useful for businesses that have grown in an opportunistic and haphazard way. The concept forces them to focus on what they do best. Properly facilitated, it normally enables the business to create new services as it applies its business competence in an open minded way. Experience shows, though, that it is enormously difficult to get managers to abandon those services which are not core, even if they are causing distraction, draining resources or increasing costs.
- The 'service value chain': based on research by Heskeett, Sasser and Schlesinger, the value chain identifies all aspects of a service company that contribute to earnings and growth. Properly used, it can improve profitability by focussing employees on the main functions of the business and discarding extraneous activities. It can be made relevant to employees at different levels in the organisation using the 'balanced score card' process.

Purists would argue (probably correctly) that each of these has complexity and has different functions in a firm. Some would suggest that a large business developing a well-rounded strategy should cover them all. For the busy business leader, though, any one can be used as a banner to rally the business around one clear purpose. In tightening markets this, in itself, will improve performance.

By contrast, leaders of large corporate businesses needing to improve the performance of a jumble of different service businesses will probably find the 'portfolio planning' tools are the most useful to them. The most famous of these is the 'Boston matrix' (shown in Figure 2.4) which was developed, by the Boston Consulting Group, around the experience curve concept. A business might be at various points on the experience curve, depending on its maturity and the accumulated investment in its prime area of focus. The matrix, which plots relative market share against relative growth, was an attempt to give business leaders a way of evaluating the success of different business units in different markets at different stages of development.

Businesses which have low market share in high growth markets are 'question-marks' because, as they have just started operations, the ability of the management team to improve their business competence and gain cost advantage is unproven. They have long-term potential and are being bought primarily by buyers who are willing to experiment. They need large amounts of cash if they are to be developed to their full potential because the company has to keep adding technology and people to keep up with the fast-growing market.

A 'rising star', on the other hand, is a company that has established itself in the market and is beginning to thrive. It is a leader, with high share in

Market growth	Relative market share: High	Relative market share: Low
High	'Star' • Defend leadership • Accept moderate short-term profit and negative cash flow • Consider geographic expansion • Consider line expansion • Aggressive marketing posture • Price for market share	'Question mark' • Invest heavily in selective businesses • As for 'rising star'
Low	'Cash cow' • Maintain market position • Cut less successful lines • Differentiate to maintain share of key segments • Limit discretionary marketing expenditure	'Dog' • Prune aggressively • Maximise cash flow • Minimise marketing expenditure • Maintain or raise prices at the expense of volume

Figure 2.4 The 'Boston matrix'

a high growth market. However, it requires significant investment in order to maintain or grow market share and does not necessarily yield a positive cash-flow. Stars are usually profitable, though, and can become 'cash cows'.

'Cash cows' are companies that are well established and profitable. They have high share in low growth markets. They are producing profit but unlikely to achieve any exciting or dramatic improvements. They are normally cash positive and can be used to fund other initiatives. Whereas the final group, known as 'dogs', have low share in low growth markets. These are companies who will decline and should, ultimately, be sold or closed. They are loss-makers, providing small amounts of cash if any.

The matrix can be used to develop different business strategies for each business unit. Objectives, profit targets, investment constraints and even management style are likely to be different according to their position. A multi-business company can use the analysis to create a balanced 'portfolio' of businesses, each having clarity about their role and success criteria.

Worrying for aspirant service firms, though, is the fact that the tool is based on the two axes of growth and market share which are not always the primary success criteria of a service business. An alternative portfolio technique is the directional policy matrix. It was developed by McKinsey for its client General Electric in the 1970s and is shown in Figure 2.5. Launched

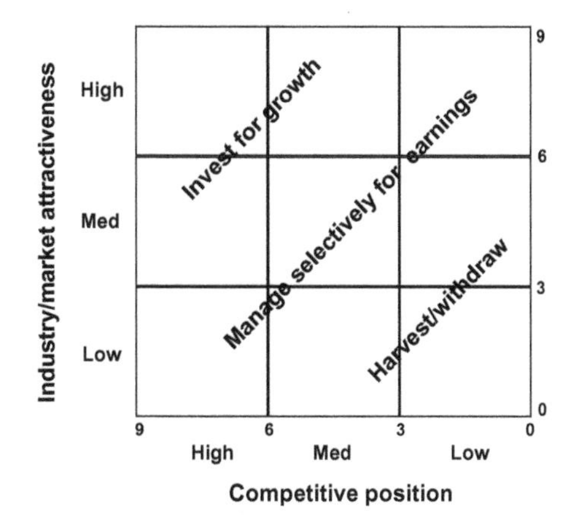

Figure 2.5 The directional policy matrix

Table 2.1 *Factors of market attractiveness and business strength used in the original GE matrix*

Market attractiveness	Business strength
Size	Size
Growth rates	Growth rate
Competitive intensity	Market share
Profitability	Profitability
Technology impacts	Margins
Social impacts	Technology position
Environnemental impacts	Strengths and weaknesses
Legal impacts	Image
Human impacts	Environmental impact
	Management

soon after the Boston matrix as a result of the inadequacies with it, it is a way of categorising businesses against markets and is more flexible than the Boston matrix because it uses criteria created by the management team themselves. It also creates a healthy and enjoyable debate among leaders of the firm about their market and business strategies. As such it is more relevant to the individual strategic position of a service business in its market place. The grid plots 'market attractiveness' against 'business strength' and allows management to prioritise resources accordingly.

The power of this technique lies in the ability of the management team to create their own criteria for the attractiveness of a market and the strength of a business. The original GE matrix used the factors which are listed in Table 2.1 because the GE management team believed that, taken together, they had the most influence on return on investment. However, this list should be modified for each company according to its own particular circumstances and the judgement of its own leaders.

Strategy for each business can be deduced from its position on the matrix. For instance, where a business unit scores high or medium on business strength or market attractiveness the firm should maintain or grow investment, whereas those businesses that score low/low or low/medium should be cut back. If possible, cash should be harvested from them. Units scoring high/low or medium/medium should be examined to see if selective investment can increase earnings.

This is a really powerful way to reach consensus among a group of business leaders about the strategic intent and investment levels needed for each

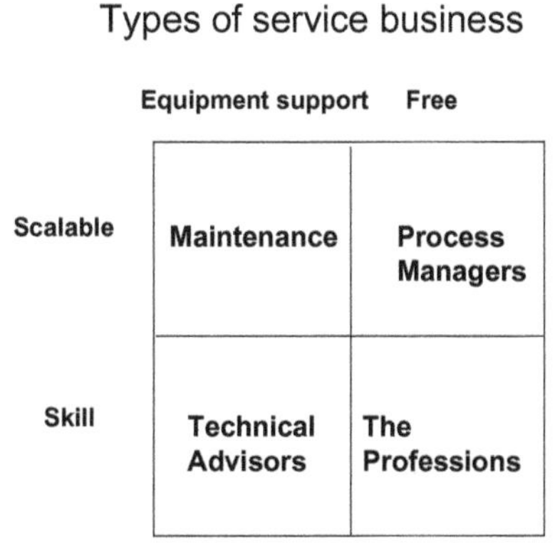

Figure 2.6 Using the forces of service success to clarify the shape of service businesses

business. The definition of business units, the agreement of common criteria and, particularly, the joint scoring exercise stimulate debate which is very valuable. Experience suggests that it is therefore a tool which is very relevant to firms with multiple service businesses.

One final method of shaping a range of service businesses is based on the dynamics of different service offers. Are they supporting equipment or not? Are they scalable, process-based, services or high-margin professional services? A representation of these different forces, which is an adaptation of a proposal by McKinsey (see Auguste, Harmon and Pandit, 2006), is shown in Figure 2.6. Debate among the leaders of a firm about where each service unit fits on these axes of different success criteria will produce clarity of purpose.

Summary

In response to the forces outlined in Chapter 1, businesses in many different parts of the developed economies have created service offers. These range from maintenance and process-based support, through systems integration and 'solution sales' to high end professional service or financial offers. They are frequently more profitable for the companies that initiate them than the commoditised products that they produce. Some of these service businesses are created by well funded programmes, at the request of top business leaders. But many are not.

Product companies moving into service business often fail to understand the different success criteria or purpose of different service initiatives. As a result, newcomers to the service economy often struggle to make real returns once markets tighten or efficient competition arrives. At some stage, then (and despite modern scepticism of strategic tools or analytical approaches), the firm should clarify the strategic intent of its service businesses; either investing in or withdrawing from opportunities.

3

The degree of change needed to set up a service business

Introduction and overview

A move from product manufacturing to service provision is a profound change for most businesses. Yet the degree of change depends on the extent of the move and the type of service business adopted. Some merely seek to supplement declining product revenues, while others offer their long-standing product offer through a service experience and still others move so far into services that they drop products altogether. So how different are service businesses and what parts of a product company need to change if it is to succeed in this different form of business?

Change management techniques have been explored, researched and published by numerous management specialists. Yet those companies which have successfully moved into service have, in reality, adopted a range of approaches, from the hidden, gradual encroachment of the 'skunk works' to the dramatic gesture of a major acquisition. These methods and their necessity are explored in this chapter.

Just how different is service business?

A significant strategic consideration for a manufacturer moving into service is how different the proposed service business is from the firm's established modus operandi. The word service itself implies a difference, referring to personal support for others. As Professor Levitt pointed out:

> The concept of 'service' evokes, from the opaque recesses of the mind, time worn images of personal ministration and attendance. It refers generally to deeds one individual performs personally for another. It carries historical connotations of charity, gallantry, and selflessness, or of obedience, subordination and subjugation (Levitt, 1972).

So the culture of a service environment is assumed to be very different to manufacturing where the focus is on efficient production, not attendance on people. In some cases, the difference is dramatic and obvious. A manufacturer trying to move into a strategic consultancy market similar to, say, McKinsey's, would soon become aware of how completely different the business dynamics are. For instance, the main 'unit of production' would then be the skill and experience of its people; highly trained and educated world-class specialists with all the benefits and drawbacks that come with managing such individualistic prima donnas. In other areas it's not so clear. The streamlined, technology-based operation of an internet service is, for example, similar to software manufacturing and distribution. In fact, the similarity has drawn several software specialists into this business.

In the past, there was an assumption that the hierarchical, systematic business practices which were commonplace (such as automation and closely supervised work broken down into small components) should be applied to service businesses. Theodore Levitt, for example, lauded the 'industrialisation' of service (Levitt, 1976). He argued for the application of the manufacturing style of thinking to 'people-intensive offers'. He pointed out that rail services, among others, have tried to adopt the 'replicable, systematic and reliable process management recognised by manufacturers'. He argued that a large manufacturing organisation has many people employed in it who perform similar functions to large service organisations. In other words, 'everybody is in service' and many elements of service delivery are very similar to that of manufactured products.

Although modern thinking about service business is predominantly different to this view, the approach still applies to much self service and service automation being pioneered today. A business which offers customers an infrastructure on which to perform tasks must be as accessible, reliable and easy to use as manufacturers' systems. Its quality perception is built on dependability and its economics on the efficiency of, technology dependent, processes.

Yet most people who have tried to run both take the view that service businesses are very different from product manufacturing. Typical, for instance, is Louis V. Gerstner, IBM's CEO during the 1990s. In his book *Who Says Elephants Can't Dance? Inside IBM's historic turnaround* he says:

> . . . I have worked in service companies (McKinsey and American Express) and product companies (RJR Nabisco and IBM). I will state unequivocally that service businesses are much more difficult to manage. In services you don't make a product and then sell it. You sell capability. You sell knowledge. You create it at the same time you deliver it. The business is different. The economics are entirely different (Gerstner, 2002).

So experience suggests that the methods to create, run, communicate and grow a service business are different from those used to handle a product business. But exactly how different and how can these differences be planned into the project to set up any new business model? The major differences reported by managers working in the field and by researchers who have studied it are:

1. Services are intangible

Pure services are intangible. They have no physical presence and cannot be experienced or detected by the five senses, so it is not possible to taste, feel, see, hear or smell them. As a result, they are communicated, sold and bought in the customer's imagination.

The ground-breaking article on this subject was written by a manager in a leading service firm, G. Lynn Shostack (Shostack, 1977). She was then vice president of Citibank and said:

> It is wrong to imply that services are just like products except for intangibility. By such logic, apples are just like oranges except for their 'appleness'. Intangibility is not a modifier; it is a state. Intangibles may come with tangible wrappings but no amount of money can buy physical ownership of . . . experience . . . time . . . or process. Tangible means palpable and material. Intangible is . . . impalpable and not corporeal. This distinction has profound implications.

The intangibility of services affects much of a service business, distinguishing it from manufacturing. A product company will have to change packaging, sales, branding and communication if it wants to move successfully into it. For instance, many people find it hard to imagine something before it is placed in front of them. They need to see it and touch it to understand it. When these people are potential customers of a service business they need help if they are to understand and grasp the offer. They will seek the opinion of people they respect before purchase and will buy again only if their initial experience of the service is good. So the reputation of the service, the quality of the experience, the ability to offer free trials and the appeal of the packaging are all very important. The supplier needs to make its intangible service seem both tangible and testable.

Also, as there is no product, salespeople cannot emphasise its 'benefits' but must communicate the experience and outcome of the service process. The selling of service must therefore be very different from products. In fact, if the routine closing techniques of product sales are used to clinch service deals, due to intangibility, the buyers tend to feel coerced or cheated and, as a result, might challenge the price or have second thoughts. In fact, the deal can unravel altogether.

Moreover, the intangibility of services exaggerates the effect of a phenomenon called 'post-purchase distress'. This is experienced if the purchase of any item, product or service, is emotionally challenging or expensive. Worry or anxiety, caused by a large or important purchase, is often allayed by the buyer admiring the purchased product or showing it to others. However, as services are intangible, there is nothing to offset this anxiety. Business buyers may be concerned about the effect on their budgets, the effort to justify the item to others, damage to their credibility or risk to their political capital. Also, this anxiety is increased if the supplier is operating in unfamiliar territory. The person who buys a service from a product company, however well known and long established, may become anxious due more to the risk of using a familiar supplier in unfamiliar circumstances. If this anxiety is not managed, then problems occur.

As a result, methods of summarising the emotional relief of a well executed project have evolved in many service markets. For instance, the 'tombstones' routinely created and distributed after mergers or acquisitions embody the achievement of a well-completed, possibly worrisome, project. They are a tangible representation of the deal and a small example of attempts by suppliers to make the intangible tangible, relieving 'post purchase distress'.

Finally, as it is often not possible to patent intangible services, suppliers have to find other mechanisms to protect their investment. Failure to do so will mean that the offer will commoditise quickly and markets will be dominated by price wars. Successful service companies therefore create powerful brands, like Virgin or Wal-Mart, which cannot be copied. Product companies that are not skilful at brand creation and management, like many in the IT industry, have damaged their business by moving into service with very little means of maintaining differentiation.

2. The variability (or heterogeneity) of services

Once a product has been designed and the manufacturing process set up, it will be produced time and again by a factory with little variation. Customers know what they are buying and it is consistently delivered. Any aberrations in product quality tend to be few and easily (or relatively easily!) driven out by quality control and improvement processes.

Services, though, are rarely as consistently produced as manufactured products. Even those service businesses that try to industrialise their offer through efficient and robust processes find it hard to deliver reliable, consistent service. For instance, one of the essential components of many services is the people who serve customers. But people tend to think for themselves, adjusting behaviours and outcomes to suit unique circumstances. Moreover, in some circumstances, customers are involved in the process of service production. As people (whether they are the supplier's employees or the customers) take initiative and change or customise the service, it is unusual for one service experience to be identical to another.

This has implications to strategy, financial controls, management, human resource processes and operations. For instance, people need to be given clear guidelines on how much they can vary the service. Some businesses want little variation and give their employees little discretion. Others, 'mass service shops' like Burger King, for example, see competitive advantage in allowing a degree of customisation but are aware that too much will damage the economics of their business. Operations planners therefore need to design processes which streamline as much as possible but allow people to vary delivery and anticipate failures. At the same time, the firm's marketing team need to work to set expectations and communicate the quality that customers might expect because they are unable to judge the likely quality in advance.

3. The 'simultaneous consumption' of services

A product can be manufactured and stored or passed through a distribution system until it is bought. Once bought, it can then be stored by the customer and used at a later date. By far the majority of services, however, have to be used as they are created. They cannot be stored by either the supplier or buyer. As Donald Cowell said as long ago as 1984: 'Goods are produced, sold and consumed whereas services are sold and then produced and consumed' (Cowell, 1984).

In order to deliver, though, resources must be prepared and deployed ready for erratic demand. A maintenance service, for instance, must have computer systems able to receive fault reports, trained technicians with appropriate tools able to tackle faults, and carefully calculated caches of spare parts. A merchant bank, on the other hand, must have centres of expertise in various parts of the world, with knowledge of industries and deep client contacts, plus links to specialist contractors (ranging from lawyers and accountants to secure printers) able to engage in demanding projects at short notice. Moreover, much of this investment can be unseen by the customer before, during or after the service experience. This means that service companies need to develop techniques which communicate the value of this stored investment.

As the service is produced while the buyer uses it, the customer is 'in the factory', able to see the production process and unable to see the finished result. This has implications to service operations and the service environment because the production process must be well prepared and tested, able to host customers and engage them professionally without causing anxiety due to poor planning. In fact, one mistake made by many product companies moving into service is their failure to sufficiently plan or design the process through which their customers will move.

Simultaneous consumption also affects sales and marketing because the firm must manage expectations. It must explain the key steps in the service process and any tasks that the customer must undertake. Finally, it has implications to quality management because recovery must happen in real time. Quality processes cannot be the same as manufacturers' post production sampling and correction because any error will be immediately experienced by the customer.

4. In the customer's mind it is difficult to separate services from the people who provide them

Credible academic researchers (see, for instance, Zeithaml & Bitner, 2003) suggest that, in the customer's mind, most services cannot be separated from the person they encounter when they buy and use them. So people are not only important to the design and management of a service, they are part of the service itself. Their motivation, behaviour and appearance are part of the benefit package offered to customers. In many ways they are an essential element in the value that customers seek, part of the bought service, and their behaviour affects the customers' perceptions of price and quality. They are so intimately involved in delivering the service experience that their body language and appearance will communicate messages to the customers as much as their words or the firm's marketing claims.

So, at the front line of interaction with the customers, a firm's employees must embody its intentions and, as a result, the appropriate treatment of employees is very important to service businesses. If employees of a production company are treated as mechanised 'units of production' their dehumanised boredom or dissatisfaction will not be passed on to the buyers. But in a service business it will. If their leaders treat them badly then it will be communicated, even if they try to be professional and disguise their unease. Conversely, if they are treated like human beings there is a strong chance that the customers will be too.

Managing employee behaviour in line with changing customer expectations is therefore a major focus and challenge for service businesses. Good service managers understand that front line people can cause customers to turn to or turn away from a service. Many put real effort, investment and resources into programmes designed to raise the impressions caused by their people. In fact, it is probably no exaggeration to say that service companies invest in this 'intangible asset' the way manufacturers invest in tangible assets.

5. Services are perishable

Generally services cannot be stored or saved for other occasions. Once an empty airline seat has flown over the ocean or a hotel room remained vacant for a night, the service is passed. The moment cannot be recaptured. As a result, the demand forecasting of a service business has to be more accurate than a product company that can store excess items in a factory until they are used. Maximum capacity must be carefully calculated, balancing the highest anticipated demand against the cost of investment. Also, service businesses must use pricing programmes to affect demand in the days before the service happens. As a result, airlines offer a bewildering array of fare options and hotels give special rates for conferences, weekend vacations and frequent users.

As services are time bound, the management of time, through operations, is an important task of a service business. In fact, one researcher (see Ruskin Brown, 2005) suggests that there are several 'flavours of time' that service managers need to consider: punctuality, duration, availability, speed of response and speed of innovation. Of these, 'punctuality' or 'reliability', in the sense of delivering the service when promised, has been shown in many studies to be one of the most important factors in the way customers judge the operational quality of a service.

6. The fact that ownership of a service does not pass to the buyer

When people buy a product, ownership of it passes to them. They can store it, use it or give it away. That does not often occur with service though. The people who are part of a training or consultancy service cannot be purchased or owned by the buyer. Nor are restaurants, airline seats or taxis bought; they are rented for a moment in time as part of the service. Payment is for use, access or hire of items. People will talk as if there is a sense of ownership ('my flight', 'my pension' or 'our training') yet there is not the same sense of possession as with a product purchase.

As a result, the service firm has to dramatise the moment of contract and find mechanisms to emphasise value as the service progresses. Unless this is tackled by a product company moving into service they will struggle continually with price pressure. The lack of ownership will cause buyers to question value and price. They will look for greater added value or ask for price reductions.

7. The existence of the service process

One of the major differences between the purchase of a product and the experience of a service is the process through which the buyer moves. Products are entities which are bought through a process but are independent of it. When someone buys one, they are in control of it and can do whatever they like with it. They can use it, break it, give it away, or ignore the instructions. However, services have a process inherent in their design through which the customer must pass. So when people use a service they must submit themselves to the service provider's process.

One of the world's leading researchers in this field, Finland's Christian Grönroos, has put great emphasis on the importance of the service process (see Grönroos, 2003). For him, services *are* processes. He says: 'Services are processes consisting of activities or a series of activities rather than things.' He goes on to suggest that this has profound implications to service management, customer relationships, operations, quality functions and marketing:

> In order to understand service management and the marketing of services it is critical that one realises that the consumption of a service is process consumption rather than outcome consumption. The consumer perceives the service process (or production process) as part of the service consumption, not simply the outcome of that process, as in traditional marketing of physical goods . . . the consumption process leads to an outcome for the customer, which is the result of the service process. Thus, the consumption of the service process is a critical part of the service experience.

A product company moving into services must plan the service process in detail and educate its customers in the parts of the service they will experience. It must organise itself to deliver satisfactory experiences for customers as they use the service. This frequently involves adopting a process, rather than a functional, organisational structure, so that all employees focus on quality of delivery. Eventually this can lead to conflict between a growing service business in a large product company and other functions. Its need to chart its user's experiences causes it to take a longer-term, relationship approach to customers, challenging any erratic or short-term behaviour, such as the sale of inappropriate products to achieve quarterly sales targets. The journey into service has, for some firms, ended in a complete reorganisation which recognises that everyone is involved in service and value delivery to the customer.

8. The phenomenon of control

When a customer buys a product, they normally have complete control as to when and how to use it. They might keep it, use it immediately or give it to someone else. They even have the choice as to whether to comply with the manufacturer's instructions or not. When they buy services, though, they do not have such choice and freedom. They must surrender themselves to the service delivery process which the supplier has designed for them. In doing this they cede control of themselves to the service provider. And human beings hate being out of control. The purchase and use of a service therefore invades their personal space and raises emotional issues which service suppliers must learn to tackle (see Bateson, 1999 and 1985).

This lack of control means that new customers must be reassured by mechanisms such as helpful people, a familiar brand or a clear, well sign-posted service process. Many of the well known customer service and after care techniques must be used to allay fears and criticisms arising from this underlying emotion of lack of control. However, if customers use the service repeatedly they assert an unconscious need to regain control. They try to cut corners, look to serve themselves and get irritated if the process is inflexible. In fact they can become annoyed with the simple, clear steps that they first found so enticing.

Service for the experienced user is therefore very different to that for the new customer. It must be a streamlined club, similar to frequent flyer programmes, which allows as much self service as possible. This has profound implications to service design, operations, process management, marketing and technology deployment which product companies must consider if they are to move effectively into services. In fact, in some markets, the arrival of a supplier offering, for the first time, a service designed for the experienced user has had major strategic impact.

9. The service environment

For many services the environment in which they are experienced by customers is an important component. The design and ambience of a restaurant and the layout and style of an airline cabin set expectations of quality and value. Retailers, hoteliers and managers of holiday resorts are just a few of the service businesses who have to think carefully about the physical setting of their service. It affects the behaviour of employees, sets the expectations of buyers and can be a source of differentiation.

There is a wealth of research on the affect of the physical setting on the health of a service business. A complex and sophisticated process is involved in creating a new one because the supplier must take into account and balance a range of factors including: 'sight appeals', 'size perception', shape, colour, sound, scent, spatial layout, flexibility, brand and signs or symbols. It must also calculate operational factors such as capacity, crowding and queuing. In fact, some businesses use the complex statistical techniques of queuing theory (that are used to design sophisticated communications and computer equipment) on the flow of people through their premises. Yet they also have to allow for subtle cultural preferences which influence a range of ambient and behavioural factors.

For those services where the physical setting is important, these complex considerations are unavoidable because they affect buying behaviour. Credible experiments have demonstrated the affect of these different factors on sales. People buy more, for instance, if different music is played, if different colours are used and even if different smells are deployed. A manufacturer moving into service must therefore consider the affect of any physical setting on the success of the proposed business. This will involve operations, sales, human resource management, marketing and design.

Some services, though, are experienced in more subtle and flexible environments: the virtual vagaries of the internet or the customers' imaginations. Yet, just as in a real, physical environment, impressions need to be created which set expectations of value. This needs careful design and marketing if it is going to influence sales and price perceptions.

10. Services are performed

Services tend to occur at a moment in time and involve the attention of one person on another. Many are 'performed', not produced. Moreover, the style of the performance influences the price that can be charged and the degree of customer satisfaction. From representation in negotiation, to service at the restaurant table, people perform a service for others and the style of performance affects the customers' views of both quality and value. As a result, the service industry puts great emphasis on the 'service encounter'; that 'moment of truth' when the supplier's employees interact with the buyers. It is a moment when the firm has a chance to impress and deepen a relationship with a buyer, in addition to delivering the promised benefits.

Understanding and planning the degree of change

Not all services will have elements of all these differences to the same degree, nor will they all be faced by companies moving into service businesses. For example, while some services are completely intangible, others rely on a tangible product (e.g. telephone services or car maintenance) while others (such as retailing) make a tangible product available. Also, a number of products (such as food and fresh flowers) are as time bound as services and lost if the opportunity to sell them passes. So product companies in those categories will be equipped for this aspect of service business.

These shades of grey in the differences between product and service offers affect the degree of change that a product company entering a service business needs to tackle. In self service businesses, for example, there will be less reason to manage and motivate front line people, whereas in a business consultancy there will be little emphasis on a service environment. A software supplier might find it relatively easy to move into the former and a business-to-business supplier easier to move into the latter. A detailed understanding of the elements of the different service businesses and their similarity to an existing product business makes the transition easier to plan.

There are two practical ways in which managers can understand the different nature of a proposed service business so that they can structure their thinking and plan the degree of change. The first uses a concept called 'service categorisation'.

Academics have argued that, whenever comparisons between services and physical goods are made, the comparisons must be appropriate, comparing like with like. For instance, a service aimed at a mass market should be compared with a mass market product business and a highly customised business-to-business service compared to tailored business products. A number of different ways of categorising services have been suggested. Each will give useful insight into the dynamics of a proposed service business. They are:

- **Customised services versus industrialised services.** The margins, approach to market, degree of engagement with buyers and personnel used, vary enormously between these two types of offers.
- **Infrastructure-based services versus added value services.** Some services are based on an infrastructure, a technology or a network. They include water supply, computer 'platforms' in major companies, telecommunications networks, networks of airline slots or sets of maintenance contacts. The issues, development and degree of reliance on that infrastructure affect the nature and the content of those services. Very often there is a core service ('communications' in telecommunication companies, 'support' in computer maintenance companies and 'power supply' in utilities) and opportunities for added value services, as illustrated in Figure 3.1.
- **Product-based services versus free services.** Some services are adjuncts to product propositions and are therefore intimately tied to the value,

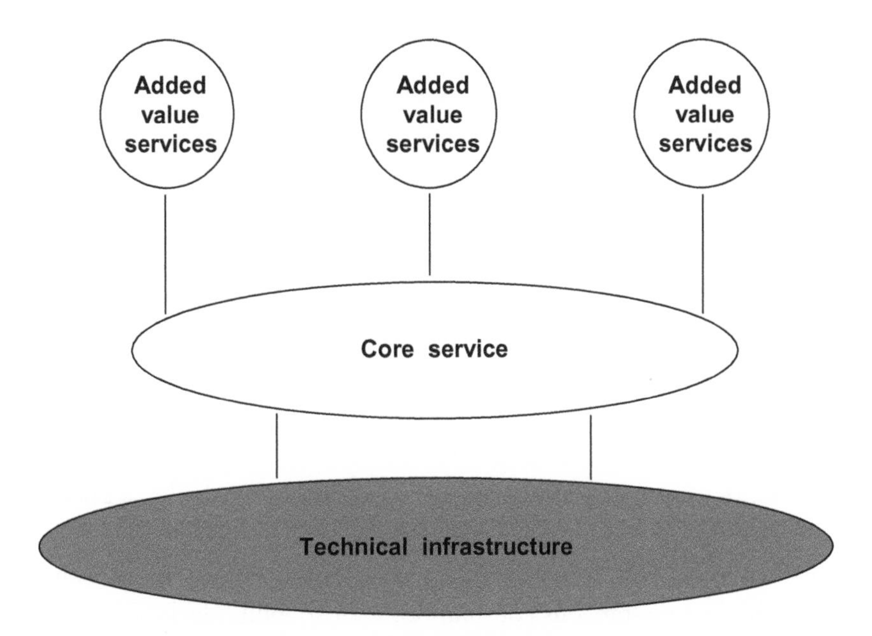

Figure 3.1 Infrastructure services and added value services

development and pricing of that product. Other services are unique propositions in their own right which stand alone in the market place.

- **Discrete (project) services versus continuously rendered (annuity) services.** Some services, such as consultancy, are one-off discrete projects whereas others, like financial audit, are recurring contractual relationships. This difference affects pricing, customer relationship techniques, margins and business structures.
- **Technology-based services versus people-based services (high tech versus high touch).** Some services (extranets for business buyers, for example) comprise technology through which customers are served. Other services are predominantly reliant on the skills of people. In some cases, the difference is based simply around the buyers' preferences. In others it is linked to market evolution. A supplier in a market where service by people is the norm might introduce a technological innovation whereby customers can undertake some work themselves.
- **Self-service versus performed service.** Some services are performed on behalf of a buyer, whereas others provide the means by which they can perform the service themselves.
- **A membership relationship versus anonymity.** This classification suggests differences according to the relationship of the buyer to the supplier. Membership may range from formal paid-for inclusion in a club to an emotional attachment to the group or community at whom the service is targeted. However, in some circumstances, buyers prefer anonymity or simple functionality and resist suppliers' attempts to form an intrusive relationship.
- **Transactional versus interaction services.** Some services are short term 'transactions'. They are often low value and commoditised purchases. 'Inter-actions', though (a relatively new definition), are higher value, mutually profitable exchanges between a customer and a supplier over a long term.

Figure 3.2 demonstrates how managers can think through the applicability of the generic differences between products and services to each type of service business they propose to move into. A 'self service' is, for example, 'very high' on simultaneous consumption, perishability, lack of ownership,

	A self service				A professional service			
Intangible			High					Very high
Variability	Very low							Very high
Simultaneous consumption				Very high			High	
People significance	Very low							Very high
Perishable				Very high				Very high
Ownership does not pass				Very high				Very high
Significance of service process				Very high		Low		
Control issues	Very low						High	
The service environment				Very high	Very low			
Service performance	Very low						High	

Figure 3.2 Thinking through the differences in a proposed service business

process and environment. A professional service, on the other hand, is stronger on people contribution and weaker on the significance of a service process. Having thought through the content of the proposed service business, the management team can then compare it to its own business, or business units, and identify the specific areas where major change is necessary.

The second method is to use the nature of the prime offer of the new service business to understand the degree of transition. The proposition of the firm can be service dominant with product elements or product dominant with service elements; and various propositions put to the market can be categorised at a point on a continuum between these two extremes. Lynne Shostack created the, now famous, diagram in Figure 3.3 to illustrate this (Shostack, 1977). A service designed to support a product, towards the left of the diagram, will be very different to a 'hybrid' in the centre or a pure service at the extreme right.

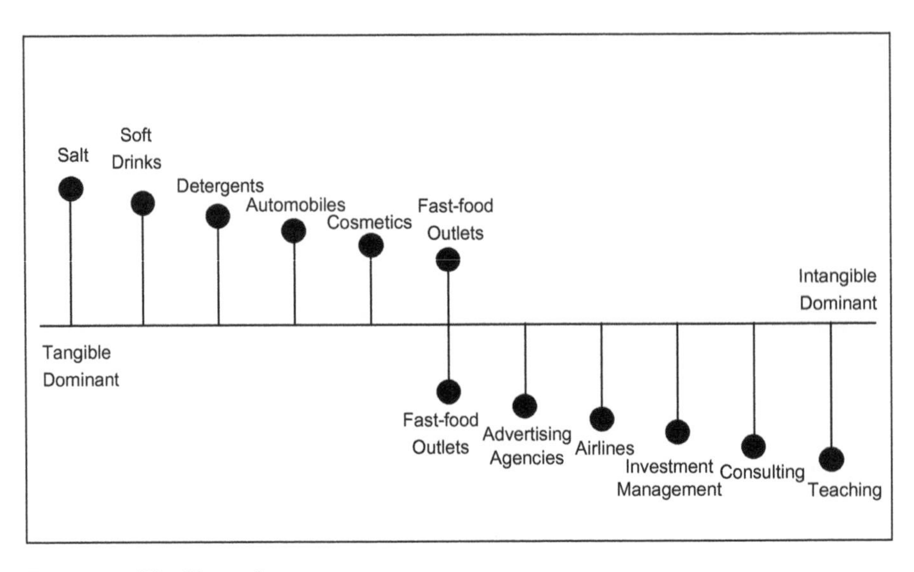

Figure 3.3 The Shostack continuum
Source: Shostack, 1977. Reproduced from G.L. Shostack, Breaking free from product marketing, Journal of Marketing, with permission of American Marketing Association.

What needs to change when a company moves into service?

As there can be so many differences between service and product businesses a wide range of functions of the firm are likely to change when a product company moves into service. They are examined in later chapters of this book and include:

Operations strategy and management

The operations of a product company will have to change as it moves into services. The nature of production, the environment of the offer and the determinants of productivity are likely to be different.

Management of people and attitudes to 'human capital'

If the proposed service involves people who will interact with buyers, they will need to be led, managed and coached carefully. They will be 'human capital': resources which produce value. The culture of any product firm will need to change so that it values these people and motivates them accordingly.

Sales

Service selling is different from product selling and few but really talented sales people can make the transition from one to the other. Moreover, a vast number of service businesses are professional services, built around knowledge and experience. The income generation in professional practices is completely different to product sales, involving the leaders of the service in such a personal way as to deny a role for separate dedicated sales people.

Brand strategy and management

A product company can create stand alone product brands in many different markets which are unrelated to its company name, reputation or corporate brand. A service company, however, needs to position its corporate brand in the markets it wishes to dominate. So brand strategy is very different for a product company moving into a service market.

Financial management and pricing

While a number of elements of financial management are similar, there are often very different financial dynamics between product and service businesses. A service company will, for example, tend to have more intangible than tangible assets and it will frequently have to treat the contribution and costs of people differently to a product company. A product company moving into a service market might well have to change its financial systems to cope with these different dynamics.

Marketing

Service marketing is different from product marketing. Not only are market dynamics different, the successful marketing of service offers has a different emphasis ('demand pull' rather than 'product push') and different techniques (thought leadership, relationship management, networking, etc). The marketing profession has missed much of this because it has been obsessed with fast moving consumer goods (FMCG) and the vast revenues that advertising agencies can earn from them. Even though, in practice, if FMCG techniques are used to market services they often fail.

IBM develops its service strategy

Twenty years ago the proportion of IBM's business categorised as 'services' as opposed to products was an estimated 5 %. Ten years later, it rose to roughly 15 % and now services account for well over half of revenues. In fact, IBM Global Services is now the world's largest business and technology services business.

The beginning

The story of how Lou Gerstner arrived at IBM in April 1993 as chairman and chief executive officer (CEO) and turned around a stumbling giant on the edge of financial collapse has been well told – not least, by himself, in his best seller, *Who Says Elephants Can't Dance?* (Gerstner, 2002). But, although it is just one chapter in his book, it was his strategic decision to re-orient the company toward services that lies at the heart of IBM's renaissance.

Gerstner made three key moves after his arrival. The first was to get costs under control. The second was to turn the company into a multi-channel sales and marketing company. The third, and probably the bravest, and riskiest, decision he made was, in his words, to place 'a big bet on services'.

After all, IBM had been the archetypal product-based IT company, with a culture rooted in successfully selling what it manufactured. But by the time Gerstner took over, he and a few of his lieutenants could sense that their market was changing fundamentally.

First, IT was becoming a commodity business, which meant that products alone would not offer the kind of growth demanded by shareholders. Moreover, business customers were getting fed up with not seeing the promised financial benefits from their expensive IT installations.

Even more importantly, as a former customer himself, he could see that demand was increasingly shifting toward IT companies supplying the answers, not the products; to integration, not the technology by itself. He called it 'the customer's overpowering desire for someone to provide integration'. As he continued:

At first that was just the integration of technologies. But as the networked computing model took hold, it created whole new dimensions around integration, forcing customers to integrate technologies with core business processes, and then to integrate processes – like pricing, fulfilment or logistics – with one another.

Overcoming obstacles

This called for a new business model. But he knew that this reorientation would not be easy; it would be 'an exquisitely difficult trick to pull off' for a number of reasons:

- It would mean that IBM would recommend other companies' products if that was the best answer to a customer's needs. And that, along with maintaining and servicing those products, would meet fierce resistance in the sales force.
- The company would have to get to grips with the economics of a services business, which are very different from those of a product-based business. For instance, a major service contract can last anywhere between six months to 12 years. This would also have big implications for sales compensation and financial management.
- A service business is much more difficult to manage, because it is human-intensive; selling capability, knowledge, and 'creating solutions' at the point of delivery.

At first he placed the embryonic service division under the regular sales force, despite realising they would strongly resist letting anyone into an account who would dare to offer a competitor's products. He spent a lot of time trying to convince the service people that the sales team could get them into the customers' doors and making the sales people realise that the service teams could develop new sources of revenue from their customers.

By 1996 the service business finally became solid enough to stand alone as IBM Global Services. As he said, if the effort to build it had failed, his vision of IBM would have failed with it.

e-business on demand

But it flourished. By the mid to late 1990s, services were growing at over 20% a quarter. By the time he handed over to Sam Palmisano in March 2002, the business was primed for the next stage in its transformation into a services-oriented business. This was critical, since the IT business itself was changing shape yet again (Cerasale & Stone, 2005), with the emergence of the network economy.

Palmisano called this strategy of marketing and selling computing as a service: 'e-business on demand'. Integral to that was the $3.9 billion acquisition in October 2002 of PwC Consulting, the biggest in IBM's history. It was combined with the existing Business Innovation Services division to form Business Consulting Services (BCS). This was a powerful blend of the specialised knowledge of the former PwC Consulting professionals with the existing services and technology expertise of IBM itself. It also, at a stroke, gave the company the manpower it needed to accelerate its penetration of the market.

Going deeper and broader

Currently IBM offers a broad spectrum of services, from high level management consulting and integration, IT related services, through to business transformation outsourcing and related services. The overall objective is to offer clients the depth and breadth of its industry and functional expertise.

For example, IBM specialist retail consultants are working with supermarkets and consumer goods companies on the development of radio frequency identification (RFID) tags, which will increase the efficiency of supply chain management.

For its part, business transformation outsourcing moves well beyond handling a company's data warehouse and sees IBM improving, redesigning and, at times, running significant parts of a client's operations; allowing them to focus on their core activities.

IBM remains convinced that the future lies in offering integrated packages of hardware, software and services that deliver measurable results for clients, along with the technology which underpins them. A key ingredient will be the implementation of a global delivery model for services. And, unlike its competitors, the company can call on its own experience of undergoing one of the biggest corporate transformations in modern business history.

The IBM experience offers a number of key lessons:

- The chief executive has to be the prime driver of change, or appoint someone to do it on their behalf.
- Making the transition to a service orientation can be very difficult, but perseverance ultimately pays off financially.
- Bringing employees along is critical. It's important to think of them as a channel to market.
- External advertising can be used just as effectively toward an internal audience; to emphasise to employees where the company is going.

Methods of change

The task of building a service business in a product company is therefore one of profound change. It is likely to challenge much of the company's ingrained attitudes and processes; and, as a result, be resisted at many levels in the firm. Sales people, for instance, will initially think that it undermines their earning potential, because service people may have to recommend competitors' equipment. Operational leaders, on the other hand, will be used to service as the 'after market', an afterthought not considered to be the centre of the business. They will be slow to give service issues prominence until they become, demonstrably, a prime requirement in customers' minds.

Companies who have successfully moved into services have used a number of approaches to initiate and manage this change. They include:

The radical business unit leader

Many senior business leaders who have wanted to move their corporation seriously into services have started by the appointment of a driven, ambitious and determined leader. One of the roles of this person is to be a 'change agent' spearheading the growth of the service business, taking on entrenched views and creating a new culture. Both Lou Gerstner at IBM and Jack Welch at GE started their transformation into service by appointing such an individual.

In a large company, the initial task is to pull together disparate service skills (generally in maintenance and after care) from across the firm. There then follows the instigation of a number of fundamental activities which are the foundation of a competitive service business. They include: creation of an asset register of the equipment that customers own, creation of realistic service contracts, including 'end of life' pricing (which focuses on margins as the offer comes to an end) in the responsibility of the firm's product managers, creating or improving effective customer reception facilities, setting up service sales capability and establishing realistic, clear accounts for service-based business units. Many of these will not have existed before or will be developed to different levels in different business units in a large corporation. A respected and politically powerful leader is needed to drive the investment and effort needed to create one, firm-wide business unit.

Top management message, endorsement and political support

At some stage in the transformation to services, top management must visibly back the project. This is not only an important message to the market; it is an important message to the firm itself. The service business is often so counter cultural that it meets stronger internal opposition than it does external competition. To quote Gerstner again:

> Still, there were fireworks. Throughout these critical early days, it seemed there was a crisis a week between services and some other IBM unit. Many of our brand executives or sales leaders went ballistic every time the services unit proposed a product solution that incorporated a competitor's product. On more than one occasion I found one of these people in my office, railing against the renegades from services. My message was always the same: 'You need to invest the resources necessary to work with the services team to ensure they understand the competitive advantages of your products. View them as a distribution channel for your products. Your competitors do!' (Gerstner, 2002).

One of the key aspects of change management is the creation of a reason to change for the people it affects. The leadership needs to create dissatisfaction with the status quo, a vision of the benefits from the intended destination and a clear message of the way to get there. Top management need to show that the move into service will yield returns and successes which their current business would find unachievable. Proper communication will engage people in the transition process.

Osmosis, middle management pressure and 'skunk works'

Very often the move into service is initiated by people at business unit level who are able to see the opportunity when top management cannot. They are caught in a dilemma. They know that a service approach is important for the future of the business but their boss or senior managers do not share their vision.

Many in these circumstances create a shielded programme aimed at starting the momentum. For example, one former service vice president of a (sales orientated and product dominated) technology company, deliberately recruited an individual who would shake up the entrenched attitudes to business. He first wrote a 'golden parachute' clause into the contract of the new hire so that he was protected when the organisation began to resist change. They then quietly sanctioned the selling of service offers, beyond their existing, tight remit and beyond product related key accounts. In parallel with this, they jointly created a 'political map' of the company, planning who was to be influenced and when by the new approach. Now, two decades and several generations of leaders on, the company claims to be a service-dominated technology supplier with more than 60 % of its worldwide revenue coming from consultancy, outsourcing and other forms of service.

Businesses are based on finance and, as economically-based organisations, people within them are competing for scarce resources. There is a competition of ideas, policies and ambitions which uses both informal and formal influences to affect the development of the firm. The service function has to successfully engage in this continual debate if it is to fulfil its role effectively. In fact, they have a responsibility to join the fray in order to achieve the outcomes that shareholders have employed them to gain.

They must participate in formal meetings and communicate effectively in one-to-one presentations to leaders. But they also have to understand internal politics. It is not unprofessional to think about how to negotiate power points to achieve the strategies and policies which, from a service perspective, will make the company successful; it is unprofessional not to. Politics is therefore neither good nor bad, it simply is. Nobody in any senior role achieved their success and pre-eminence without an awareness of how to influence organisations through both informal and formal mechanisms.

Natural growth: building on an existing business

If there is natural demand in a market, successful companies tend to innovate or flex existing offers to meet it. So, as a result of natural demand for service assistance in many business sectors, a wide range of product companies have created businesses that have service elements to their offer. They might be part of the general operations of the organisation or may be a separate business unit within it. They are, though, the basis of a more substantial business. As demand continues and grows, the service business flourishes and gains momentum. Eventually it is recognised by top management and given appropriate resources. This steady, natural growth into service markets is an appealing, low risk method of achieving strategic change, even if it takes a little longer than some of the dramatic, high profile initiatives trumpeted in the business press.

Acquisition

The experience of substantial businesses that have moved into service is that acquisition plays an important part in building the momentum of the programme. Interestingly, few start with an acquisition. Normally there are some parts of a competitive service unit that can be used as a basis for the new business. But once that, and the top team, is established, acquisition is an important tool to drive the change and build shareholder returns through service. For instance, in his book about his tenure as CEO of GE, Jack Welch (Welch, 2001) says: 'Acquisitions played a big role in service growth. From 1997 through 2000, medical systems acquired 40 service companies, power systems 31 and aircraft engines 17.' IBM also signalled the seriousness of its move into services by the acquisition of PricewaterhouseCoopers massive, worldwide consulting arm. The influx of such a large number of service people and service contracts substantially changed the centre of gravity of the corporation.

There are a number of sources of acquisitions:

- Analysis: a review of the markets the company intends to move into will identify likely targets. Merchant bankers and other specialists use recognised techniques to tease out targets and lucrative deals.
- Opportunism: an unexpected target might reveal itself or be presented by a merchant bank. In this case, although the top team may have to move very fast, the attraction of the immediate deal must not be allowed to distract from the long term strategic intent.
- Strategic aims: a target may be acquired for a new organisational competence, to stop a competitor gaining a foothold in a service market, to enter a new market or to consolidate a position in an existing market.

Michelin UK builds their service business

Michelin is the world's leading tyre company, with a 20.1 % share of the global market. It operates in more than 170 countries, with seventy-five plants in nineteen countries producing 194 million tyres a year. It also publishes nineteen million maps and guides and operates a number of digital services.

As the case study in Chapter 1 shows, over the last few years Michelin has been experimenting with new, service-oriented offers to maintain its premium position and foster closer relationships with customers. This has stemmed from a growing awareness that tyre purchase is in danger of becoming commoditised, with more buyers giving price a higher priority than value and quality.

What has been happening in the UK with trucks is a good example of the company's pioneering approach and demonstrates how the move into service can be achieved by progressively growing a business.

Changing markets

The truck industry in the UK has been very fragmented, with roughly 450 000 operators, many of them 'one-man bands'. However, the industry is consolidating, with the big getting bigger. And with that has come a growing awareness among the large fleets that while tyre management represents a small slice of their operating costs, it take up a large amount of management time and effort.

For example, when fleet operators buy the tyres themselves, it is a straightforward transaction. However, it presents them with a variety of different elements to control to ensure maximum mobility. Along with the actual purchase, they have to estimate for themselves how much they should pay for each tyre, arrange for comprehensive servicing and generally oversee all aspects of tyre health.

In addition, tyre purchase has increasingly moved out of the engineering department and is being overseen by purchasing professionals who want a more transparent process; one where they have control over costs and cash flow to be able to plan their own pricing structures.

For small fleets, with ten trucks or fewer, this is not such a big issue. However, with fleets which run into the hundred and thousands of vehicles, this becomes a more complicated operation, with the amount of time and resources that need to be applied disproportionate to overall operating costs.

Testing the waters

For nearly ninety years Michelin has offered bus companies a 'total mobility solution' where the companies contract the tyre supply and servicing to Michelin and pay on the basis of pence per mile. For that, the company installs a fitter in the bus workshop to maintain the stock, including daily tyre checks and repairs. The company currently has 32 000 of the 40 000 buses in the UK under this direct mileage contract.

In the early 1990s Michelin began to experiment with offering this tried and tested model to large fleets with expenditure on tyres of over £500 000. The company said to prospective customers: 'pay us a certain amount of money regularly and we will look after the tyres and their servicing'. This would transfer much of the complexity of tyre management to the experts and, in the process, make it much more evident why choosing a premium product pays off over time.

There were risks involved. For instance, although the company had such a depth of experience using this model with buses, there were big differences. Buses operate in a controlled environment, returning to their garage each evening where problems can be dealt by a Michelin technician. Trucks, on the other hand, can be anywhere.

Secondly, the challenge for Michelin would be, not only to estimate costs as precisely as possible over the three year period of the contract (which tends to be the minimum period for effective tyre planning), but also to educate the fleet operators about the benefits of professional tyre management. The strongest argument was and still is the tyre pressure/cost of fuel equation: a tyre which is 10 % under-inflated can cause a 1 % rise in the fuel bill.

Finally, this wasn't a two-way relationship between Michelin and the fleet operator but also included an additional player in the mix: the tyre distributor who would do the actual servicing. That meant there were two contracts: between Michelin and the customers, and between Michelin and the tyre distributors who would provide the service to the customer on Michelin's behalf. They would have to be motivated by payment for quality of service. (In the UK, distributors are divided between manufacturer-owned and independents.)

A different approach

Despite all these potential pitfalls, the business built up such a solid base that by 2000 Michelin decided to formalise what was already happening by giving it a name (Michelin Fleet Solutions, MFS). This emphasised the shift away from just selling tyres to large fleets, toward offering 'solutions to customers' mobility problems.

This shift involved a number of changes in the company's approach to the market. First, it had to persuade customers of the importance of continuous good tyre management. There was a danger that, in handing over tyre management to a third party, fleet operators might become less assiduous in taking care of their tyres. However, Michelin's teams had already a lot of experience in educating smaller customers about the benefits of good tyre management.

Secondly, it called for a distinct change in sales force motivation and measurement since there is a difference between rewarding a sales person for the number of tyres sold and successfully managing the customer's tyre needs. The answer was to set in place account managers, who were given full responsibility for the customer's business, including overseeing the contract and delivery from the service provider.

This called for quite a cultural shift in terms of both managing and measuring results. For instance, account managers are now seen more as business people than sales people. They have to have a good understanding of the businesses their customers operate in. For instance, while petrol tanker fleets want to discuss safety, environmental issues and mobility, a waste management company is more interested in damage resistance and getting back on the road after a breakdown. Whereas previously they were 80% sales-oriented and 20% business-oriented, with MFS that proportion is reversed.

Gaining ground

By 2006, up to 55% of the UK target market had embraced the MFS approach and that proportion continues to grow as customers come to appreciate the benefits of consistent tyre management throughout their fleet. Even more important, up to 95% of customers renew after the contract ends.

But the market is still immature. So the company continues to educate customers about the offer and its managerial and financial benefits. For example, in the bus industry, it took a number of years for the system to bed down and claims of mobility, security, safety and fuel efficiency to be proven. The marketing reflects this objective, focusing on the benefits other customers have experienced. Public relations and word-of-mouth, as well as advertising in the trade press, play a big role.

The relationship between the account managers and customers is equally critical. Account managers have to be both persuasive and credible in order to convince a customer to commit to a three-year contract. However, getting a signature on a contract is where the real work starts. The account manager has to make sure that customer satisfaction remains high, while at the same time arbitrating between the possibly conflicting needs of Michelin, the service provider and the customer.

Financial calculations

Getting the right contract for the right customer, and one which ensures Michelin makes the appropriate profit, is a complex process. So the company has built up an extensive database to be able to work out as precisely as possible the price-per-mile it should charge. It does this by calculating a whole range of factors, such as what tyres the fleet is running on and their condition.

Upfront investment may be necessary, if those tyres need up-grading; as might be the management of competitors' tyres for a customer. While the vehicles will migrate to Michelin tyres over time, MFS still has to manage what's in place from the beginning of the contract.

This has led to a complete reorganisation of back office processes, since there are far more details that have to be managed, including how many tyres a customer has fitted, when they were fitted, and so on. At the same time, however, it makes life far simpler for customers, since their financial planning becomes more straightforward. By delegating responsibility to MFS they gain control of their tyre budgets, reduce administration costs, receive customised reports and have an identified price-per-mile.

The competition is fierce. But Michelin can take advantage of its strong brand and what it stands for. Moreover, this experience has enabled the company to broaden its understanding of what is involved in the shift to a more service-oriented approach.

Specialised tools and ideas to help with planning change

The change of a business into a service company, or into a corporation offering its products through a service experience, must be carefully planned. Even if the culture and market of the firm is fast-paced and demanding, time should be taken to think through the steps needed to succeed. Fortunately, as in many other areas of business, techniques exist to help plan this fundamental change, saving time and reducing risk. They are based on the experience of companies who have initiated change in many different sectors and help to guide novices through a change programme. It is sensible to use them in planning.

For example, the Johnson and Scholes 'cultural web', illustrated in Figure 3.4, is just one respected and practical example (see Johnson & Scholes, 2004). It identifies the elements of an organisation which need to be taken into account when planning major strategic change. They are:

- The 'paradigm': the way the organisation views the world. This may have a number of facets such as the sector or segment it concentrates on, its products or its competitors.
- 'Organisational structure': the way people inter-relate in the firm.
- 'Power structures': this acknowledges the authority that people have in the organisation and how they use it. It covers both formal and informal power.
- 'Control systems' are built into the structure of the firm to ensure that objectives are met. They might be processes, systems or measures.
- 'Routines and rituals' may not be overtly described by the firm or part of its acknowledged policies, but they can be very powerful nonetheless. Very often they are the real functions of the organisation.

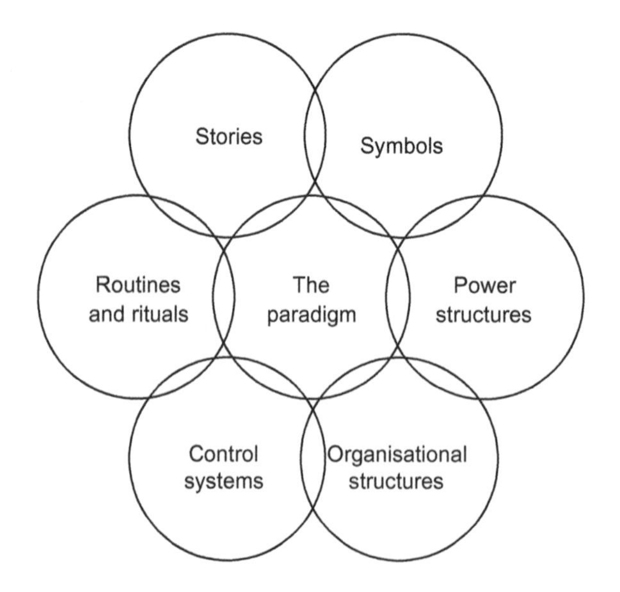

Figure 3.4 The cultural web
Source: Johnson & Scholes, 2004.

- 'Symbols' are physical evidence of past victories, failures, moments of history or power. They are very influential and can cause deep emotion to be stirred.
- 'Stories' circulate in an organisation and affect behaviour.

The components of the web indicate the full range of activities that need to be considered if change is to be effective. It allows business leaders to round out and construct a comprehensive change plan.

Towards a plan for a move into service

Figure 3.5 dramatises the debate that has been generated among many management teams who have been faced by business pressures which make them consider a move into service. The external pressures reduce margins and expose costs, some of which are service or after care costs. The leadership team needs to decide, firstly, whether it is going to make the move into service or not; secondly, the rate at which it will move; and thirdly, the way in which it will grow its competence in service management. Otherwise, the health of the whole business could be damaged.

Some move away from a service offer toward more efficient product manufacture. In some sectors, computing for example, commentators have suggested that there is a natural evolution 'from products through services

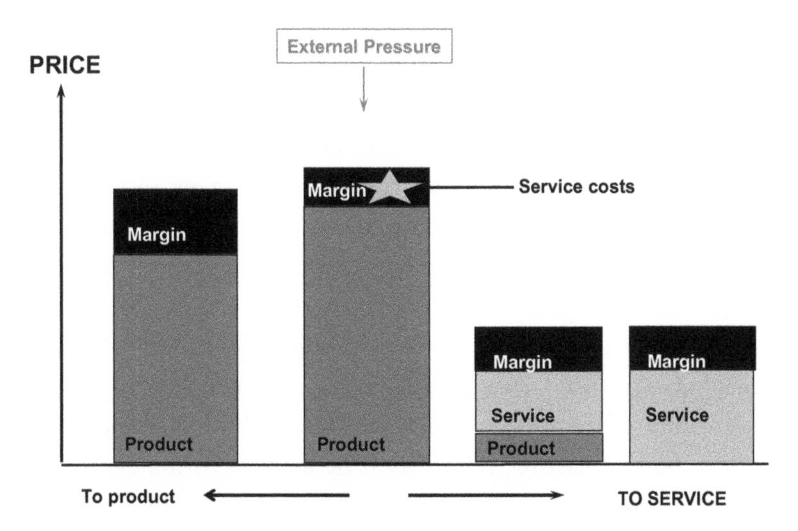

Figure 3.5 Response to margin pressure

to solutions.' Yet this is simply not true in many sectors of manufacturing. Businesses continue to thrive in developed economies by achieving unprecedented gains in productivity and finding healthy markets for their products. They succeed without becoming a service or a 'solutions' business.

They may try to reduce manufacturing costs by switching factories to areas of the world where labour costs less. They may invest in new machinery in order to reduce the labour element in production or they may rearrange logistics costs. They are likely to see service as a cost to be reduced to a level which is bearable without damaging brand, product reputation or customers' repurchase intent.

They may try to reduce the number of service engineers or the quality of support to customers. Some have taken the view that they are successful product companies and they will therefore try to strip out the cost of service entirely. In the 1990s, Microsoft Europe, for example, outsourced all its service capability to people they called 'solution partners'. Their view was that they should concentrate on the production and sale of good quality product, allowing others to serve the customer. Companies who take this approach must, however, control the quality of service through third parties so that customers do not perceive a drop in quality. Any reduction in quality of support is likely to affect customers' views of product quality, damaging future sales.

Other companies have taken a totally different view and a different strategy. Their approach begins with discussions about whether service can 'add value' or whether they can 'productise' it. They try to move from a product to a service orientation, in the belief that customers will pay for services. In the telecommunications equipment market, for example, the massive Swedish telephone supplier, Ericsson, decided to move to a more service orientation. This involved the creation of new services (such as systems integration) or charging customers for advice that had previously been funded from the product margin, called in the trade 'from free to fee'.

Still others move so far into service that they move, almost entirely, out of manufacturing. IBM's long journey from its traumas at the end of the twentieth century has made it one of the world's biggest service businesses with, at the time of writing, relatively little manufacturing capability.

There is, though, a serious warning in the experience of companies that have faced this dilemma. Those which do not move when their industry is going through profound change end up in trouble. The now defunct computer giant, Digital Equipment Corporation, for example, had a long standing policy on service. Yet it failed to change its orientation and was, eventually, bought by a young upstart, Compaq, with a very different culture. It is not enough to understand trends and discuss which strategy should be implemented. Once an industry faces a traumatic and fundamental challenge to product margins, suppliers have to take action to change their direction.

Managers need to consider the strategic significance of service to their business. Will they move to be a service-orientated supplier or will they focus on manufacturing, perhaps stripping out service altogether? The way this is tackled is likely to have a profound effect on the health of their company.

The steps that should be considered are:

Step 1 Determine the factors causing a rise in service demand or price pressure to see whether these are long-term phenomena. It is crucial to understand whether this is a change in the underlying structures of the market (for example, customers wanting service rather than product) or just a temporary phase.

Step 2 Examine all margin elements to discover the value and price of service. (In many companies, wide margins have allowed these to be ignored in the past.) At the same time, research customers to see if there is underlying demand and perceived value for service. This will make it possible to determine whether customers will be receptive to paying for new packaged services.

Step 3 Take a hard-headed decision about the organisation's ability to cope with change. The move into service is vast and involves fundamental change. It may be too much.

Step 4 Decide whether to move towards product orientation or to move towards more of a service offer. This is a fundamental decision, which needs careful assessment.

Step 5 If a move into service is agreed, construct a clear, well-articulated business plan, over the medium term, for each service business.

Step 6 Create a change management programme which includes: the reason to change, investment levels (including funds needed for acquisitions), resources allocated, timings and key milestones. Then execute this plan over a realistic period of time. It has taken many companies several years to succeed with the transition to services.

Summary

Service businesses are different from product businesses on many levels. A move into service means the firm will have to change: operations, finance, people management, sales and marketing. The degree of change depends on the extent of the move and the degree of difference from the established business. Those that have successfully achieved this change have done it through serious, and carefully crafted, change programmes involving leaders who are change agents together with a significant acquisition programme.

4

First base: gaining a clear perspective of service markets

Introduction and overview

Fundamental to the success of any business are the conditions of the market in which it operates and the position it holds within it. Profit, cash flow and shareholder earnings can be damaged if the leadership takes wrong decisions due to a lack of understanding of its experience of market dynamics. While fast decisions and 'gut feel' can be successful in markets where business leaders have spent the majority of their career, they can be extremely risky in unfamiliar markets; and service markets can have singular characteristics which need to be understood if the move is to be successful. So, before investing in a service business or moving an existing business into unfamiliar service markets, leaders ought to step back and take stock of the market in which that proposed business will operate.

This chapter outlines a number of tools and techniques which can help firms gain an objective perspective of service markets (such as a 'market audit' and 'scenario planning') and the main issues (like 'market maturity' and 'positioning') to look for. It also looks at methods to turn that knowledge into a basis for making decisions about exploiting opportunities revealed by the analysis.

Why market understanding is essential

Whether a firm is a large, sophisticated and international organisation or a small specialised unit, whether it is highly rational and procedural in its approach to business, or largely intuitive, its leaders need to understand the market it proposes to enter if they are to make sound investment decisions which safeguard the future health of their business. There is a vulnerability here that arises from what is generally the greatest strength of service firms: closeness to the customer.

Front-line service personnel are in close contact with their customers, responding to them every day. This experience dominates the culture of their business, influencing leadership decisions and policy formulation. So it is natural for them to assume that they know the market in which they operate. However, one group of buyers or one large customer does not necessarily reflect the trends and forces at work across a market as a whole.

Also, if market conditions are changing, existing assumptions about what succeeds are dangerous. Poor decision-making or erratic leadership, as people change priorities in the light of the latest encounter, can result from a myopic perspective based on direct experience of a limited number of buyers. So it is essential that the leaders step back and take stock of the proposed market using sound, objective, analytical techniques.

It is particularly important to get an analytical perspective on any new market which the firm intends to move into and it is sensible to use a recognised business process which collects a range of data in order to provide as objective a view as possible. There are straightforward methods to collect relevant information and garner market-based insights which need not take long to complete. Some take an economic perspective of markets and some a 'behavioural' approach, but each yields valuable insights which business leaders can exploit and use to reduce risks.

Important market dynamics to understand

1. Market definition

The first and most fundamental issue that leaders need to think about is how they define the market they are to operate in. This may sound simple, and it is, but there are examples of businesses being destroyed because their owners had not defined their target market properly. It is important because there is an assumption built into the fabric of a business that gives direction to its activities. If this assumption is not aligned to the market, the business will, ultimately, fail.

Theodore Levitt (Levitt, 1960) called this phenomenon 'Marketing Myopia'. For instance, the US railway companies (the computer companies of their age) were handling a stunning new technology that would revolutionise life in the nineteenth century as much as (perhaps even more than) computer power did in the twentieth. This was the first time in human history that mankind could travel faster than a galloping horse and, within decades, the industry had created new towns, new jobs and new concepts (among others, the idea of holidays).

By the end of the nineteenth century there were hundreds of thousands of miles of track in the USA alone, some crossing the entire country. The railway companies then earned huge profits. So anyone approaching the chief executive of one of these companies, in, say, 1910, and predicting that there were major new threats to the business that could see them virtually bankrupt by the 1930s/1940s, would be dismissed out of hand. And yet, thanks to the development of the car and the airplane, that is exactly what happened. According to Levitt the American railway companies struggled because they defined their businesses as 'trains' rather than 'transportation'. Had they focussed their businesses on the 'transportation market' they would have invested in these new technologies and moved their businesses in new directions.

So leaders of potential service businesses must define for their company the market on which they will focus. This must be done in clear, customer-centric terms. A computer maintenance service, for example, is in the business of ensuring that computer power remains available; whereas a corporate law firm is likely to be in the business of limiting risk. Experience shows that this can be enormously difficult to clarify but, once agreed, gives direction to innovation, leadership, investment and service quality. It can also give a newcomer real advantage if it is entering an established market, which is dominated by complacent suppliers who all have a common view of the market need. The new entrant can quickly gain share by defining its offer more closely to customer needs.

2. Insights from phases in the growth of a market

The phenomenon of market maturity, which reflects changing patterns in demand and supply, was introduced in Chapter 1 (see Figure 1.2, pages 12–16) and occurs when there are multiple suppliers and multiple buyers. This is a learning process between suppliers and buyers which develops over time. When the offer is first made, buyers need to be shown how to use it and how it is relevant to their lives, but, as time goes by, they become familiar with it and adapt it for different uses. Suppliers observe this behaviour and adjust their offer accordingly. This, in turn, causes other people to buy it and adapt it to their lifestyle.

Normally, suppliers in a market are buffeted by the forces at play in each phase of development. However, if leaders understand what phase the intended service market is in, they can set strategic direction for their firm in the light of that insight and enter it more effectively. For instance, at the time of writing, 'executive coaching' is a service which is at the 'introductory' phase of its development. Suppliers therefore need to educate the market in the concept and grow their business by inducing customers to try it. In this phase of a market's life, costs are likely to be high and firms can be unprofitable. As a result, it may be wise for any product firms wanting to enter a service market at this stage of development to wait for upstarts to burn investment and establish the concept. They can then enter by buying them out.

By contrast, some service industries, like aspects of financial advice in the West and personal telecommunications in the East, are still in the 'growth' phase of their market. There is strong natural demand for their service and, in many cases, work just 'walks through the door'. In this phase the firm has to concentrate on servicing demand, so established suppliers will be focused upon obtaining and deploying skilled resources. They must also ensure that there are efficient processes to capture and meet orders. It is possible to concentrate on internal needs, ignoring competitor moves because there is sufficient demand for all. As a result these markets are relatively easy to enter in a low risk way. In fact, natural growth from a small venture is probably the best method of entry, particularly if a supplier has a well known brand or a large number of existing customers who are likely to want the service offer.

On the other hand, many services (such as financial audit, outsourcing, advertising and some aspects of consultancy) now operate in mature markets. Although established businesses may be struggling, this is a good time for new entrants to gain a foothold by attracting the attention of buyers through offering a service experience which is truly different. The Virgin group, for example, has earned much of its fortune by entering service markets (like air transport, financial services and telecommunications) where unexciting mature suppliers exist. They shake up the market by creating a profoundly different offer which attracts customers who buy them in other markets, together with new buyers.

So leaders of potential service firms must take a view of where the intended market, however they define it, has reached in its maturity. From this they can deduce strategic options which can form part of their ultimate business and market entry plans.

3. Market segmentation

The segmentation of markets into groups of buyers which can be easily reached by suppliers is a powerful concept which has improved the profit of many businesses. It suggests that buyers can be grouped around common needs. Then, by customising the firm's offer to meet those common needs, suppliers can both gain competitive advantage and save costs because they are only addressing a portion of the market. Periodically, as markets change or fragment, this becomes a major strategic issue which affects the way suppliers relate to markets. In the past, different means of segmenting markets have been developed in different industries and produced demonstrable competitive advantage for some suppliers.

They include:

Demographics and socioeconomics: The grouping of people according to physical characteristics (age, sex) or circumstances (income, occupation or education). This is commonly used in developed nations. In the US and Europe, for example, there is currently much emphasis on the design of products for ageing populations.

Life stage: This is a more precise form of demographics. It groups buyers according to the phase they have reached in their life such as 'married', 'home building' or 'retired'. They might become 'freedom seekers', 'drop-outs' or 'traditionalists' according to their phase of life.

Psychographics: The grouping of people according to various personal characteristics such as personality or social class. In the 1980s, for instance, the 'British National Readership Survey' categorised the population as 'A' (higher marginal), 'B' (middle class), 'C' (lower middle class) and 'D' (working class). However, this is now breaking down.

Geographic/location: Grouping people according to their country of birth or area of residence. This can focus on the region, population density and climate. It can involve county, town or even street.

Behavioural or attitudinal: Grouping according to a particular behaviour which may affect product usage or price sensitivity, or values and attitudes. A good example was created by the marketing agency McCann-Erickson in the latter half of the twentieth century. It identified: 'avant guardians' (concerned with change and well being), 'pontificators' (who have strongly held traditional views) and 'self-exploiters' (who have high self-esteem).

'Tribal': A specific example of behavioural segmentation which groups customers according to the social groups or cultures with which they identify. For example, in the 1990s, one of Europe's premier television companies started to commission programmes for tribes in society (such as young, independent women) based on how they communicate and live.

Benefits sought: The grouping of people according to the advantages they are seeking from the product or service. For instance, as early as 1968, Russell Haley (Haley, 1968) published segmentation for the toothpaste market based on this approach. Customers were in the 'sensory' segment (seeking flavour or product appearance) or the 'sociable' segment (seeking brightness of teeth) or the 'worriers' (seeking decay prevention).

Lifestyle: Grouping customers by a common approach to life. One famous example of this type of segmentation was developed by Young & Rubican in the 1980s. It was this advertising agency which developed, among others, the famous, but now defunct term, 'YUPPIE' (Young Urban Professional). Incidentally, this also illustrates an important point about customer segmentation: it dates easily. Whereas people revelled in being a Yuppie in the early 1980s, it is now considered out of date and unattractive.

Context: Proposed by Dr Paul Fifield in the early 1990s (Fifield, 1998), this method groups customers according to the context in which they use a product or service. It focuses attention on things that bring people together, exploiting shared interests. For instance, one cursory glance at people on a fishing bank will show that they have little in common other than the sport itself.

Business-to-business segmentation types include:

Industry sector: Grouping businesses according to the industry in which they specialise. These sectors are often formally set by government economists as a means of defining and recording activities in different areas of the economy.

Organisation style: Grouping businesses according to the culture or prevailing climate of the company. They may be centralised or decentralised or 'innovative' versus 'conservative'. The Myers Briggs organisational types ('fraternal', 'collegial', 'bureaucratic' or 'entrepreneurial') have, for example, been used as a basis for segmentation.

Organisational size: Grouping businesses according to the number of employees, assets or revenue.

Company life cycle: Companies, like product groups, have a 'life cycle' through which they evolve. They go from birth to death at different rates, struggling to get through 'inflection points' to increase revenue and margin. They have similar characteristics (e.g. management style) in each phase and this has been used as a basis for segmentation.

Industry maturity: Industries also move through different phases. For instance, in developed economies, their agricultural or manufacturing industries are at a different phase of evolution to, say, biotechnology. The phase of growth affects the behaviour of suppliers in it and has also been used as a basis for segmentation.

Context: As with consumers, grouping businesses according to the context in which they use the product or service.

Needs/benefits based: This is based on underlying needs or benefits sought by the company from its suppliers.

Some of these methods are rudimentary and limited. A number of companies, for instance, simply group their buyers around the products and services they have bought. But a 'small system' buyer might be a big buyer of other firms' products and may become a bigger buyer if approached in a more relevant way. On the other hand, many companies categorise their buyers according to size; as: global accounts, corporate business, small-to-medium-enterprises (SME) and consumer. Yet it is virtually impossible to identify useful common needs from such a broad categorisation.

For example, grouping all businesses under a certain revenue level as 'SME' fails to recognise the different buying motivations of these businesses. The growth rate, management talent and business strategy of small businesses are as diverse as the ideas they are built on. The needs of an IT start-up with venture capital backing are very different from those of a local, independent pharmacy, even if their initial revenues are similar.

Industrial sectors are another frequently used segmentation type. Many companies, of all shapes and sizes, have 'line of business' or 'industry' specialists who focus on an industrial sector; trying to understand issues within them and customise the firm's offer to companies operating in them. However, even these groupings can be limiting. For instance, many industry sectors are breaking down as new technologies change categorisation. As a result, it is increasingly difficult to tell which company is in which industry sector. Some retailers are moving into banking, so are they now in the financial services sector? And, with the convergence of telecommunications and computing, exactly what sectors are internet retailers or publishing companies in?

Often, the definition of industrial groups to handle these changes is so broad as to make it meaningless in terms of common, useful issues. In addition, not all businesses within the same industry sector will have the same requirements. For example, a service firm trying to sell training, or management consultancy might concentrate on 'innovative' companies receptive to new ideas. Yet this promising segment could be in any industry sector.

Good market segmentation is a means of grouping buyers by their common needs, wants or aspirations, emphasising their humanity in a way which encourages them to respond to an offer. Whether the supplier is operating in the business-to-business or business-to-consumer environment, it is important to consider the characteristics of the people targeted. Properly done, it can be predictive, highlighting the future buying intent of the people in each group. However, although human beings are unpredictable, difficult and irrational, they tend to group naturally. In the real world, markets segment themselves.

Clear tests have been developed to check whether a particular segmentation is appropriate for a particular company in a particular market. They include:

- ***Homogeneity:*** To what extent will the members of the segment act in the same way?
- ***Measurability:*** How big and valuable is the segment?
- ***Accessibility:*** Is it possible to reach the segment with marketing or sales programmes?
- ***Profitability:*** Is the segment substantial enough for the supplier to profit from?
- ***Attractiveness or relevance:*** Is the segment something customers will want to identify with?

The last point is particularly powerful. If the target group can be expanded by people who aspire to belong, demand for the proposition will be increased.

As each firm has a distinct culture and its own distinct market position, it should develop its own segmentation. It is likely to be more effective to use a process to create its own particular approach to segmentation than to steal a previously designed segmentation type. The process outlined below has been drawn from academia and tested in the reality of several projects conducted in service businesses over the past years. It has produced, for the firms involved, a practical method of segmentation which has given them competitive advantage through a singular approach to their customers. Suppliers can use it to understand potential buyer groups in the service market they want to enter.

A method of segmentation

Step 1 – Review all known segmentation methods. A group of experienced leaders should be drawn together to discuss segmentation as a subject and the types previously created, their benefits and drawbacks.

Step 2 – Create a hypothesis. In discussion, the team will create an idea of how they think their market might segment. If they have existing customers in the market, they will need to think about how they behave. They may have to customise or examine market research or industry reports to get to the heart of this. In particular, they will need to discuss different attitudes or behaviours that they have observed. Eventually they will reach an idea of which previous segmentation type best fits their view of buyers in the market and how it might be adapted to their market. In doing this they are creating a hypothesis which can be tested.

Step 3 – Create segmentation dimensions. Segmentation dimensions are the ways in which the buyers will behave towards the firm and its services. As far as possible, they should be values, beliefs or cultural biases (whether in consumers or organisations) because they determine behaviour. If the segmentation is effective, each group will exhibit these in different ways.

Through discussion, the team should create a set of segmentation dimensions by which these differences will manifest themselves. These can then be scaled using sensible scoring of the extremes. For example, if a supplier was segmenting a business-to-business market on the basis of 'organisation style', they might hypothesise that there are centralised and de-centralised segments. This would manifest itself in different business practices, one of which would be purchasing style and this would become a 'segmentation dimension'. For a centralised organisation, buying would be controlled by a central purchasing department, whereas in a de-centralised organisation it would be devolved to business units.

Step 4 – First Test: Use data to test the segment dimensions. By examining any existing customers and scoring their behaviour against segmentation dimensions, it is possible to conduct a fast, inexpensive test of the validity of the dimensions and where different clusters appear. If no clustering appears in this first test, then new dimensions, or maybe a new hypothesis, need to be created.

Step 5 – Second Test: Research. Any clustering should then be confirmed with direct research. This is best conducted in two phases: first, a qualitative phase, testing the dimension in depth with a few potential customers; second, a large quantitative project using a trade-off technique such as conjoint research. Through this method different clusters of potential buyer groups will become evident. Again, if clustering does not appear, the team should revisit its initial hypothesis.

Step 6 – Third Test: Test marketing programmes. Research itself is probably not sufficient to confirm such an important subject as customer segmentation. Potential segments can also be confirmed in a more practical way, imitating as far as possible the rough and tumble of the real marketplace. A number of test marketing programmes could be designed in order to ensure that the buyers identify with the proposed groups that they are in and respond to propositions specifically designed for them.

Step 7 – Create a full investment and market entry plan. Segmentation has implications to: the market proposition for each group, customer service methods for each group, the ideal method of marketing communication, sales strategy, IT systems, operational processes and pricing. Taken seriously, it affects every aspect of the way the firm approaches its intended market. Each aspect needs to be carefully thought through, costed and built into the market entry plan.

Step 8 – Gain approval for the investment. This needs to be treated like any other hard-headed investment strategy. The pros and cons, benefits and return on investment need to be assessed and drawn together into the market entry plan, which should be submitted to the appropriate leadership team for formal approval.

Step 9 – Implementation. As part of implementation of the plan, everyone in the new service organisation will eventually need to be familiar with the new segments and how they should be handled.

4. Positioning the business

The 'position' of firms in a market is based on buyers' perceptions of the value of their offer and is often clearer after segmentation analysis has been completed. By gaining and holding a clear position in a market, a firm can maximise its margins. Just as importantly, a clear position communicates to the recruitment market, attracting high calibre service staff which, in turn, enhances quality and margins.

Figure 4.1 represents the scattering of different buyers as they seek different mixes of features and price in a market. The horizontal axis is 'perceived price', and the vertical 'perceived quality'; both of which are components of value. Some, for example, will want a 'no-frills', least-cost service, whereas others a features rich experience. A shopper at Harrod's food hall in London will think the quality of product justifies the higher prices, whereas someone who shops at a local market, because they are more interested in lower prices, will be just as satisfied. Both think that they get value for money. This scattering occurs in any given market and allows suppliers to create different offers at different prices.

Figure 4.2 is a 'perceptual map' of a service market, showing the positions that different suppliers take as they seek to command the attention of different buyer groups. To take an effective position in a new market, the firm has to understand their potential buyers' perceptions of value in this way, rather than make assumptions about what they want.

Each company, either by design or default, eventually commands its own position in a market by serving one group of customers with a particular value proposition. It might be as a 'market leader' (like IBM, Accenture,

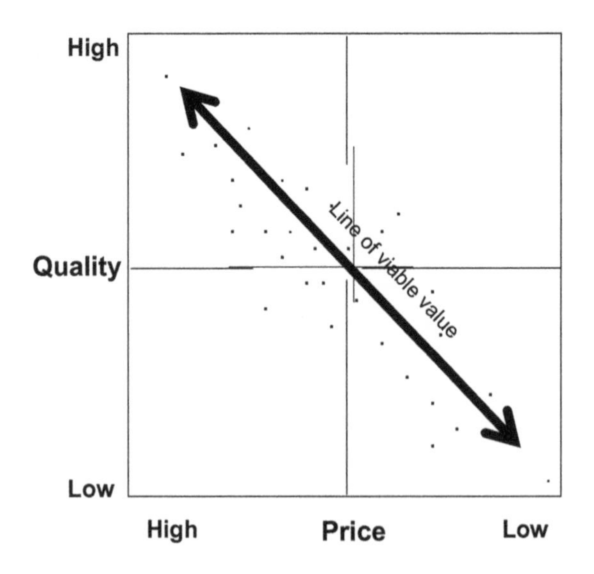

Figure 4.1 The different values sought by buyers

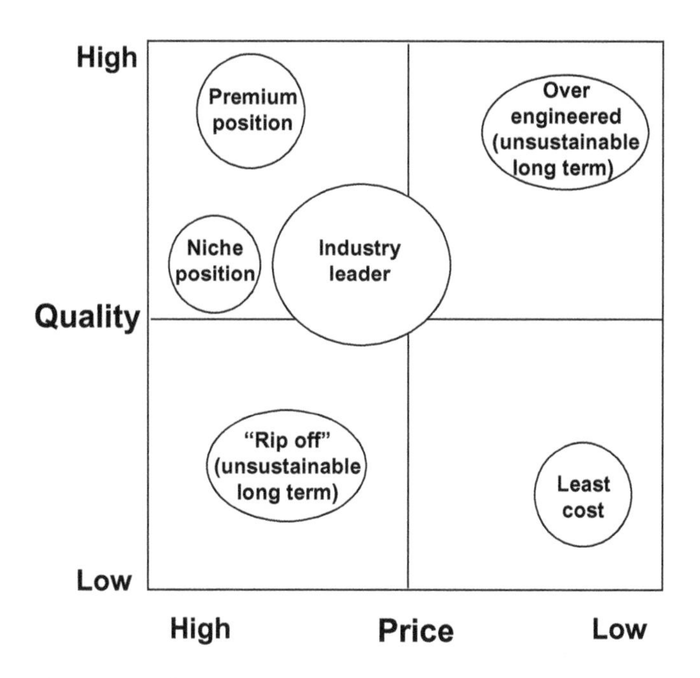

Figure 4.2 The perceptual/positioning map

BA, PricewaterhouseCoopers and Microsoft) with dominant share and the ability to influence the rules of engagement. These companies serve the majority of buyers and, as a result, set both price expectations and service standards for the whole market. Or it might be as a 'follower' (like KPMG, Virgin Atlantic or Allen & Overy) which is smaller than the market leader and able to earn a profitable existence by providing a healthy alternative either in terms of price or the features of the service involved.

Other sustainable competitive positions are: 'least cost' (Easyjet), 'premium' (McKinsey) or 'niche' (Interbrand and Bain). The two unsustainable positions are in the top right and bottom left corners. Low price and high quality mean that the service is over-engineered and won't survive in the long term. On the other hand, the combination of high prices and low quality in the lower left quadrant is often caused by a distortion in the market, such as a monopoly, which means these buyers can't make clear comparisons.

The position taken represents the competitive position of the whole firm and ought to be the orientation of everyone in it. Also, the price and features of its service offers ought to suit that position and be different from others.

For example, the service of a least-cost supplier ought to be very different to that of a features-rich premium supplier because each makes money in a different way from different groups of buyers.

The perceptual map can be used in several ways. Firstly, it can be a catalyst for debate about strategic positioning in the intended service market and the firm's entry strategy can then be based on it. The tool can be used to determine the number of buyers the firm should expect and what the value proposition should be. For instance, a firm may find that, through acquisition, it can become the volume market leader of an industry. However, to maintain that position, it must adopt the behaviour of a market leader, taking a stance on price, quality and leading industry issues. Alternatively, a firm might find that it can maximise margins by entering as a niche provider. In this case it needs to determine exactly how its service experience will be different from the market leader, communicating that to buyers.

It can also be used to understand competitive forces, the likely manoeuvres of firms already in the market, to work out competitive strategy. Markets are not static. It is dangerous, for example, for the market leader to assume its position is inviolable, since niche providers can progressively capture segments of the market and mount a challenge for leadership. Or a 'follower', which finds itself number two in a market with a vulnerable market leader, might decide to mount a challenge. So this tool can be used to anticipate the likely reaction of competitors when the firm makes its move into the proposed service market.

5. Understanding the standard of after care and service quality in a market

The perceptual map can be used to set the style and quality of 'after care' service or 'bedside manner' which is appropriate for the firm's intended strategic position. Often a business aims for the 'best quality' or the 'highest performance' whatever its market position. It is not uncommon for a profitable niche supplier to have a quality plan aimed at promoting the 'best' service in the industry or 'delighting' all customers. This is a stance which is likely to be as damaging as it is inappropriate. It is as costly as it is ridiculous to offer the same bland after care service as all other suppliers. The style of support must match the competitive position and strategic intent of the firm.

It is surprising how many companies, that consider the quality of their after care service to be an important part of their offer, do not think through the place of service in their market entry strategy. Service programmes are often imprecise and vague, thereby losing any potential advantage. It is much more effective to develop a clear idea of the nature of the after care service which matches the general business strategy and reflects the intended market position. If the firm is to be a least cost, premium or niche supplier, its competitive position is reinforced if it's after care service is undertaken in a style similar to that positioning.

As important is to recognise the moments in the evolution of a market when there is an opportunity to gain ground by offering a new standard of after care service, as described in Chapter 1. Industries appear to develop through an evolution of thought and strategy with regard to service standards and some suppliers have reaped enormous rewards when taking advantage of those moments.

For instance, service in some industries is below the standard expected by the general population, a national 'par' for quality. This is assumed, ill-defined and emotionally-based, but is a common value nonetheless. Service quality which is below this national par may have been caused by a historic monopoly or legislative distortion but it will eventually become the subject of public ridicule. It will become the target of comedians and journalists because they recognise that there is a common national experience which can be exploited.

In an industry where all suppliers are criticised, the first supplier to move to meet national par will gain market share. This has happened in numerous industries in both a national and international context. The example given in Chapter 1 is the radical improvement made by BA in the 1980s, which gained market share and grew for nearly two decades after, while other international carriers floundered. It moved to meet the service expectations of buyers when others in the industry did not. As a result it attracted new buyers, gaining competitive advantage.

Another example of competitive advantage derived from service quality is the difference between naïve and experienced segments of buyers. In an industry where all services are designed for naïve clients, the service standard comprises: good client care, clear process, smiling people and a reassuring brand. However, because of the need for emotional control, frequent purchasers can become frustrated with this approach. For them, good service is self-service and streamlined processes. So, by constructing a service which has, at its heart, a sense of privilege, of joining a club, the supplier can provide better quality service at less cost. If a supplier enters a market dominated by offers to naïve buyers, it can gain share by offering a new standard of service designed specifically for experienced buyers. It will attract frustrated, experienced buyers from other providers, gaining share as it enters the market.

6. Critical success factors

Any market has established rules of engagement by which the participants in the market survive or prosper. These rules may be imposed by regulatory or market pressures; and usually by a combination of the two. For example, in a professional services industry all of the participants must meet the necessary legal or industry standards of qualifications and behaviour in order to be able to participate. Meeting these criteria is a critical success factor as it is not possible to trade without them.

Beyond these basic requirements for being 'in the game', service providers also face certain criteria which enable them to succeed in the marketplace. However, the critical success factors for this are commercial imperatives resulting from the evolution of forces within the market. For example, a fast-moving market may call for the ability to bring new services to market quickly.

7. Distortions and false markets

There is probably no such thing as a perfect market with perfect competition affecting supply and demand as taught by economists. Distortions occur in nearly every market, caused by things like dominant market share, strong reputations, regulation, law and long standing brands. The heritage of the 'magic circle' law firms and the brand of premier consultancy McKinsey allow them, for example, to command higher than average prices.

Distortion can also be caused by some form of monopolistic or oligopolistic grip on the market. The African mining company, De Beers, has, for example, had a grip on the international diamond market for several centuries and the 'big four' accountancy partnerships command nearly 95 % of financial audits of leading American and British public companies.

Another distortion might arise from a misunderstanding of demand or preconceived ideas in the industry, distorting the services on offer. For example, a good proportion of the demand for service in the computer industry over recent decades has been caused by complexity of product and poor interoperability between components in company technologies. Companies have had to pay for skills to make new products works effectively. It would be possible to undermine this false service market by engineering reliable and simple products, rather than 'becoming a service solutions supplier'.

Understanding these issues in depth can allow new entrants to take a share of a market quickly by undercutting or altering the balance of market dynamics. On the other hand, misunderstanding them can cause the venture to fail altogether.

Structural issues specific to service markets

There are a number of issues which specifically affect the structure of service markets that need to be considered in addition to the more generally recognised market factors covered above. These yield unique insights into the dynamics of these markets and can ensure a more effective entry. Clearly, if others are unaware of them, service suppliers can gain unique competitive advantage by countering their effect.

1. Asymmetry of information

Service markets, particularly professional service markets like consultancy, are structured around asymmetry of information: the fact that the supplier knows more than the buyer about the service. The market might, for example, exist because the supplier has technical knowledge that the buyer needs to pay for. The value of this knowledge, the price the supplier can charge, depends on the scarcity of the skill, its perceived quality and how critical the service is to the customer. But superiority of knowledge also extends to the industry dynamics and the performance of suppliers, both of which affect the nature and structure of the market.

When buyers approach service markets for the first time, they lack knowledge of the various suppliers and are unable to test quality and value in advance. This causes the buyer two risks: 'adverse selection' (they may choose a poor or expensive supplier) and 'moral hazard' (poor behaviour by dubious suppliers, like post-contract opportunism). Service markets must therefore evolve mechanisms to induce trust and counter these problems. They include: regulation, personal reputation of prominent individuals, industry associations and the firms' reputations or brands.

The buying process itself might also mitigate the risks of this lack of knowledge. For instance, many businesses use a selection process which asks firms to present their credentials and proposed approach to a task. During this, suppliers can explain their understanding of the problem and explore different methods to tackle it. This will enhance the knowledge and the decision-making of the buyer.

Asymmetry of knowledge is at the heart of an unarticulated tussle between the buyer and the service provider. At its most simple, this is reflected in the changing attitude of the general population in the developed economies to professionals over the past few decades. Since the 1950s, reverence for professionals, particularly medical practitioners, has been eroded as society in general has become better educated and used tools like the internet to become better informed. Buyers are much more willing to question professionals, challenge prices and get second opinions.

Perhaps more importantly buyers are likely to pay different fee levels due to this asymmetry of knowledge. If the buyer is unfamiliar with the industry and is confronted with a small number of elite suppliers, fees are likely to be high. If, however, the market contains a plethora of competing suppliers offering a familiar and easily understood process, prices are likely to drop and services commoditise.

As buyers become familiar with a sector of the service industry through repeat purchase, they also become familiar with the individuals, processes and characteristics of competing firms. They then seek to get better value for money by cutting parts of the process, facilitating competition or doing some work themselves. The ultimate expression of this is the introduction of specialists into the buying process. They are more able to judge the nature of the technical skill offered and its value to the buyer's firm. When an HR director buys training or recruitment; when in-house counsel buys legal services; when a marketing director buys research or advertising; when a purchasing manager negotiates a formal contract; prices will tend to go down and quality up.

So it is in the interests of service suppliers to maintain a degree of mystery and restraint about themselves and their approach. This is a balance.

The suppliers need to give clues as to their quality while retaining their intellectual property and competitive advantage. As a result, certain industries and certain firms seek to maintain a mystique about themselves and their processes. By guarding their publicity and controlling communications, they exploit the buyers' lack of knowledge, within ethical boundaries, thus maintaining a price differential. Brand is a device which does this for many firms. A member of a large, branded service business is able to allude to industry knowledge or technical skill which would be questioned more closely if operating as a sole practitioner.

So the leaders of a firm which is to move into a service market should ensure that careful research is conducted into asymmetry of information. By segmenting buyers according to their insight into the industry, the basis of differential pricing can be understood.

2. The market as relationships or networks

Relationship marketing theory began to develop in the 1980s as the importance of human relationships in the buying process began to be more fully understood. As this thinking was applied to business-to-business markets, research focussed upon the inter-connection of business relationships in a network. Researchers and theorists were beginning to substantiate the experience of many service suppliers in developing profitable business relationships. For instance, their work has covered the fact that, in a project-based industry, working relationships may only occur during the duration of a project whereas personal relationships have to continue over time. They distinguished between 'bonds' between key participants, links over activities and ties over resources.

This is a behavioural view of markets and is discussed in more detail further on. It sees a market as, primarily, a set of personal networks within which these mutually profitable business relationships occur and suggests that firms can use existing customer relationships as a means of entering a new service market. They can examine their markets by profiling these relationships and methods to build on them – for example, by encouraging referrals. In fact, for business-to-business services, a market profile based on a relationship or network profile could yield better strategic insights than some of the more accepted economic approaches developed by theorists.

3. Segmentation dynamics specific to service markets

The differences between services and products raise several issues which may be used as a basis of segmentation in service markets. These include:

- **The differences between new and experienced buyers.** As discussed in Chapter 3 (page 80), one of the major differences between the purchase of a product and the experience of a service is the process through which the buyer moves. When they use a service they must submit themselves to the service provider's process; ceding control of themselves. As a result of this, new customers, using a service for the first time, become anxious and look for reassurance. It can come from the reputation or brand of the firm providing the service, the simplicity of the service process or the behaviour of people who are part of it.

  However, once the client has experienced the service process a few times, the situation alters altogether. Experienced clients try to take short cuts and try to improve on the service supplier's process. Their emotional dislike of being out of control drives this need (Bateson & Hoffman, 1999). Frequent business flyers show how different the values and expectations of the experienced service user are. Service for experienced clients is more likely to be about streamlined processes or even self-service. The secret to excellent service is to allow them to do more, rather than to perform the service for them. For the customer this is better service and for the supplier it reduces costs.
- **High tech, high touch.** Some people prefer a service which is 'high touch' because they like contact with people. They gravitate towards services which are highly customised and use human beings as part of the service offer. Often they are attracted by the fact that the people involved give them high status during the service. Other people prefer a technology-based service. They like to use technology or tools to investigate and deliver their needs. They are self-reliant and prefer to meet their own needs. So, in many developed economies, while the majority of the population is willing to use ATM technology for their banking services, some niche banks thrive by providing personal service to retirees or rural communities who tend to resist machines.
- **Mind sets.** Customers have different 'mind sets' when they approach a service. Their attitude will be different if they regard it as 'day-to-day use'

or 'an emergency'. Some people, for instance, regard a taxi service as a normal part of their day-to-day life. Others use it only in dire need, when other modes of transport have let them down.

- **Ambience.** People have different styles they prefer from services. Some people like an elegant restaurant and others a noisy, fast bar.
- **Willingness/ability to co-operate in getting service.** Many people are pleased to share the service task and to participate in the service process. Others are not. Some might diagnose faults themselves, while others regard it as a performed service that saves their time.

Each of these differences means that segmentation can be based on issues unique to service markets.

Means of gaining an objective market perspective

Figure 4.3 represents the perspective that a business needs to gain on a market; showing most of the issues relevant for an effective market entry. There are several different approaches to gaining these market insights, each of which has advantages and disadvantages. They are:

- the market research study;
- the market audit;
- scenario planning;
- relationship profiling.

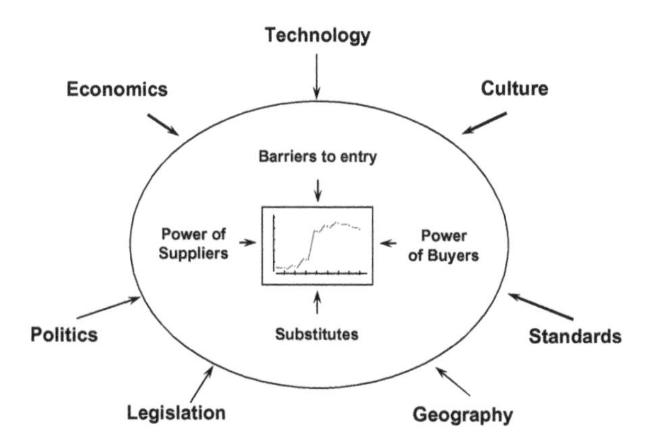

Figure 4.3 Market perspective

1. The market research study

Research projects can give insights into changes in a market, buyer needs and business opportunities but, to be successful, they must be properly managed. An ideal process is outlined below but, whatever steps are taken, the leadership team should be engaged at an early stage. They should be consulted before the project is started and be involved in selection of interviewees. They are then more likely to support the insights revealed by the research and consequent actions. However, research understands only one aspect of market dynamics. Other forces, such as regulation or technological change, also affect the market. Limiting analysis to just field research will miss the potential insights from a broader analysis.

The market research process

1. Agree objectives and research needs.
2. Write brief for agencies. Brief includes:
   - research objectives;
   - summary description of the market;
   - description of the research problem and desired output;
   - description of existing knowledge and previous research;
   - budget constraints;
   - time scales;
   - report requirements;
   - constraints (e.g. interviews must be arranged via customer relationship managers).
3. Shortlist potential agencies.
4. Contact and invite to pitch.
5. Create selection criteria. These might include:
   - technical skills;
   - previous experience;
   - interpretation of the brief;
   - proposed approach;
   - team fit (will the firm's people be able to work with them?).
6. Hold presentations by agencies to selection team.
7. Choose and confirm agency.
8. Negotiate contract.

2. The market audit

A more thorough and objective way to gain an economic perspective on a market is to carry out a full market audit; a concept pioneered largely by Malcolm McDonald (McDonald, 2002). Properly conducted, it is as objective and thorough as a financial audit, and provides a firm basis for planning. The process can take between two and three months to complete but provides very detailed analysis and, more importantly, valuable insights.

Data about the market is gathered under key headings, using analytical techniques to tease out insights which can be the basis for strategic direction and competitive advantage. The information needed is surprisingly easy to obtain. In addition to generic web searches, within business libraries, professional institutes and government departments, there is a gold mine of valuable information, on almost any market in the world, which can be obtained at relatively low cost. In fact, with the advent of the internet and search engines, the main cost is personal effort and time.

How to complete a market audit

Step 1. Analysis of external forces affecting the market

This helps the firm to understand the macro-economic forces shaping markets which are creating or destroying opportunities within them. They include:

- The raw forces affecting the market. Changes in economics, social demography and technology affect the prosperity of the market and there is little the firm can do to influence them.
- 'Moderating forces'. Politics, law and industry-specific regulation moderate the impact of raw forces on the market. These can be influenced by the firm.

By trawling through published data on these issues and drawing them into a perspective on change, surprisingly powerful insights can be found. They could, for instance, highlight an issue on which firms might need to lobby regulators.

Step 2. Understand market structure

- Decide the market's definition.
- Plot the maturity of the market.
- Determine purchasing power. What is the balance of power between suppliers and buyers?
- Examine competition. Who are they and what are their strategies?
- Analyse substitutes. Can buyers get the benefits of the service in any other way?
- Segment the market.

Step 3. Detailed buyer analysis and research

This involves analysis of research into the needs and aspirations of existing and intended buyers. It is wise to start by collecting all published research and previously-conducted research projects in order to identify gaps in knowledge. The team may then come to the conclusion that a specific research study is needed to fill important gaps in knowledge. If so, this is likely to be the most costly and longest aspect of the audit, yet the most valuable. Reassess segmentation, the service offer, pricing and communication approaches in the light of this research.

Step 4. Internal analysis

This is about understanding the internal position of the firm within its market by detailed analysis of both the firm's own competencies and the profile of its buyers. It includes the source of business, revenue and income trends and the potential for growth. This analysis can yield surprising insights. Some firms, for example, believe that their buyers are chief executives, when analysis shows them to be lower level specialists. Others have been surprised to find that larger corporate accounts are less profitable than mid-market, smaller customers. Such insights can yield real benefit for the firm's approach to its market.

The market audit can be conducted by a specialist engaged by the firm or, with assistance, by a sensible, experienced employee. If the culture of the firm is resistant to an analysis of the market, and it is not prepared to spend time gathering data, the process can be run as an interactive session with the leadership team. A half, or one-day session, working through the various subject areas, in data-assisted discussions, is likely to yield insights which can improve the quality of subsequent strategic decisions.

3. Scenario planning

Scenario planning is another analytical tool. It helps firms to think about potential futures in the light of change, complexity and uncertainty. Less linear than the market audit, it allows management teams to explore likely scenarios which might develop from current market forces. With its roots in the military and first developed successfully as a management tool in the strategy process of oil giant Shell, scenario planning creates a framework in which potential strategies can be developed and tested in the light of future uncertainties.

Scenarios can be thought of as stories which help managers to develop different potential futures based on both knowledge and people's assumptions about the present. They are not forecasts, but help provide a common perspective and language (Ringland, 1997).

Usually, a team comprising people from across the firm is formed to construct scenarios. In a session, led by someone experienced in the process, the participants brainstorm potential futures for their firm. Input to their debate might include evidence from futurologists, buyers' views and other pertinent data. The team is normally encouraged to think widely before scenarios are grouped and ranked. A firm moving into a service market can create different scenarios of how that market might develop and how competitors might react to their entry. These different scenarios can then be worked into a market entry plan which anticipates risk.

Ericsson develops service scenarios

Ericsson is a leading provider of telecommunications equipment and related services to mobile and fixed network operators across the world, operating in over 140 countries with over 130 000 employees. At the end of the twentieth century, while at the top of its market, Ericsson recognised that to maintain its leadership, it would need to shift from a totally product-oriented to a more service-driven culture. Further, this culture must be prepared to compete in an increasingly complex, and therefore uncertain, convergent technology industry.

Background

Growing beyond its relatively small, local market in Sweden, Ericsson had developed into a truly global firm before most American companies. As a result, Ericsson developed a culture that accommodated a reasonable degree of local-market, organisational input. Still, like other telecom equipment manufacturers, it had succeeded in part because it had established an efficiently streamlined, centralised command structure. The organisation and culture were geared to the logistics of product manufacturing and distribution.

However, as the communications industry converged with the information technology industry, Ericsson was increasingly required to deal with more complex and faster changing products and markets. For instance, Ericsson's traditional 'fixed-lines', or 'wire-line', business had been augmented and changed by its mobile business; and the company had been required to establish a position in the Internet Protocol (IP) networking market.

These products required the company to provide increasingly sophisticated and varied support at its many, different customer locations. To maintain its competitiveness, Ericsson believed that it needed to change its culture, particularly to make it more distributed and responsive in its decision-making. Because scenario planning is undertaken to engage employees throughout an organisation in open-minded thought about possible, uncertain futures, the scenario-planning process was deemed an especially appropriate vehicle for Ericsson's work.

The process gets under way

Employee involvement was considered to be the most important element in Ericsson's planning process – and for that process to be of greater importance than any specific predictions or ideas that might come from it. Not only was broad employee participation actively sought, but the team also solicited outside ideas and perspectives to enrich the scenario planning. However, external input was kept in check so that the initiative and results of the project belonged to the company and its employees. The process also involved discussions and considerations of:

- elements of the wider environment, including global, social and economic factors;
- certain and uncertain factors.

In addition, Ericsson identified eight driving forces that it judged to be certain and critical factors within its future market:

- Increasingly capable microelectronics.
- Computer paradigm expansion.
- The internet.
- Consumer orientation.
- Globalization and internationalization.
- Mobility.
- Continuing deregulation of telecommunications.
- Increasingly blurred boundaries between the fields of telecommunications, media and data.

However, Ericsson considered the timing and specific direction of these forces to be uncertain and variable, particularly in different geographic regions.

One baseline assumption that Ericsson had made was strongly reinforced by all this evaluation. The telecom, IT and media industries were universally expected to continue converging into one combined industry, which Ericsson called the 'Infocom' industry.

The next step was to classify those trends that were possible – but not certain – within three clusters of direction in which it believed its industry could develop. Each of these three 'scenarios' formed an internally consistent world as it might evolve. Interestingly, Ericsson did not believe that any one of these scenarios would prevail completely. Rather, it believed that some mixture of these three trends would manifest itself, and, that that mix would vary by product segment, geographic region and time. However, services played an important and growing role in each of the three scenarios that Ericsson developed.

The three scenarios

Each of the three 'scenarios' formed an internally consistent world as it might evolve. These scenarios would form the platform for further work within the planning process. They were:

'Service Mania'

In this scenario, end users – individuals as well as companies – would turn to a broker for help in gaining access to an appropriate package containing information and interactive services. Professional users would prefer to draw up contracts with specialised communications networks. The TV channels with entertainment and information would successfully defend their positions against the Internet.

In this world, the end user 'belonged to' the broker, who in turn contracted with 'content providers'. Perhaps the broker would also supply customers with suitable terminal equipment. Customers would be offered different methods, by which they could link up with the network, depending on the service package they had selected. The network operators would function as suppliers to the broker.

In this scenario, the content and service providers would be the financial winners. However, a large percentage of the revenues would also be transferred to the distribution segment, mostly as a result of the expected strong growth in mobile networks. End users would be unaware of this, as they would be paying for content and service rather than for bit transport.

'Gran Tradizione'

It has been said that mankind is basically conservative. If this trait controlled developments, the present way of behaving in business and private life would persist. The end customer would rely on his or her traditional operator to provide the basic services he or she considered essential, and purchase the necessary terminal equipment. Underlying this behaviour is a strong tendency on the part of people, notably in the Western world, to value family and the environment more highly than new technology.

In this scenario, the internet had not achieved the impact that many had predicted but the price of communications services was still expected to decline. However, this would be compensated by increased traffic and the continuing cost-rationalisation measures taken by telecommunications operators. The result of this trend would be a sharp decline in the number of operators in the market; however, those who survived would be strong companies that offered both wireless and fixed communications services.

To satisfy their demand for electronic information services, end users would turn, to an increasing but still limited degree, directly to the content providers. In this scenario, the end user would pay primarily for communications. Accordingly, it would be possible for operators to make heavy investments in traditional networks, particularly in developing countries where providing wireless access to networks has proved to be a cost-effective way of expanding them.

'Up and Away – Full Speed Ahead'

In this scenario, end users would gain access to advanced communications systems virtually free of charge, but, as a rule, they would pay only for the terminal equipment. The manufacturers of the equipment would pay for the communications and for end users' access to the communications network.

Advertising would cover the cost of the content as well as gateways. End users would have accepted, for example, the fact that advertising messages were displayed on their terminals either whenever they used them, or when they logged on to any of the information banks, entertainment services or similar facilities offered through the networks. End users with plenty of money would gladly pay extra to gain access to premium content and advanced gateways to 'exclusive' parts of the 'Futurenet', the worldwide communications system that would have succeeded the Internet.

This 'Futurenet', a broadband network, would handle everything: multimedia, video, television broadcasts, ordinary telephone calls, etc. A significant percentage of end users would prefer wireless access to the Futurenet, since this will not involve any limitation either of the services offered or of the system's 'functionality'.

Technical developments would have made communications simple and inexpensive. Many traditional suppliers would have disappeared from the market, leaving only a few regionally based operators. With the new technology, large financial investments in networks would no longer be required. The manufacturers of terminals and other devices for end users will reap most of the profits in the industry.

Strategic and organisational direction

On the strategic level, Ericsson identified itself as a 'total solutions' firm, and accordingly repositioned itself on the industry's value chain:

- By the turn of the century Ericsson had positioned itself as a full-service telecom outsourcer in selected markets, with its greatest success to date posted in its Enterprise Systems business unit.
- The company had taken steps to divest itself of a number of manufacturing functions (e.g., outsourcing cable assembly tasks to Volex and a number of circuit-board manufacturing responsibilities to Flextronics).
- Ericsson had identified mobile internet access as a core capability by which to leverage the firm's mobile strengths within an IP world.
- The company had formed a consortium with other key players to develop the Wireless Application Protocol (WAP) for furthering the development of mobile Internet capabilities. By 1999 the WAP Forum had more than 100 industry members.

The company also took a number of organisational steps to foster its fledgling services initiatives. It had twice restructured the firm to accommodate its service initiatives. First, as a result of its 'Spinnaker' service-specific planning project that was based on the 'Ericsson 2005' initiative, the company established two services business units: one for maintenance services, the other for professional services. Then, to coordinate these services better, the company subsequently consolidated the units within a single structure.

Ericsson added service staff to its local, customer-level marketing teams and oversaw an initiative within its Enterprise Solutions business unit to provide its customers with 'complete outsourcing solutions'. Then, the company sheltered this still small, far-flung service staff under the supportive umbrella of a corporate-wide 'service committee' that provided a needed unity and focus to its new service efforts. As important as finding common approaches across business units, however, was the committee's role in systematising an understanding as to where the business models of its various units differed and how services initiatives had to be applied differently.

Results

By revenue and culture, Ericsson was still very much a traditional, telecom product provider as it entered the twenty-first century. However, through the 'Ericsson 2005' initiative, the company believed it had made substantial advances in adjusting its culture and strategy. Ericsson was becoming a services-oriented, 'solutions' provider in an uncertain, but rapidly converging, technology and media industry. And, as the company approached the halfway point of its original 10-year horizon, it found its original scenarios to have been remarkably valid.

Early results from Ericsson's 'total solutions' outsourcing were especially promising. Its Enterprise Solutions unit found that shifting from a product to a solutions orientation increased its share of customers' relevant budgets from 12% to 60% of budget. With its 'solutions offerings', Ericsson was winning contracts not only of much larger size, but also tending toward longer duration. Most importantly, the nature of the business was bringing Ericsson in much closer day-to-day partnership with its customers.

This case study is published with the permission of ITSMA.

4. Relationship profiling

Those suppliers who take a behavioural, rather than an economic view of their market can audit the strength and depths of relationships between suppliers and buyers. They can understand the degree of trust, the intimacy of relationship and the effect on buyer behaviour. They can then use this information to strengthen relationships or plan 'viral marketing' campaigns which spread 'word of mouth' messages through interconnected networks in the market.

A tool which can be used to do this is the 'ARR' model. The 'actors–activities–resources' model was developed during the early 1980s, by researchers and theorists interested in both business to business marketing and network marketing. Yet it appears to be a tool that can also be used in practical business contexts as well as just pure theoretical research.

The model divides business relationships into three layers:

(i) 'Actor bonds'. These occur when two business people interact through some professional process. Theorists suggest that there are three components necessary for them to develop. The first is reciprocity during the process, ensuring that both sides give something to the interaction, even if one is a customer. The second is commitment and the third is trust. As people interact they form perceptions of each other about: capability, limitations, commitment and trust. If the relationship develops, these perceptions influence the degree and clarity with which the two communicate; and also the degree to which they involve each other in their own professional network.

(ii) The term 'Activity links' captures the work, or other activity, which is involved in the interaction and business process. These vary with the depth of relationship. They range from simple technical projects through to two firms meshing or adapting their systems and business processes to become more efficient. The latter has created exciting business opportunities in areas such as outsourcing.

(iii) 'Resource ties' are items used by people during business interactions. Resources might include: software, intellectual capital, skilled staff,

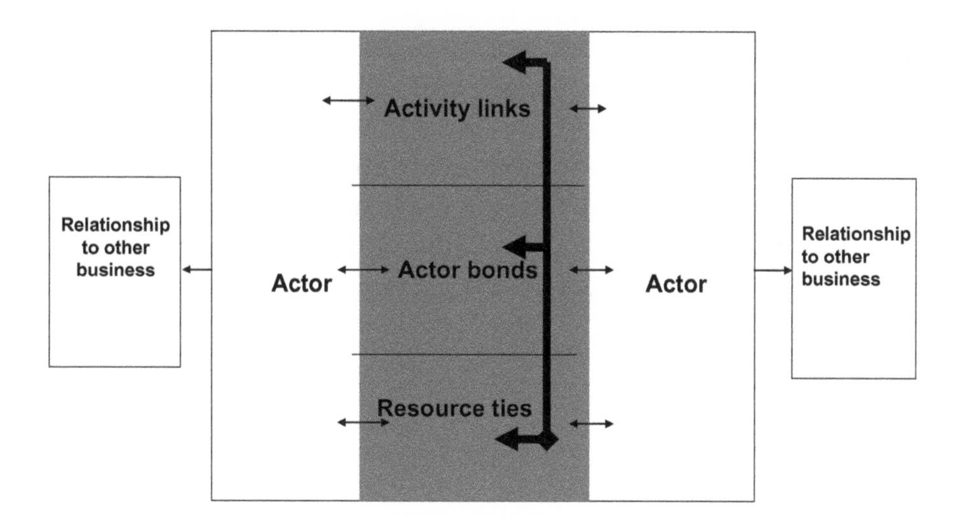

Figure 4.4 The ARR relationship profiling model

knowledge, experience and expertise. People who have resources, or control over them, have greater power in professional networks.

At its very simplest the model can be used as a basis of discussion with internal colleagues to map relationships in a network. They can be asked to complete formats of their client relationships using the three levels of the model. Actions arising from discussion (e.g. creating more opportunities for non-task related exchange or making different resources, such as knowledge, available) to strengthen relationships can be put into account plans.

It can also be used as a basis of detailed analysis and research. A hypothesis of the professional relationships that exist in a market, and the types of interaction, can be created using the terms of the model. It can then be used as a guide to designing a research sample and questionnaires. A two-step, qualitative and quantitative research process is then likely to reveal powerful insights into the relationships clients have with the firm and its competitors.

Opportunity analysis

The reason for undertaking an analysis of a market is to gain insights into new opportunities or to find justifications for closing down declining areas of business. It is then necessary to draw the analysis into an agreed view of the opportunities facing the firm to which resources need to be allocated. In this area, above all else, it is essential to combine such analysis with market insights and the experiential judgement of the leadership team. While a powerful perspective can be gained from informal discussion, there are a number of formal tools which can be used to structure thinking and debate. Used properly, they lead to a consensus and healthy perspective. They are:

- the SWOT analysis;
- the Ansoff matrix;
- the directional policy matrix.

1. SWOT analysis

The best known and most straightforward tool is the 'SWOT' analysis shown in Figure 4.5, which helps a firm to summanise internal strengths (S) and weaknesses (W) along with external opportunities (O) and threats (T). This information can be used to construct the SWOT matrix by plotting the opportunities and threats against the strengths and weaknesses. It can be done interactively, in discussion with the leadership team. However, it is more useful when it is used in conjunction with market analysis for reference. A surprising number of management teams start out with a 'SWOT' brainstorming session and no analysis. Yet if they have a distorted or mistaken perspective on their market, this is counter-productive, since it builds

Strengths	Weaknesses
Opportunities	Threats

Figure 4.5 'SWOT' analysis

that entrenched view of competitive position into the firm's strategy. Moreover, if they are considering an unfamiliar market (such as when a manufacturer considers a service market) the lack of analysis is even more risky because they have very little experience on which to base their judgement.

For the more systematically-minded, the 'TOWS' prioritisation method is useful. This enables the team to match opportunities with strengths and construct clear strategy in a systematic way. Each item in the SWOT matrix is numbered. Then each threat is compared against each weakness and each opportunity against each strength, in a systematic search for strategic options. As the strengths and weaknesses arise from debate about the firm's competencies, the planner is, in fact, checking these against market opportunity through this process.

2. The Ansoff matrix

Corporate strategy pioneer, Igor Ansoff (Ansoff, 1957), developed this matrix, represented in Figure 4.6, to help businesses examine both current and potential offers in current and potential markets. He based it on very detailed, long term research that he conducted into American company behaviours. The matrix helps leaders think through four different growth strategies, which are listed below in ascending order of risk:

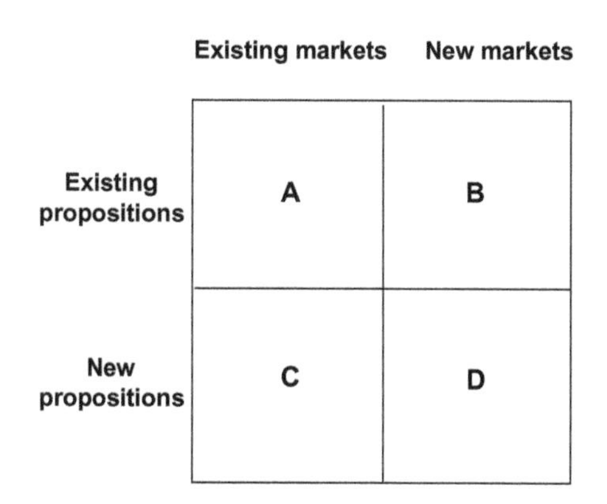

Figure 4.6 The Ansoff matrix
Source: Ansott, 1957.

A Market penetration, or increasing market share with existing propositions to current markets.
B Market extension, or targeting existing propositions at new markets.
C Product development, or developing new propositions for existing segments.
D Diversification, or growing new businesses with new propositions for new markets.

The matrix helps to clarify leaders' thinking and to illustrate the very different strategic approaches needed for each of the four strategies. Ideally, a plan should be constructed for each strategic option that is approved.

3. The directional policy matrix

This tool was introduced in chapter two (see Figure 2.5, page 67). It helps the firm balance its strengths against the attractiveness of a market. Its power lies in the ability to create criteria unique to the firm, which can form the basis for prioritisation of opportunities. For example, it could be that a particular market offers potential growth, or that it contains customers willing to pay high prices, or is easy for the firm to access.

These tools and techniques help create a framework to structure the leadership team's thinking about its markets by developing a common language, by testing assumptions and by helping to reach consensus. Using these tools won't guarantee success or eliminate risk. But they will provide the basis for a more thoughtful and potentially lucrative approach to market entry issues. They will also reduce risk and improve the quality of decision-making.

Summary

It is sensible for the leaders of firms intending to enter a service market to gain a thorough and objective view of it. They need to understand the competitive forces and any opportunities (or dangers) it offers. This chapter has discussed a number of tools and techniques available to help do this which need not be too costly or take too long. Used properly, they provide leaders with a deeper understanding of the potential market and insights which will help with market entry. More importantly, perhaps, they do so by giving leaders a common language with which to debate and discuss the move.

5

Creating the services to be sold in the new market

Introduction and overview

Manufacturing companies have different ways of producing the goods they sell. Some are geared to researching and developing new technology, whereas others improve on a range of offers that were once innovations. Still others adopt sophisticated management processes to research, create and launch branded items for carefully targeted groups of customers. Called new product development (NPD), this is one of the most well understood and substantiated areas of business. But the move into services means that this all has to change. The company now has to make offers that have service content or that are primarily services. Yet, although less well known, there are also well-established tools and techniques which can turn a firm's expertise into appealing, profitable services. In fact, services can be researched, developed, improved and launched much like products. The approach, new service design (NSD), can also help revive services which are in danger of becoming undifferentiated commodities. This chapter discusses NSD in depth and outlines a comprehensive, practical guide to the service design process.

Lessons from new product development

Many companies start business with a product that is an adaptation of, or improvement on, an existing, well understood, product group. Others create a totally new technology for which they have a patent and this becomes the focus of the whole company. Some move their business into a promising new area, opening up new revenue streams and, sometimes, this becomes the main offer of the company. IBM, for instance, existed before it manufactured computers and Nokia before mobile phones. These innovations opened up rich, new markets and went on to dominate their whole business.

As years go by, however, many firms find themselves settling into the steady improvement of one type of product range and can flounder when dramatic change is needed. The computer industry of the 1980s, for example, had become obsessed with enhancing the performance and speed of its main frame and mid range systems primarily for its installed base (that is, customers who had bought their proprietary equipment before and would find it too costly to change). As a result, when real change was needed, due to new 'open' standards and upstart competitors like Microsoft, reputable brands like Digital Equipment Corporation were consigned to history and IBM needed to be saved.

As a survival mechanism, some firms facing radical market change have developed the skill of creating and launching range after range of new products. This proactive creation of new products has been established practice for many years in a number of different manufacturing sectors. Leading organisations in those markets where this approach to new product innovation is a critical business skill have developed highly sophisticated processes which are managed at a senior level in the company. They aim to present many appealing new products to a fast changing market, knowing that at least some will be successful.

As a result, the processes and concepts behind NPD are well-established and known to provide demonstrable value. Research has shown, for example, that a new product design process reduces both the risk of product failure and the costs of innovation.

The widely-recognised factors which contribute to the success of new product design include:

- senior management involvement and control;
- a clear and managed new product design process;
- superiority over existing products;
- investment in understanding the market;
- the proficiency of marketing operations;

- degree of business fit;
- effective interaction between R&D and marketing;
- a supportive management environment;
- effective project management.

Many companies in many sectors now have in place clear and formalised new product creation processes, portfolio management techniques and dedicated product managers; and these can be applied to NSD.

The growing role of new service design and development

In 1991, Canada's Ulrike de Bretani (de Bretani, 1991) conducted research designed to apply the 'conceptual and research paradigms that have evolved from studies of new manufactured goods to services'. His analysis suggested that the issues facing service organisations were similar to those product companies have used NPD techniques to solve. While the technology and steps of the NSD process may be different from those of NPD, the underlying concepts behind their use are not. Both involve creating as many good ideas as possible and then reducing their number by careful screening to ensure that only those with the best chances of success get into the marketplace.

Service offers can be changed, improved, marketed and withdrawn just like physical products. In fact, many NPD techniques can be adapted and adjusted to the service sector in order to improve the likelihood of success. With the growth of the service sector, a more widespread understanding of the importance of NSD to continuing success and growth has developed, with an increasing number of firms generating revenue by either enhancing their core service or creating entirely new services. Their experiments with NSD and exploration of related techniques, along with the confirmation by theorists and researchers of many of the success factors, have contributed to a growing body of knowledge as to what works and what does not. Consequently, NSD is becoming as recognised a function in service companies as NPD is in product companies. Both apply theory, process and experience to the company's need to create new offers. As a result, it is a function which is crucial to the success of any move into service markets by companies with few pre-existing service offers.

The reasons for new service design

The main thrust of this book is the experience of companies which move from manufacturing to services; from selling products to intangibles. Apart from those attempting this transition, there are, in fact, several reasons why companies need to create or refresh the services that they offer to their customers:

1. **Revenue creation**: service ideas are launched simply to increase revenue. A business needs something to sell. NSD is a rational process to create service offers and bring in cash.
2. **Obsolescence of old services**: the need to create new services to replace old ones which no longer appeal to buyers.
3. **Commoditisation of services**: if buyers have lost a sense of value due to bad pricing practices by the suppliers, services can be repositioned and re-launched with a new pricing regime and greater margins. Many modern managers seem to believe that the commoditisation of products and services is inevitable. It isn't. Companies can learn to turn a commodity into a value proposition with healthy margins.
4. **The desire to take advantage of new opportunities**: a company may spot a gap in a market and seek to take advantage of the opportunity.
5. **Increased competition**: services may be created to copy or stay ahead of competitors' offers.
6. **Spare capacity**: services may be launched to use up spare capacity due to troughs in demand.
7. **Seasonal effects**: some services are subject to seasonal changes in demand so new ones might be created to compensate.
8. **Risk reduction**: new services are launched to balance a portfolio reliant on one service.

Common mistakes in service design

In the same way that some new products do not sell, there are many services which do not generate revenue or profit for the businesses that created them. Common mistakes in the approach to NSD include:

1. A lack of differentiation

Many services look the same as competitor offers so that the only basis on which customers can choose is price. As a result they beat down suppliers to the lowest possible level.

2. Allowing the service to become a commodity

A commodity is a product or service which is not valued by potential buyers. They see it as a cheap necessity and are not prepared to pay what they consider to be a high price for the offer. Yet offers only become commodities because suppliers allow them to. It is quite possible to turn commodities into value propositions with the right approach.

3. A poor understanding of buyer needs

One disservice that the gurus of customer care have done is to imply that, by simply asking buyers what they want and meeting or exceeding those desires, firms will engender customer loyalty and create profit. In fact, people generally do not know exactly what they want and cannot envisage new propositions, so their vision will often be limited to improvements on an existing proposition. They may ask for it to be provided faster or cheaper (a course which will drive a supplier progressively out of business) but it is very rare that they will suggest creative new insights.

This is because they can be unaware of the possibilities that new technologies have opened up or they may be unable to articulate their needs. As a result, they will rarely be a source of valuable new ideas for new propositions unless specialised research techniques are used. A good example of this is Coca-Cola. If researchers, at the end of the 19th century, had asked people if they required 'a black drink, full of caffeine and sugar' they would have received very few positive responses. But once the proposition was placed in front of customers, in a way that was attractive, one of the most successful marketing propositions of the twentieth century was born.

Moreover, if suppliers take a technical, superficial approach to the analysis of their customers' needs they will be misled. There are a range of needs beyond the purely technical. Suppliers must use research techniques to understand the true benefits sought by buyers. For instance, the underlying emotions or unarticulated needs are just as important. An insight into these might open up a totally new approach. Research which can uncover such possibilities needs to be explorative or observational.

4. Misapplying the 'solutions' concept

As discussed in detail later, this concept has arisen in the past two decades in several technology industries. It suggests that suppliers offer a 'solution' to customers instead of pre-packaged products or services. Its strength is to challenge suppliers to move beyond pushing a predefined product or service without cognisance of the customers specific needs.

At the time that it first appeared, in the computer industry, the suppliers were selling their machines mainly on the basis of enhanced speed or processing capacity. The 'solutions' concept caused many to take a more analytical, customised approach. They set out to help their buyers articulate their needs and then compare their total existing technology (even if bought from other suppliers) against those needs. As a result they would often put more effort into areas such as network configuration or software design than upgrading specific machines, producing a customised 'solution'.

At heart the 'solutions approach' was a sales technique adapting some software design methods. Account managers and sales people were encouraged to ensure that they used methods to understand customers' requirements and then design a mix of hardware, software and services to meet the need, just as software specialists had analysed departmental needs to specify new computers. Essentially it was an argument to be more responsive to individual customers and to customise technology projects to their needs.

There are two difficulties with this, though. First, the approach generally results in a lack of a clear value proposition. Successful businesses create propositions that customers value through a meeting of mind between suppliers and buyers. The supplier crafts a proposition in the light of customer insight, creating something new which attracts buyers. 'Solutions', by contrast are normally a project by project method to meet the immediate demands of a pressing need.

The second difficulty is that, in industries where the predominant pricing method is 'cost plus' and where there is a tendency to discount to win business, this approach leads to the erosion of margin and profit by endorsing a discount-led culture. Experience suggests that it frequently destroys value. In other industries (cars and tailoring for example) customisation is more expensive than pre-packaged items. A 'solution' ought to be a premium-priced adaptation of technology.

5. Over-reliance on industry reports

Another common mistake is to rely too much on industry-produced reports as a means of gaining market perspective for new service design. In many industries there are specialist research companies which dedicate themselves to tracking buyer and supplier behaviour. Very often these research companies are staffed by technical specialists from the industry rather than skilled researchers and, in order to maintain their own margin, conduct trend analysis based on their previous reports. Their general approach is to take briefs from suppliers and then talk to specialist buyers inside large companies.

These buyers themselves are often influenced by industry magazines and conferences which cover their area of technical expertise rather than their own firm's business needs. They therefore reflect back ideas developed from these media and reinforce emergent beliefs. In this way the members of the industry convince themselves of trends they have heard from the same sources. There is therefore a huge danger that industry research reports are used by internal management and sales people to justify a preconceived notion about what services are wanted, so that industry mediocrity becomes a self-fulfilling prophecy.

6. The 'one-off' service

This is a phenomenon seen in many different businesses. The one-off service seems to arise from a need expressed by a customer to a senior manager. A project team is drawn together comprising various functional experts from across the organisation that creates a unique, unusual answer to the customer's needs. As it is an individual project to meet a specific need, there is much effort involved and costs are high. In addition, because these projects are unusual, they attract attention.

If successful, they are presented to others in the company as potential ideas that might dominate its future portfolio. They are seen as a 'future direction for the company'. However, this relies on an ability to replicate (to industrialise) services. As companies rarely have established processes to turn ideas into replicable services, the costs of turning individual customised projects into firm-wide offers are often prohibitive and the attempt fails.

7. 'Over-claim'

The sales literature of many firms claims that their service is 'leading edge', 'world-class' or 'the best'. Yet there is rarely any objective measure or justification for this claim. In fact, the service is often the same as that of peers. Whereas it is accepted that product companies can be niche or least-cost suppliers, producing different products and encouraging choice, this is less common in service markets. Many exaggerate the benefit of their service and thus create cynicism among their customers.

8. The lack of a clear value proposition

A good number of service offers, particularly in business-to-business industries, are unclear and complex. The suppliers fail to create a simple value proposition which appeals to buyers over others. They should present their offers in a way that stimulates their customers' imagination and helps them to clarify their needs by assessing the benefits of that proposition. Over the decades, simple value propositions as different as Heinz Ketchup, French Champagne and Nike trainers have made huge profit by appealing to different groups of human beings. Suppliers need to do exactly the same with services.

9. A 'product-led' approach

Most industries have evolved through a sales boom. As explained in Chapter 1 (pp 12–16), this is a period of powerful natural demand when suppliers have difficulty simply servicing demand by creating sufficient reliable product and making it available through their sales channel. During this wonderful phase the industry is supply-driven and 'product-led', but it eventually comes to an end.

When the market matures, this successful behaviour can lead to mistakes. Firms which are primarily production machines are then exposed to huge costly errors if they have no NSD management process. They do not have the organisational focus on adjusting their offer to changed market opportunity.

10. Servility rather than service

Customer orientation and responsiveness are vital to the success of service support specialists. However, years of client service creates something akin to servility in some. They undervalue themselves, their firm and their services. It leads to discounting and, eventually, declining revenues. Managers with a servile attitude should be kept away from pricing work because they will tend to undervalue the offer.

11. Inadequate component design

As services are intangible, companies can offer them to the market with too little preparation or design. They are therefore lacking in coherence and disappoint customers.

Clearly, for companies to create real value out of the services that they are designing, they must introduce techniques, skills and practices to minimise the mistakes listed above. The NSD methods and approaches are geared to institutionalise the creation of effective, competitive services and do just that.

Where NSD can be applied

NSD can be used to change the firm's core service or to create added value services and completely new offers.

The 'core' service offer

Many companies claim that they have been 'creating service for years'. By this they mean that they have invested resources, processes, training and skilled people into the systematic improvement of the core service that they offer to the market. They are moving down the 'experience curve' so that, over time, costs systematically decrease and enhancements are made to the service. This is a natural evolution which can be helped by more structured NSD techniques.

An NSD approach is particularly important if a company's core service is a commodity and needs to be turned into a value proposition to stop the erosion of profits. The firm needs to create a new perception of value for its core service by positioning the service differently in different markets. First, the supplier must create different versions of the core service for different segments of buyers. Secondly, NSD techniques can be used to create ideas which enhance the existing service, and improve its perceived value over time. This is illustrated in Figure 5.1.

Through research and innovation processes, the supplier identifies improvements to the core service which will appeal to buyers. These are launched as a 'premium' service for which an extra price is charged and the enhanced service earns extra revenue from some customers. However, over time, customer perceptions change so that these premium features become a market standard. They fall into the core service and this new package replaces the old basic offer. The perceived value of the core service either increases in value or holds steady. The supplier now has to create a new premium offer in order to maintain the value position over time.

A product analogy illustrates this evolution well. The basic car offered by a manufacturer establishes value expectations in one segment of the market. This also sets a benchmark that defines the features for which spe-

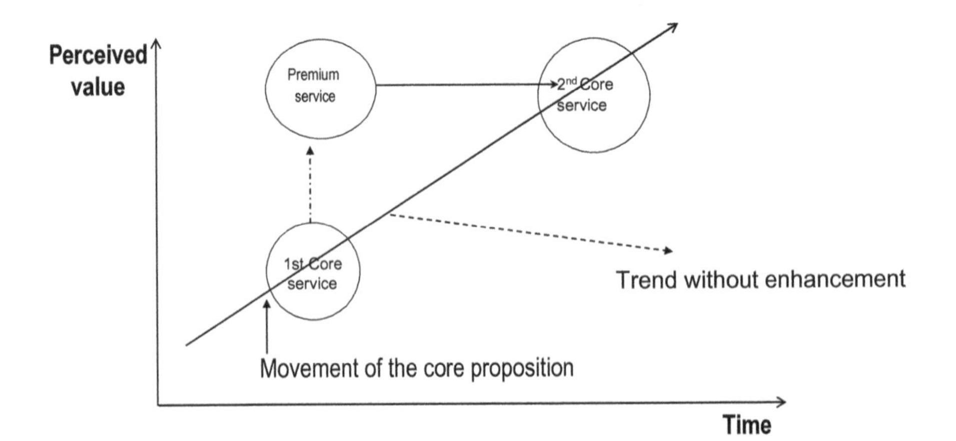

Figure 5.1 Method to maintain service value

cific groups of buyers will pay extra; the 'GTI' or 'Supra' model. Yet, over time, car buyers begin to expect a different package of features to be included 'as standard' with the basic car. This is caused by both a general rise in the expectation of buyers and the actions of competitors.

The car with the enhanced features then becomes the standard offer and a new benchmark becomes the norm. As a result, the bundle of features offered by the car industry some twenty years ago (i.e. a low performance engine with no sun roof and manual windows) would be unacceptable to the modern buyer. Over time the core offer has increased in value through the introduction of added value features. This management of features is highly sophisticated and requires an institutionalised approach to NPD or NSD.

Interestingly, experienced manufacturers do not put into the standard offer all the features that they know customers will want. There might be one feature (such as, at the time of writing, coffee cup holders, satellite navigation or a DVD player for the rear seats) which they deliberately put into the premium offer. Customers who buy the basic offer notice that there is something in the premium offer that they want and this causes them to consider buying it next time. In this way the supplier creates aspiration and repeat purchases.

Through the application of creativity to the core service it is quite possible, then, to turn a commodity into a value proposition. Services offered by utilities, banks and high technology companies can be rescued from crisis and commoditisation in this way. This is one of the primary roles for service design in the single service company.

The application of service design to 'added value' services

In many industries, added value services such as maintenance and warranties have been created which increase revenue and profit from product propositions where no service content has existed before. They maintain the value of the proposition, generating extra revenue and profit. They also enhance the relationship to customers and create knowledge of future needs through more regular contact with them.

Service designers need to apply NSD techniques to added value services. This implies that proactive service creation needs to be undertaken whether the added value proposition is:

- a complaints department or warranty service;
- a maintenance or support service;
- a proposition wrapped around a product sale;
- a service component of a product sale which now needs independent value.

The creation of unique, new services

This is the focus of much of the research, theory and writing on NSD. It demonstrates that it is possible to create new service propositions that have their own value and succeed in the market. They may be delivered electronically, through people or via physical channels. Either way, it is clear that the proactive creation of service, and techniques to make this effective, are an important competence that companies need to foster, especially if changing from product manufacturers.

Shaping different service offers

The offers of companies are often a mix of physical parts and intangible service components. Yet, whether the service offer is the 'core service', a 'support service to a product' or an 'added value service', these components can be planned, identified, adjusted and mixed to appeal to different groups of buyers. Whether they are physical, technical, process-based, artistic, human or emotional, they should be planned carefully. If product designers need to use detailed design and planning systems to adjust physical product features (because manufacturing or packaging processes need detailed specifications) then they should also be applied to service propositions. These different offers can be identified and precisely planned using Lynn Shostack's 'goods/services spectrum' of offers. It is shown in Figure 5.2 as it was modified by Leonard Berry (Berry & Parasuraman, 1991).

The detailed planning of the components of each of these offers can be based on a method used by marketing specialists to understand the components of products, as illustrated in Figure 5.3. This suggests that every proposition offered to a market has three types of features. They are 'core', augmented and emotional.

- 'The core feature'. This is the hub of the offer and is the prime benefit to buyers. In the case of a briefcase it will be to 'carry documents', in the

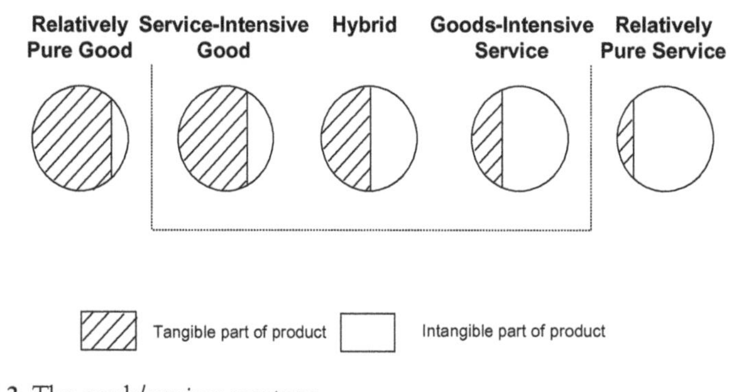

Figure 5.2 The goods/services spectrum
Source: Berry & Parasuraman, 1991.

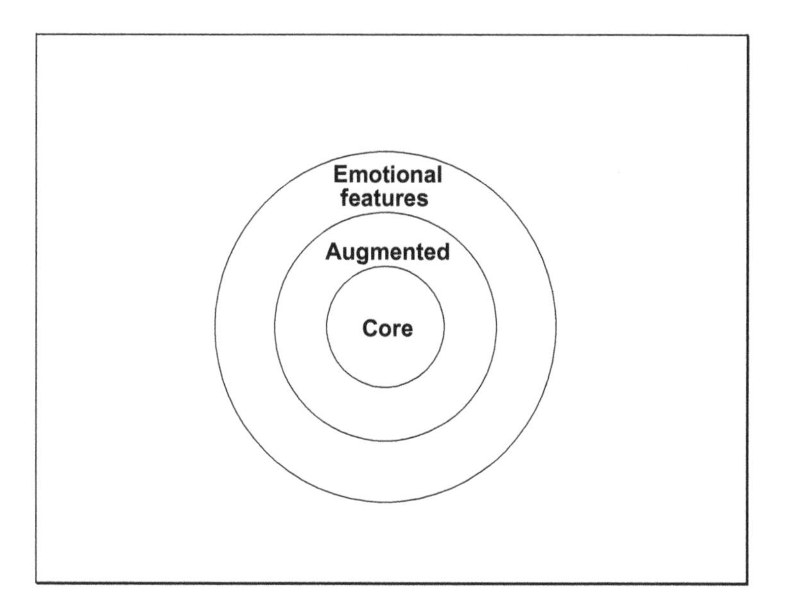

Figure 5.3 The elements of a pure product

case of a car it will be 'personal transportation'. Experience shows this to be one of the most difficult aspects of product and service design. Designers frequently find it difficult to settle on the core proposition; yet it gives meaning to the entire offer.

- 'Augmented features'. These are the physical components of the product through which the designer chooses to express the core feature. In the case of a briefcase it would include the choice of leather, latches, nature of stitching, internal construction, etc. In the case of a car it would include the engine, the bodywork, the colour and the physical layout of the car. This is the design and assembly of physical components around identified customer need.

- 'Emotional features'. These are designed to appeal to the buyers' underlying, often unknown and unarticulated, emotional requirements and they can be the most influential aspect of the proposition to the buyer. They particularly affect perceptions of value and, without them, many offers become commodities. Although they are actually offered through the physical (augmented) features, the emotional ring of the planning tool is there to remind designers to proactively plan their presence. They are particularly tied to the firm's brand values. For example, the emotional promise of a briefcase that is labelled 'Gucci' will give a different message, to one which is labelled 'Woolworths'.

  Incidentally, the importance of emotion in the planning of a business-to-business proposition is just as critical as it is in consumer propositions. Business-to-business buying is not, in reality, much more 'rational' than consumer buying, despite the formal buying processes that exist. Business buyers are human beings who experience emotions at work. In fact, many business decisions are based almost entirely on emotion or belief. The degree of risk, personal enhancement or political effort in a purchase, particularly a service purchase, can be decisive.

It is the proactive management of this mix of features that allows managers to design increasingly sophisticated versions of their product in the light of feedback from markets. This allows the suppliers to profit through the evolution of differentiated offers.

If Figure 5.3 represents a pure product at the far left of the goods/services spectrum, then Figure 5.4 represents a product with a maintenance, guarantee, warranty or 'service support' package which is a little further toward the centre of the spectrum. The core proposition is a physical product in which the supplier has accepted, generally because it is based on new technology, that faults will occur. Service has to be provided as an emotional reassurance to the purchaser of the enduring provision of those benefits. So the service component is primarily an emotional reassurance to accompany a product offer. The promise is: 'don't worry, if it goes wrong we'll repair it quickly'. This form of service support has been provided in many product categories over the years, from washing machines and cars through to airplanes and elevators.

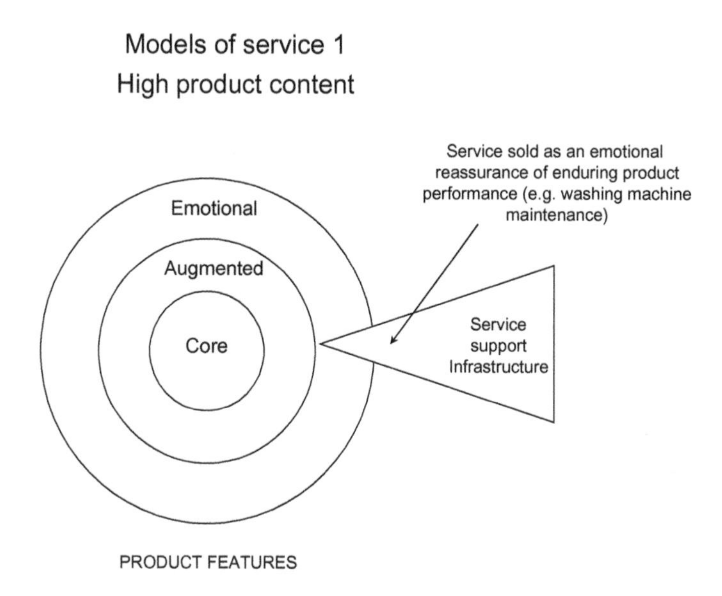

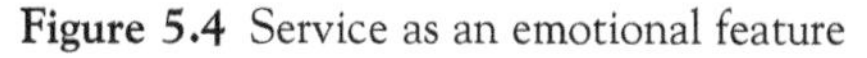
Figure 5.4 Service as an emotional feature

Models of service 2

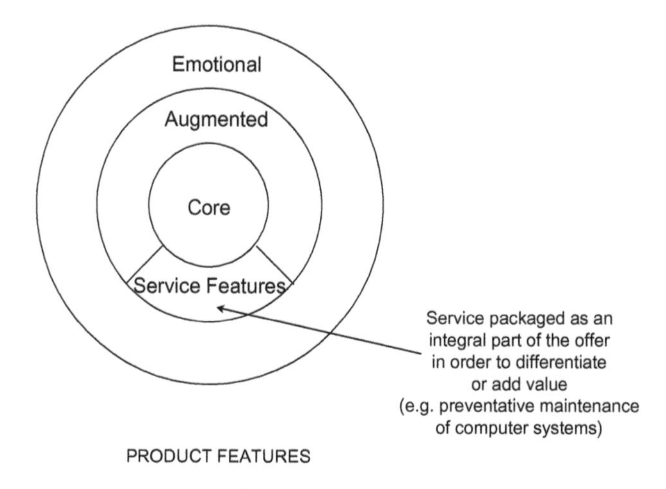

Figure 5.5 Service as an augmented feature

Figure 5.5 represents an evolution in a market where suppliers begin to build service into the product concept. It occurred, for example, in the computer industry during the latter half of the twentieth century. Suppliers began to provide preventative maintenance through a monitored service involving people, procedures and technology. It was sold as part of the product offer so that computers failed less due to self-diagnostic technology and preventative maintenance. This was an entirely different proposition to the previous maintenance contracts, promising almost complete availability of the product's benefits and gave competitive advantage to the first suppliers in different product groups to offer it.

In this model, service has become an augmented component of the product offer. The promise is: 'we have engineered service into our product so that it will almost always be available to use'.

Figure 5.6, by contrast, represents a position at the centre of the goods/services spectrum. It is a hybrid in which people are buying a mix of service and product and is common in industries which offer a high volume, low margin product. The fast food industry, for example, uses service to sell a cheap product. The brand, environmental design, product range, technology support, people behaviour, method of accessing the service and the process through which the service is provided are all integrated into a holistic experience which people buy. This is the core service of fast food retailers and has evolved over a long period of time. Yet the hybrid model can also be used to design complex business services such as systems integration projects

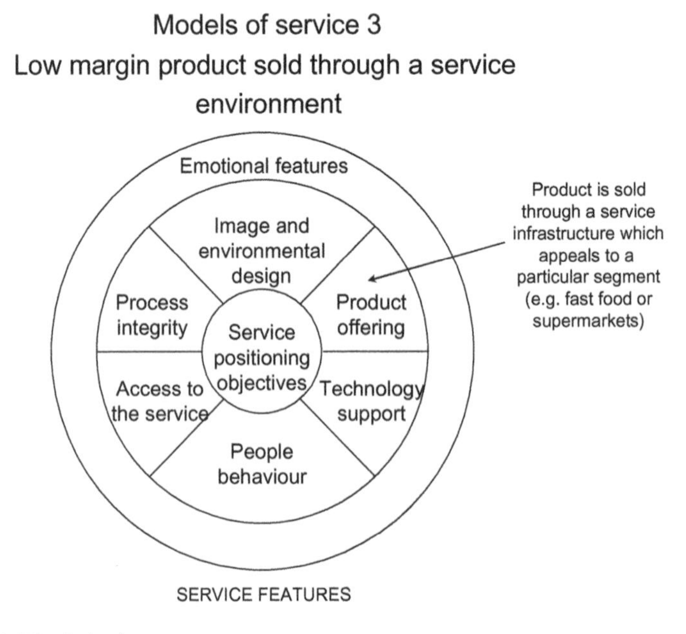

Figure 5.6 The hybrid

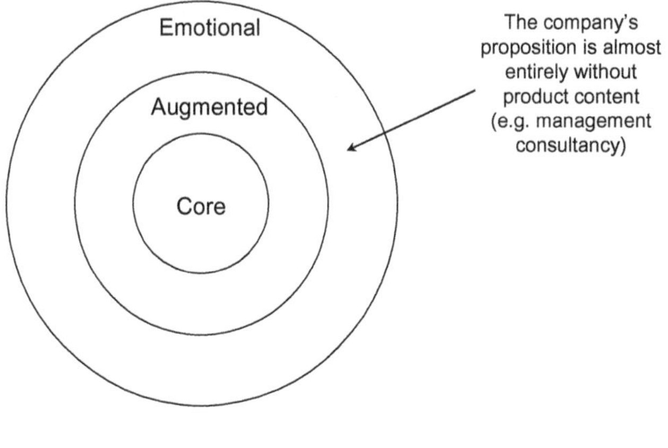

Figure 5.7 The intangible service

and outsourcing. Interestingly, in this model, any products (from hamburgers to software and servers) are augmented components of the overall service. The other service components, such as the behaviour of service people, are just as important in delivering the benefit of the offer.

Figure 5.7 represents an almost pure service offer at the far right of the goods/services spectrum which has very little physical or product content. An example would be management consultancy where any physical components (such as bound reports) are merely a reassurance to the buyer that quality and value exist in the offer. The tangible elements are a reassurance of the intangible benefit. As explained elsewhere, suppliers need to make the intangible offer more tangible to buyers and users by the deft integration of physical elements into the offer. 'Product' has become an emotional component of the offer.

Full circle: back to products

It would be a mistake to give the impression that the evolution of offers in a market are only from left to right on the Shostack spectrum; from product to service. There are many examples of the reverse happening, so that products or technologies replace services.

One example is the replacement of some service tasks by self-service technology. This ranges from very simple propositions, like the replacement of laundry services by automatic washing machines, to more complex modern services, like self-service check-in at airlines and many web-based services on the internet. This substitution effect is dependent on two things: the difference in the perceived cost of changing to new technology and the education of the user to adopt the new technology.

Despite the subliminal, emotional need to regain control, explained elsewhere, there is a natural reluctance to move toward self-service which suppliers must plan to overcome. Customers have to have a strong incentive to learn, an easy socialisation process or training. So the success of self-service technology is critically dependent on the customer being trained in its use. This might be an explicit training experience or a subtle socialisation process. Most modern consumers did not notice, for instance, how they were shown the process (of similar complexity and public exposure) of putting petrol in their car or taking money from an ATM, even if they may still have difficulty with the equally simple process of programming their video/DVD player.

Designing the tangible and intangible linkages

Having decided on the detailed nature of the proposed service offer, it is sensible to plan the linkage of the different tangible and intangible components. 'Molecular modelling' is a technique which allows planners to do this.

The method breaks down the offer into 'tangible' and 'intangible' elements. In Figure 5.8 tangible elements are represented by a firm circle whereas intangible elements are represented by dotted lines. The outer rings represent various aspects of marketing such as price, distribution and positioning. Lines interconnecting the various elements show the interrelationship of processes which deliver the service.

The classic representation of the technique (for airlines) is reproduced in Figure 5.8. In this case the intangible core service (flight) is carried in a tangible product (the cabin) but contains an intangible added value service (in flight care) which is judged on some tangible components (the meal). The benefit of this technique is that it allows the service designer to vary components to match the requirements of different customer groups,

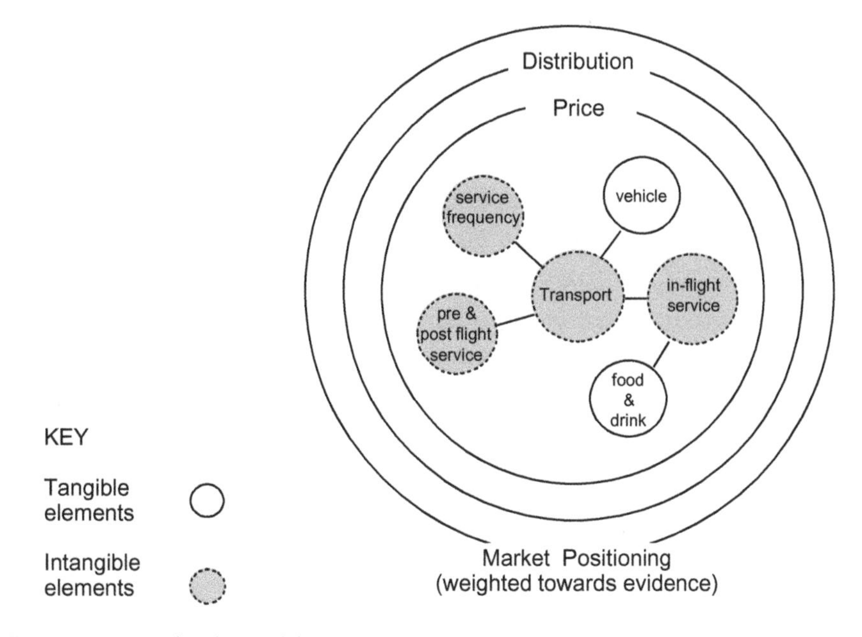

Figure 5.8 A molecular model of an airline
Source: Shostack, 1977.

adjusting the different elements to match needs which are important to them.

The steps to completing a molecular model are:

(i) Identify the 'nucleus' of the proposition.
(ii) Identify physical and intangible elements.
(iii) Link the elements.
(iv) Ring the total entity and define it by its price.
(v) Clarify its distribution method, so that its relationship to the customers is obvious.
(vi) Describe its brand positioning or 'public face'.

Thinking through and designing the customers' experience

As discussed in Chapter 3 (page 79), one of the major differences between the purchase of a product and the experience of a service is the process through which the buyer moves. This has an impact on the customers' experience of the service and their reaction to it. In many cases it is a major influence on repurchase intent. Some industries call it 'the customer journey', reflecting the way it controls the customers' experience and affects repurchase intent. It has several components: the sales process, the contract, the delivery and completion. It needs to be thought through and each phase carefully designed. A technique which can be used to do this, to map the customer process, is 'service blueprinting'. Using this, the process through which buyers move can be mapped and designed. It is an important step in pro-ducing effective services and is represented, in Figure 5.9, using Lynn Shostack's example of a simple shoe shine service.

The approach uses recognised flow diagram techniques to chart the course of the customers through the service process. However, it clearly differentiates between processes that the customers see and those that they don't.

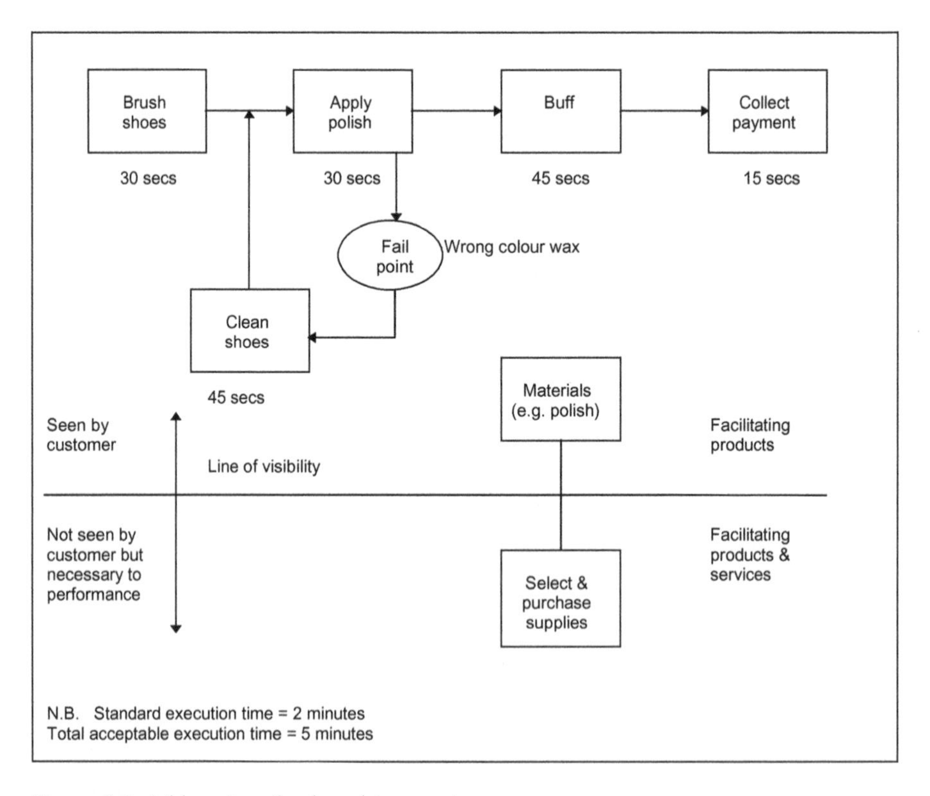

Figure 5.9 A blueprint of a shoe shine service
Source: Shostack, 1982.

This is called the 'line of visibility'. This separation has been important to many service businesses. The separation of 'front office' and 'back office' processes has been especially helpful in retail banking, for example. It has allowed the firms to streamline and centralise back office processes, improving their productivity. At the same time, they have been able to recruit people, whose strength is relating to other people, into their front office.

An important part of the blueprinting technique is the timing of each step that the customer experiences. By isolating and timing them, tolerances can be measured and adjustments made. In some cultures, for instance, speed is the essence of good service and unnecessary delays can drive customers elsewhere. On the other hand, it can be a negative. Some telephone services have found, for instance, that an instantaneous answer with no ring tone irritates customers who value a few seconds of ring tone to collect their thoughts. Blueprinting allows the planner to get the balance right for each customer group.

A final, but important step in blueprinting is to design emergency procedures or likely responses to failure. In Lynn Shostack's example, it was how to recover from the wrong polish being applied to shoes. All organisations and all human beings experience errors. It is sensible to think of likely errors and build recovery from them into the service process. It is also important to give front line service employees clear guidelines as to the latitude they have in correcting errors of customising the process. Too little will cause immense customer dissatisfaction, whereas too much will add costs, perhaps prohibitively.

Generally the service process must encourage customers to receive the benefits they are seeking. It must be designed to help them and to allay any fears they have. Any hiccup in the process or lack of forethought will cause them to become disaffected and buy elsewhere.

Making sure that the service is a true value proposition

A value proposition is an offer to buyers which meets most of their buying criteria at a price which they regard, however unfairly they form that judgement, as value for money. Contrary to popular belief in many industries, price, or more accurately, cheapness is not a buyer's prime consideration. Sometimes they are willing to pay more for a particular item and sometimes they deliberately choose an 'expensive' offer. It depends on the value of the offer to them.

However, in reality, most effective value propositions have evolved naturally over time. Suppliers create an offer to which buyers respond. The supplier then adjusts the offer in response to how they see it being used and launches an adjusted mix of components. Yet evidence exists that neither the supplier nor the buyer frequently understand what is happening. Human beings make many of their decisions based on belief, emotion or impulse. They frequently do not know, or cannot articulate what they want or why a particular offer appeals to them. It may resonate with past memories or vague, unarticulated aspirations. Similarly, the individuals in the supply organisation might be unaware of the reason their offer resonates, particularly if they have no regard for research or methods to understand the mind of their target market.

Moreover, some new services fail to make money, not through poor planning of the service concept or its components, but because it is misrepresented in the market place. The marketing and sales literature is merely a description of the various components of the service. It would be ridiculous, for example, to describe a fast food outlet as follows: 'Our service contains people in a carefully designed uniform who prepare food very quickly using the latest technology to cook a limited range of food so that it is both hot and ready to eat very quickly.' Buyers would be bored by the time they reached the end. Yet this is exactly what many service firms do, particularly in the business-to-business sector. As a result, they waste many forests of expensively produced brochures. Instead, an attractive proposition, which summarises the offer in clear terms, must be put to the market.

Companies fail at this because the creation of a value proposition is frequently fragmented. A project team will create the components of the service, a finance leader will agree pricing, a sales or account manager will work out benefits to buyers and an advertising agency if used, will create a one sentence proposition. It would be better if this crucially important function was managed in an integrated way. A dynamic model is needed to turn the raw components of the service into a unique proposition. This is represented in Figure 5.10, which suggests that the supplier thinks through several elements to the creation of a true value proposition:

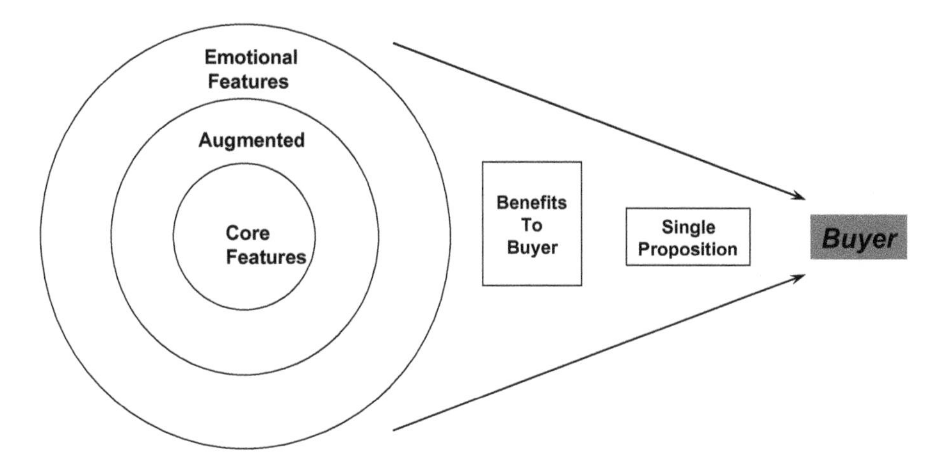

Figure 5.10 Dynamic model of a value proposition

- A clear understanding of the buyers it is aimed at, their rational and emotional needs.
- An integrated view of the practical, design and emotional components of the offer, and their value to the buyers.
- A clear view of the benefits of the proposition.
- A short market-based description of the offer.

The service design process

De Bretani's research (de Bretani, 1991) showed that the existence of a service design process was a good indicator of a firm's proficiency in service design and ultimately of its competitive success. It also demonstrated that, by using a rational design process, it is possible to create new service-based propositions proactively.

The general NPD process can be adapted to service design, with certain elements added or heavily modified. The world's leading software companies have found, for instance, that they have been able to apply their rigorous software development processes to their support services with real success. As a general rule, those services that are high-volume, low-margin and easily replicable can be developed more easily using a rigorous development plan than those that are highly customised (like professional services). The process suggested in Table 5.1 contains the tasks necessary to develop services.

Table 5.1 *An NSD process*

A service design process	
Step 1	Analysis: business backdrop and buyer analysis.
Step 2	Idea generation.
Step 3	Prioritisation of ideas against the firm's criteria.
Step 4	Detailed component design.
Step 5	Create the value proposition.
Quality check: are the unique considerations of services thought through?	
Step 6	Create the concept representation.
Step 7	Research: Focus groups with buyers to test the concept.
Step 8	Write the 'product' plan.
Step 9	α and β trials.
Step 10	Launch.

The process starts with the creation of ideas. Many service firms develop an attractive idea without first stopping to consider if there is an alternative which will have greater appeal to the market. This tendency is exacerbated if there is pressure to generate funds. It is sensible, however, to step back and stimulate ideas from people within the business before putting effort into new service creation.

Once a list of potential ideas has been created they need to be prioritised. A variety of criteria can be created which might be related to the objectives of the firm, the need to generate more funds from existing customers or the need to develop a new area of expertise. The criteria must be specific to the firm and practical.

The process then moves on to the design of the detailed components of the new service and the translation of those into a value proposition. Finally, each aspect of the service, including marketing materials, sales process and service delivery are summarised into a detailed business plan, which will test the viability of the service, through financial rigour and research before launch.

Creating and managing a balanced portfolio of service offers

In order to stay competitive, a business must continue to offer an up-to-date and broad range of products or services in a relevant way to a particular market. Yet all propositions (whether product, service or hybrid) have different levels of success. Even the most profitable might earn low margins when first launched or when reaching the end of their 'life'. Most need some sort of adjustment during their lifecycle and, if not managed properly, can cause real damage. If a company is offering a range of products which are, for example, all reaching the end of their life, then its survival is threatened. A successful company is therefore likely to have a range of offers and it is sensible to ensure that it is balanced, with offers at different stages of development.

There are various tools which help think this through. They are:

(i) The 'Boston matrix'

The Boston matrix (see Chapter 2, p 66–67) is commonly used to discuss a portfolio of products or services.

Managers can be heard to talk of their products as either being a 'cash cow' or a 'dog'. This misuse of the concept is dangerous, because the phenomenon on which the tool is based rarely relates to the volume sales history of an individual product or service. Often called the 'product life cycle', this concept is still unreliable and controversial. Yet managers often assume that an old product is at the 'mature' phase of its 'life cycle' and therefore, a 'cash cow'. In addition, one of the fundamental assumptions of the matrix is that market share is a measure of success. This is based on the experience of consumer product industries, where the likes of Coca-Cola and Pepsi, or Unilever and Procter & Gamble, may fight over tiny percentage increases in share. However, market share is not necessarily a critical issue for service businesses.

An example of this is the executive search market, where high-quality suppliers operate an 'off limits' rule. This means that, if they are contracted to find senior executives on behalf of a client, they agree not to approach their employees as candidates for other searches. Clearly if they had a high share of one business sector this would restrict the number of companies available in which they could search for candidates, and thus limit their ability to deliver the service. Market share is not, therefore, a measure of success in this market.

(ii) The directional policy matrix

Portfolio strategy can be deduced from the 'GE/McKinsey' (see Chapter 2, pages 67–69) matrix. For example, a product or service in a highly attractive market which is weak clearly needs investment, whereas one that is weak in an unattractive market needs to be with drawn or sold.

This tool has been used by various service organisations to help them prioritise resources and to approach new markets. In each case it has proved to be useful in creating viable, practical service strategies. It is particularly powerful at creating a consensus among the leadership team during the ranking of criteria and the rating of individual practices.

(iii) Line extension

Another way of developing a service portfolio is 'product line extension'. This categorises products according to a 'range' or a 'line', like a manufacturing line. Designers look for applications based around the service competence that produces them, and then try to apply them to new markets or different segments within a market. Theorists argue that the range should have 'width and depth'. 'Width' refers to the number of different 'lines' offered, while 'depth' refers to the assortment of offers.

(iv) Using Lynn Shostack's product/service spectrum

A drawback of recognised portfolio planning techniques is they do not help managers to think through the product/service mix of their propositions. However, the modified model originally created by Lynn Shostack, in Figure 5.2, can be a particularly useful and practical method of planning the strategic direction of a portfolio. Changes in the strategic direction and positioning of the company, or changes in demand, can be incorporated into this diagram and used to plan the structure of the company's 'proposition portfolio' (i.e. the mix of products and services).

Management issues

(i) The creation of 'product managers' for services

Manufacturing companies frequently create a 'product manager' for their most important products. This individual is a senior manager who is dedicated to the management of the features and benefits of a product and its success in the market. Product managers often have worldwide responsibility for the creation of new products, the adjustment of existing products and the deletion of products from the range. They are invariably people who have either a technical background and/or a deep knowledge of the organisation. They are trained in new product creation techniques and have responsibility for the business plan of the product, for understanding the requirements of buyers and for the profitability of the whole range.

Clearly if the creation of new services is important to organisations moving from products to services, they should consider creating dedicated 'service managers' who have equal weight and responsibility to product management. The role of a 'new service development manager', modelled on the product approach, would be to:

- create new services;
- adjust the features mix of existing services;
- withdraw old services;
- prepare and manage the business plan for a particular service;
- be responsible for the profit of the service being brought to market;
- establish all processes necessary to launch the service successfully and generate revenue from it.

(ii) Senior champions

One of the criteria for success in NPD is senior management sponsorship, often from a board committee. Product companies which have moved into services have had to create 'service champions', individuals responsible for the spread of a new service concept through the organisation. These tend to be senior managers with weight in the organisation who take on the role of 'political champions' for the concept of that service.

This role is necessary because of the difficulty of selling new service concepts inside a product or sales-orientated organisation. The need to get buy-in from so many different functions and individuals means that internal marketing is critical to the success of the service. A service champion also needs the skill to encourage the members of a project team to perform at their optimum level and achieve the NSD objectives. He or she must lead the team, smooth over disagreements and, particularly, give support to the new service concept at all levels in the organisation.

One difficulty in NSD is how to achieve the necessary level of integration between headquarters functions and field groups, particularly if the latter are delegated business units or different geographic businesses in an international organisation. Representatives of each unit need to be drawn together and co-ordinated by an individual with a firm-wide and, often, an inter-national perspective. Service champions must lead this, overcoming any dislocation between the local and global perspective. They should manage project teams of individuals to take each idea and establish it as part of the common service range.

(iii) Investment controls ('development gates')

Experienced product manufacturers build control points into their NPD process (often called 'gates'), which manage the rate of investment in a new idea. At the first gate, product managers are given a budget to complete initial feasibility and research. They are then required to return to the management group for authorisation for further funds to go to the next phase. Some financial service companies are as disciplined in this as manufacturers and build as many as eight gates into their NSD process. Controls of this kind would save other service firms from wasting investment.

(iv) Measurement of NSD

Leaders ought to establish criteria by which new services are considered to be effective. The measurements put in place by top management give signals to the organisation as to what is important and what gets priority. If the creation of new services is important to a company, appropriate success measures must be created. De Bretani's research identified a number that are used in American and Canadian firms:

- Sales performance.
- Competitive performance.
- Cost performance.
- 'Other booster' (i.e. how it affects other offers or other costs).

Tackling future needs: the management of service creativity and innovation

There are well researched projects and many anecdotal stories about the need to bring innovation to new product development. In fact, some researchers have suggested that the ability to innovate new products and services is the key to survival for some companies operating in a number of fast changing markets.

The management of innovation in those product companies is often a clearly defined discipline, whose principles are well understood. Some manage innovation and creativity by keeping the organisation small and by ensuring the management team stays focused on the creation of new opportunities. This has generally been the strategy followed, for example, by Virgin Group. Its founder and head, Sir Richard Branson, said at a conference of the UK's Institute of Directors, that as soon as a business unit gets to a certain size, he breaks it down to retain the benefit of small company innovation inside a large brand. Other companies have turned from large bureaucratic organisations to smaller, innovative cells in response to a near disaster which meant missing an opportunity. This is reported to be the experience of 3M after its initial lack of response to the original idea of 'Post it' notes.

Some other product companies have managed creativity by using an external agency. These agencies, which came to prominence in the 1970s, are known as 'new product development companies'. They take a brief from managers in the same way that advertising agencies or research companies take briefs from marketing departments. These briefs contain requirements to produce new products, offering benefits to new markets for whatever reason.

The then drinks company, IDV used, for example, a small creative agency to develop the famous 'Bailey's Irish Cream' (since bought by others). The requirement was to produce an 'apparently traditional' product, originally to use spare production capacity, with typically Irish ingredients like whisky and cream. These agencies have specialist processes to explore the target market, to design the offer and to specify manufacturing and packaging. They return to the company a researched concept which can be taken, through a detailed business plan, into manufacture.

Some service companies use similar innovation techniques. Yet it is rare for them to have established idea generation processes and it is relatively rare for them to set about the creation of ideas proactively. Formal schemes, such as they are, generally consist of a method of recording ideas, or an escalation route to a manager or 'ideas' group for assessment of potential. Most service companies encourage their employees to submit ideas, but following up the resultant propositions is often a weak point at which the process can break down. In short, the rational and proactive management of innovation in much of the Western service sectors appears to be weak, leading to an inability to industrialise potential ideas.

Summary

The success of a move into services hinges on the ability to generate funds from viable service propositions; and there are recognised processes and techniques by which service firms can create effective new services. Understanding the management issues and techniques involved in developing new services and breathing new life into existing ones should be of far greater importance to aspiring service firms than it currently is. The processes and concepts behind new service development have been shown to provide demonstrable value. They can teach firms valuable lessons about how to turn expertise into a much more lucrative competitive service offer, whether with firm's core service, added value services or brand new offers. This demands the development of a far more formal approach to new service design. Getting to grips with this critical part of the business should be high on the leadership's change agenda.

6

Altering the operations of a product company to provide services

Introduction and overview

Operations are at the heart of a manufacturing company. They are the means by which all the raw materials that the company buys are changed into saleable products. The efficiency, success and improvement of these activities can make or break a firm, particularly if moving into an unfamiliar market. As a result, the operations people are often its backbone, providing the talent pool for future leaders.

In the past, there was a widespread view that it was the production line that actually ran manufacturing firms because, if it stopped for any reason, senior managers were quickly on the floor trying to sort out the problems. However, many modern businesses have outsourced aspects of their operations, including manufacturing. In fact, some of the world's leading Western production companies now design, assemble and distribute product but do little actual raw manufacturing. That is outsourced to cheap, often Third World, suppliers. Yet, even in these circumstances, operations managers have to oversee and control the detail of the end-to-end processes if the firm is to thrive.

The efficient design, build and management of manufacturing operations are a speciality and science in themselves. Over many years, production companies have developed, learned and refined methods to control and run these critical activities. Called

'operations management', it provides a study of concepts, techniques and processes by which production companies can systematically improve performance and profit.

Yet 'service operations' are as important to the effectiveness of service companies as manufacturing operations are to product companies. As a result despite the emphasis on manufacturing in this discipline, many companies in the service sectors have adopted, adjusted and used aspects of operations management to improve the productivity of their businesses. However, the nature of these operations varies according to the characteristics of the service firm. The operations of a professional services firm, for instance, are focused on the efficient deployment and 'utilisation rate' of competent people. Consumer services companies, by contrast, are a fusion of process, technology and environment concerned with giving large volumes of consumers a pleasant experience.

What is indisputable, though, is that setting up effective service operations is a critical aspect of the move from products to services. Firms on this journey have to understand the nature of the service operations they will plan, build and run. Failure to do this will make them incapable of delivering the proposed service to buyers. This chapter explores the relevant aspects of service operations and the changes necessary as a company moves more fully into services.

The role and scope of operations

The operations function of a company creates, builds and delivers its offer to buyers. It is responsible for all the activities that make the company's products and services, even if subcontracted or outsourced. In many senses, this function defines what the firm itself is about. Operations in Microsoft, for example, make and distribute software, while operations at Ford build and ship cars. Although rarely seen by customers or presented to them at marketing or sales events, they are the firm's prime source of competitive advantage and success. If operations specialists do their job well, the customers will like and buy the offer. If not, reputation, sales and revenue will decline.

The operations function plans, manufactures, distributes, organises and implements. Its responsibility runs through the organisation, focusing upon the efficient assembly of components, whether tangible or intangible. It takes various inputs (such as components, machinery, information, human capabilities and money) and, by changing them during the operational activities of the company, produces its outputs (including waste and other by-products, in addition to the intended goods or services). The function's processes can include production, assembly, finishing, packaging and distribution. In other words, it does whatever is necessary to produce the finished offer of the company.

As a result, the work of operations management is often the source of the company's enduring competitive advantage. It ensures, for instance, that low cost airlines (like Easyjet) can continue to offer cheap fares or that freight companies (like FedEx) carry on delivering speedily and that first-rate professional partnerships (like PricewaterhouseCoopers) maintain excellent advisory services.

Just as importantly, operations managers are often an important source of profit improvement as they innovate and invest in different aspects of their work to improve productivity. This applies as much to service companies as manufacturing companies, where the operations function will try to understand how people-intensive offers can be changed in order to improve productivity. As Theodore Levitt said of service businesses as far back as 1972 (Levitt, 1972):

> They will ask: What technologies and systems are employable here? How can things be designed so we can use machines instead of people, systems instead of serendipity?

In fact, productivity gains and operational efficiency might be central to the survival of companies in many future service markets. A range of these markets (from professional services to IT support) have been protected by historical distortions. For example, the 'big four' accountants have been protected by their dominance of audit, some law firms by their 'magic circle' status and the big computer companies by their installed base. However, these advantages are being eroded by better informed customers, regulatory changes and more efficient competition. Suppliers will need to become more efficient to stay in these markets, particularly if international service competition increases. This is likely to stimulate major productivity advances in service businesses, just as the last half of the twentieth century saw huge productivity gains in manufacturing.

So, operations managers, and associated specialists, are vital to the successful strategic move by product companies into service markets. Although specialist functions (like HR, marketing or IT) will help with the design and specification of the new service, ultimately operations managers must implement any programme. They will have a range of different issues to address in this change, including:

- the importance of the organisational interface (the 'front office') with buyers;
- the 'back office' and its interface with the 'front office';
- planning and managing the role of people in the operations of the service business;
- process design and the introduction of appropriate technology to improve process efficiency;
- planning the environment in which the service will be experienced;
- forecasting, capacity planning and quality control.

The importance of the organisational interface with buyers (the 'front office')

Designing the organisation's interface with buyers is a critical first step in moving from products to services. Until relatively recently, manufacturing companies were rarely called on to relate directly with their buyers unless they were selling to high-value business customers. There were, normally, retail distribution chains or agents which handled the sale and supply of product to buyers. For instance, despite the direct approach of firms like Dell, much of the computer industry still relies on a network of dealers, value added resellers (VARS) and partners to get to low-value business buyers and consumers.

Although the internet has radically changed this in many industries, service companies have always had to focus directly on the interface with their buyers and users. It is an integral part of their business and at the heart of their operations. This boundary with customers is both the service company's factory and its 'front office'; and, as a result, its prime area of operations. The work in it is complicated by the fact that customers are 'in the factory', experiencing the creation of their service as they use it, and very often this is a major factor in their final decision to buy.

Their experience in the front office can also be a significant influence on their intention to repurchase. An attractive environment encourages them to buy and a good experience tempts them to repurchase; whereas a poor experience turns them away. So managers of service operations must regard this point of interface with their buyers as a 'moment of truth', where the service experience either reinforces the company's claim to the market or undermines it. As a result, it is an important ingredient in the future profits of the business.

So the operations managers of a prospective service firm must have a clear idea of what the intended customer interface should be like. It might be the combination of premises, ambience and style of service found in restaurants, theme parks or hotels. In these businesses, the customer facility is a major part of the service, dominating operations. On the other hand, the customer reception facility may be a thin veneer on an efficient distribution system, as in the case of American computer supplier Dell, Swedish furniture retailer Ikea and British catalogue retailer Argos.

Alternatively, it may be a business-based service where much of the work is done on the customer's premises or in the brains of the supplier's employees. Even then, however, the security clearance system and reception facilities of any office visited by clients can be an influence on their views of the service they receive. As explained further on in this chapter, Fujitsu is just one of many business-to-business suppliers which has taken care to address this as it has moved from products to services.

On the other hand, the customer reception of a service may occur in 'virtual space' on the internet. Here most of the service will be accessed by the customers themselves and will take place in their imaginations at any time of day. So both the entrance to the web site and the navigation through it need to be designed extremely carefully using reliable, technology-based processes, to back it up.

The design of the service interface needs to be based on an understanding of both the market and the company's competitive positioning, which is often provided by other functions. For instance, marketing specialists will normally specify the nature of the service and designers create its ambience. Nevertheless, it then needs to be carefully constructed by operations experts, integrating all the relevant components of service into a holistic experience. So a manufacturing company moving into a service business needs to design a 'front office' (real or virtual) that is based on this explicit grasp of its buyers' needs. This design then needs to be built by experienced operations people; a task made more complicated if they have not worked in any service business before.

All the (service) world's a stage

In setting up the 'front office', the first and main consideration is the interaction (and possible relationship) between supplier and customer in it. This interaction needs to be warm and flexible, encouraging positive interchanges between people. If a dull, mechanistic approach is taken, buyers will not respond positively to their experience and will, ultimately, move away. As important, but more difficult, this sense of spontaneity needs to continue after the honeymoon period of the initial launch of the new service. This has caused some operations people to think of the numerous encounters within the service reception facility, as dramatic moments, with the elements of a theatrical performance and following an explicit or implicit 'script'.

As Professor Leonard Berry said (Berry, 1995), after years of research into the service industry:

> Services are performances and people are the performers. From the customers' perspective, the people performing the service are the company. An incompetent insurance agent is an incompetent insurance company.

The components of this 'performance' can, as in the theatre, be planned and designed to achieve any desired outcome and maintained over a long period of time. If a play like London's 'Mousetrap' can run for decades using theatrical techniques to keep the performance of the script fresh each night for each new audience member, so can service businesses. They can be designed to give a particular style of service to a specific group of customers on each encounter. The main components of this service performance include: the environment in which the service is experienced, the behaviour of the people who are part of the service and the processes through which the dialogue moves.

What the supplier sees as a set of operational procedures can be thought of as a 'customer script', guiding interactions between the customers and the supplier's employees or equipment. In fact, there is evidence that suppliers with a creative or theatrical heritage, like Disney resorts, have achieved success by intuitively applying dramatic techniques to service businesses. (In the Disney resorts, for example, employees are largely resting actors who see signs reminding them that they are going 'on stage' as they start work.) They have demonstrated that, if a 'service script' is followed, it is likely that the quality of service will match the expectations of the buyers and the intentions of the supplier. So this script needs to be worked out carefully, communicated to buyers and, where necessary, form the basis of training for both employees and customers.

This script is also a way of giving customers a degree of control as they experience the service process because it makes them feel that the outcome is more predictable, reducing stress levels. If they learn the script properly, the service episode is, effectively, managed by them. (Of course, not all customers like a high degree of control, preferring a spontaneous style of service. In these situations an obvious script may not be necessary if each service episode is managed with close personal attention by experienced people.) The script should also make clear where the boundary lies between the server and the served. This boundary can be physical (for example, where a customer stands behind a counter to receive service) or mental (the customers' expectations of the actions required to achieve the desired service).

Uncertainties about script and boundary can be very damaging to the relationship between customer and supplier. One of the roles of employees is to know when and where they can deviate from the script and break the rules to give buyers a better service without affecting the overall efficiency of operations. So, operational procedures in a service company should 'empower' front office workers to meet any unforeseen needs by giving them the right to make concessions, within a controlled framework. 'Empowerment' is the discretion given to employees to respond to individual customer needs. This concept arose as service organisations needed to communicate their desire to respond to unforseen needs and in response to strong evidence that any inflexibility in employees' behaviour damaged both reputation and future business. John Bateson (Bateson, 1999) suggests that there are three levels to it:

- Routine discretion, where employees are given a list of alternative actions to choose from.
- Creative discretion, which requires an employee to create a list of alternatives as well as choosing between them.
- Deviant discretion, which expects people to do things which are not part of their job description or management's expectations.

The latter are normally most noticed and appreciated by buyers. Yet, if good service depends on experienced employees consistently breaking the rules, operations management has not done its job properly. They should ensure that concessions are recorded, so that the fundamental processes of the organisation can be re-examined in the light of the type and frequency of concession.

The 'back office' and the interface with the front office

Like product companies, a portion of the processes of a service company are hidden from the buyers' view. For instance, fast food chains need to deliver huge volumes of food daily to thousands of outlets around the world, retailers need to secure vast numbers of goods to sell and holiday companies need to choose a wide range of appealing resorts. Although invisible to customers these processes are crucial to delivering the service when needed. As in manufacturing they need to be as streamlined and efficient as possible, with operations managers constantly thinking about ways to increase productivity and effectiveness through them.

For example, in a maintenance organisation one of the important 'back office' functions is the forecasting, management, costing and delivery of 'logistics'. The operations management in these businesses need to ensure that spare parts are held in caches in various places of a country or continent. These stocks need to be both large enough to meet demand and small enough to be economic. The design of the processes to ensure optimum size is based on a complex calculation of the 'average time between failure' of products already being used by customers; so that, if something goes wrong, a spare part can be delivered within an agreed period of time. On the other hand in a complex business service, like a merchant bank, one of the back office functions is the statistical analysis of a market in which a target acquisition operates through building complex models. In both cases, these processes probably won't be visible in the 'front office', but it is essential that they work properly.

Engineering the optimum relationship between the front and back office is very important. In most companies there is balance to be struck between the need to deal with the erratic demand of customers and the need for efficient, predictable delivery processes. In a manufacturing industry customers may, for instance, buy a different number of products in different seasons whereas the supplier wants to produce a constant number of items. Operations people will, in these circumstances, build 'buffers' between the two parts of the company's operations, such as warehouses, as Figure 6.1 shows.

Separating the erratic and visible environment of the front office from back office processes can be even more important in service businesses. In the latter half of the twentieth century some British banks, for example, developed problems in their branches by having desk-based processing clerks visible to customers. These were often lesser qualified than the counter staff and not permitted to handle customer transactions until qualified and promoted. But customers became anxious and dissatisfied if they were queuing in a branch with one or two counter positions vacant while these desk-based

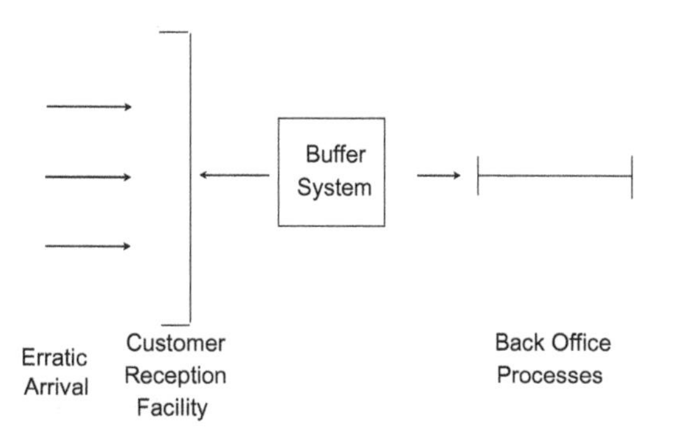

Figure 6.1 Simple systems model

people apparently ignored them. Taking large parts of the back office processes out of branches and putting them into separate offices not only led to greater efficiencies but also took away this cause of dissatisfaction. The change created a buffer between the need for back office efficiency and the delivery of good, front office service.

Fujitsu develops operational initiatives to support its move into services

Fujitsu is a leading international provider of IT systems and services. With its headquarters in Japan, it has revenues of over $40 billion. It employs 158 000 employees across the world, with sales and support operations in over seventy countries. The company is the world's third-largest IT services provider and Japan's market leader. Fujitsu and Fujitsu Siemens Computers are among the top five companies operating in the global markets for servers and PCs.

Migrating to services

Over the past few years, Fujitsu has been placing an increased emphasis on services. Spearheading this move is Fujitsu Services, its European-centred IT services arm, which employs 18 000 people in over twenty countries. It is the largest IT services provider to the UK public sector, is making notable inroads into the private sector, and is seeing steady growth in continental Europe (particularly in Finland, Ireland, Spain and Portugal). Its business model encompasses a comprehensive range of both bespoke and continuous services, including:

- desktop and distributed systems management;
- remote systems management;
- data centres, e-business hosting;
- design, build and management of call centres, help desks, service desks;
- professional services, consulting, project management.

A compelling cultural blend

The journey to becoming more services-oriented (what the company calls 'moving up the service stack') is part of a shift away from a reliance on products to services seen in most major technology businesses. There is, however, an interesting twist in the case of Fujitsu.

Traditionally, Japanese industry has focused on production excellence and has been known for its success with lean manufacturing, continuous improvement and total quality management. Fujitsu Services is now acting as the test bed for a new approach, with the services expertise of the West being merged with the Japanese experience of consistency, quality and continual refinement. The company believes that this powerful combination of Japanese heritage and Western understanding of service culture could be a distinct competitive advantage.

Rethinking its approach

Transforming itself from a product company selling technology to one that is rooted in a services environment is having major implications for the company's approach to its markets in Europe. For instance, when Fujitsu's main business was selling technology to the IT department, the key audience would be IT directors and sales were mainly transactional. However, Fujitsu Services is now increasingly involved in major deals comprising very large scale services completed over several years, and involving far more people on both sides. At the same time, more people are likely to be involved in the purchase, including, for example, representatives from the procurement department, functional directors, and, sometimes, even the chief executive.

This significantly changes the nature of the conversations taking place between the company and its customers. Customers will expect Fujitsu Services to have a good knowledge of their industries, their companies and even the particular issues the executives involved in the projects are tackling. To deal with this, the company is changing the way it analyses its markets (in order to gain much deeper insights into customers) and to learn to operate through more of a 'pull' model of marketing rather than 'push'. In other words, customers have to be persuaded, not only that Fujitsu Services understands their issues, but that it has something new to say to them, including a new way to help them deal with their business problems.

A 'services marketing mindset' is seen by the company as essential to underpinning these efforts. As a result, the service marketing function has been enlarged and now has three main responsibilities. The first is to help the company set strategic direction, the second to help build the company's reputation (Fujitsu prefers the term 'reputation' to 'brand') and the third to generate demand.

Operations initiatives to support the change

To encourage this cultural shift, the company has put in place a range of initiatives to help employees flourish in an environment where building longer-term relationships is what counts. This includes reviewing the specifications of job roles, changing the way account and sales teams are rewarded, rethinking training and developing new ways to support them. The aim is to move toward a much more in-depth, intelligence-led approach, equipping those who deal directly with customers with much better knowledge and understanding of the companies and people they are meeting.

Another example is an initiative called 'Sense and Respond' which is being applied to the call centres Fujitsu operate (both for itself and clients). Based on continuous improvement, Sense and Respond creates intelligence through constant monitoring and analysis of what issues callers want help with so that, over time, the root causes of the problems can be addressed. This not only cuts down unnecessary calls and eliminates waste, but it aligns the call centres far more closely with business goals.

The Fujitsu Services headquarters in London is another indication of the importance of continuous service improvement. The reception facilities (considered to be an important international 'front office') have been completely revamped and remodelled, emulating the operations of a first rate hotel, rather than the office of a computer company. Visitors are greeted and handled to the standards of the global hospitality industry. Information (such as their favourite drink) is gathered about them so that each subsequent visit becomes better than the previous one, creating an exceptional service environment from the moment the visitor walks in the door.

Another major initiative at Fujitsu Services is a comprehensive internal reputation programme to embed an understanding of the 'Fujitsu personality'. It consists of a long-term programme of regular workshops for everyone in the company, covering: what the company is, what makes it different, why that is important for customers and how it is displayed in employee behaviour. In the first 18 months of the programme, 15 000 employees attended up to 4 workshops each; a total of 2 700 workshops. The programme has been so successful that plans are in hand to roll it out across the entire Fujitsu group. The company's long-term intent is to apply the same high standards of quality, management and improvement to service operations as it does to manufacturing operations.

Planning and managing the role of people in the operations of a service business

Effectively deploying people who serve buyers

As a product company moves into services, it usually finds that it must drastically increase the roles and scope of people who serve customers, perhaps in a newly created front office. As explained in Chapter 3 (page 77), the way that employees are managed and deployed needs to change dramatically because they are part of the service offer and their behaviour affects future purchases. In fact, the success of a service firm often depends on the people who are part of it. Their skills, experience and motivation are seen by the customers as the main driving force of the firm and are one of its competitive advantages. They can be its production line, its sales force, its service support team and, in many ways, the product itself. They are the firm's 'human capital' and, very often, the repository of most of its intellectual capital. Their talent, behaviour, communication and output are part of the value that buyers seek.

So, the operations managers of a potential service business need to plan and manage the recruitment and deployment of people who will serve customers very carefully. Called 'boundary roles', the jobs these people will fill link the company with its external environment. They must be filled by people employed specifically because they have the skills and characteristics to deal with the outside world and the erratic, unpredictable whims of people who want to buy. These jobs range from 'subordinate service roles' to those based on 'professional experience' (see, for example, Shamir, 1980). Both need to be managed carefully but differently. For example, professionals (like lawyers, consultants and accountants) have a different status and adopt different behaviours to subordinate service workers (like waiters or toilet cleaners) because of their qualifications and the nature of their relationship to clients.

People who occupy boundary roles have different needs, characteristics and behaviours to more remote workers (employed in, say, back offices or production processes) and should be hired to use those characteristics in dealing with customers. If these people are recruited and managed successfully, they will communicate the values and aspirations of the firm to buyers, overtly and subtly, through the contacts they have every day. If not, difficulties with quality of service will occur.

At the time of writing, for example, dramatic changes in the accounting and consulting markets are causing professional service firms to ask world-class technical experts to become 'relationship managers' for the accounts they have served. Some, however, despite being successful multimillionaires, do not have the advanced social skills to succeed in that role because their career to date has been based on natural demand for their technical expertise. Using such people as boundary workers is likely to lead to difficulty.

Researchers have found that, in certain circumstances, people in boundary roles can experience stress which causes them to under-perform in their role. The causes of this stress include:

- Inequity dilemmas: feeling belittled or demeaned by putting buyers first.
- Feelings versus behaviour: the need to be professional and represent the firm means that they cannot always be honest when, for instance, buyers behave badly.
- Territorial conflict: customers intrude into personal work space (like a taxi) or privacy.
- Conflict between the organisation and buyers: where the firm's policies contrast with customers' views or needs.

- Conflict between customers: where tension between two buyers with opposing needs explodes into an embarrassing or difficult incident.
- The unarticulated fight for control: this tussle is, in fact, threefold, involving, the buyer, the service person and the firm (through its processes and policies).

Boundary workers particularly experience stress if their firm is out of step with the needs and demands of its buyers and if they sympathise more with them. If the leadership of a service firm misunderstands the market, the service will be out of touch with customers' needs. Buyers will, in turn, express this to people at the interface, and these front line employees will experience stress. This phenomenon alone can damage a product company's move into services. If it has wrongly specified or badly set up its front office, the employees in it will regularly experience the embarrassment of compensating for inadequately designed service. If they are then ignored by their leaders, their morale will plummet, exacerbating the problem further and damaging the experience of customers. These customers are then unlikely to buy again and the potential business will be ruined.

The intensity of role stress and its consequences to the behaviour of front line employees cannot be over emphasised. Some withdraw from customers by adopting 'automatic behaviour' as a protection or hiding behind inflexible company procedures ('the computer says no'). For example, one European utility found, when it was at the height of a major quality problem, that some complaint handling staff took time out to ride up and down in the company elevators to escape the avalanche of hostile, complaining customers. This, in turn, exacerbated the problem further.

Over-acting is another common coping strategy. Impulsive, natural acting can make customers feel happier about the service they are getting and diffuse difficult situations. The waitress, who pirouettes down a crowded restaurant, as a number of different tables call for her attention, is playfully saying 'I know you all want me and I'll get to you when I can'. This can cause diners to smile, laugh and be patient. So, front line employees learn, intuitively, behaviours that can help them deal with conflicts which are inherent in their role. Nevertheless, diagnosing stress in front line employees and resolving any poor quality of service resulting from it, ought to be one of the prime operational management processes in a service firm; particularly in a product company venturing into service markets. So it is sensible to listen to boundary workers and adjust the direction of the firm in the light of their feedback about buyers' experiences.

It is vital that prospective service firms attract the right people for each front line role and train them to do good, technical work in addition to handling customers well. On top of this, they have to make sure that these people reflect the values of the firm in that work; that they are the face of the firm, the embodiment of its brand in the service that the customers experience (see Chapter 9, page 314).

Keeping employees motivated to deliver the service vision

The leaders of the firm also have to develop and institutionalise strategies to retain good people so that the investment in acquiring and training them is not wasted. For instance, they should communicate effectively with employees, listening and responding, to ensure that they are supportive of the strategic positioning of the firm as it evolves. As a result, many service firms have adopted sophisticated internal communication programmes. These are important tools which help to keep employees informed of issues, while creating a common sense of purpose, contributing toward positive motivation.

However, ill-conceived, poorly planned or erratic communication can have a detrimental effect. If the leadership of the firm does not ensure that internal communication is managed well, the leaders and the people responsible for different activities or functions will copy emails, send out erratic messages and pass on ad hoc technical changes. The front line employees will then suffer from over-communication; becoming overwhelmed by a discordant cascade which conflicts and confuses. If there is no discipline, there will be a multitude of conflicting, disparate messages which will become a deluge that employees are unable to comprehend (see Chapter 8, page 278).

HR management is so important to service firms that it often becomes one of the main focuses of their leaders. They invest heavily in internal communication, reward, development, motivation and recruitment. People management becomes one of the key competences of the service firm and one of its critical success factors. The also have to focus on what Christian Grönroos (Grönroos, 2003) describes as the two components of internal marketing: attitude management and communications management. As a result, many of these firms have highly developed HR expertise, employing leading practices in the field and consistently coming at the top of surveys of most desirable employers. Any product company moving into a service business needs to develop this competence if it is going to thrive through providing human service to customers.

Process design and management

A product can be made in many different ways and so its success depends, to a very real extent, on the processes which make it. This is more true of service offers because, as explored in Chapter 3 (page 79), processes are an integral part of their nature. In fact it is often difficult to distinguish between the services offered and the processes used to deliver them. Is, for instance, the first class service of Singapore Airways or le Cirque restaurant in New York just the travel or the meal? Or is their service also dependent on the experience, en route, of an enjoyable, privileged process?

The effective design and improvement of the processes which make a service work are an important part of the company's offer to buyers. So, process design is a vital ingredient of operations management in a service company. Operations managers must plan the best process to produce a particular service and the integration of the details of the activities involved in each step. They must identify, plan and build each activity which supports the final service to customers.

Different types of processes

For a long time manufacturing was associated with mass production and continuous processes. But over the last century production specialists have learned how to design different types of processes to make different types of products both efficiently and effectively. As processes are so important to service businesses, a company moving from products to services must be even more careful to choose the right processes to suit the proposed business. There are several different types:

- **Project processes.** Each project is essentially unique, and businesses dominated by this type of work usually undertake different unique tasks by varying a common, project management, approach. Although there might be a common methodology, there is a lot of variety and little standardisation. The output is likely to be an enormous or time-consuming product which is highly customised to the buyers' specifications and releases a large number of resources when complete. Examples would be: making a single, spectacular building (like London's Wembley stadium) or high quality but individual products (like a Saville Row suit); whereas service business based on project processes might provide a unique strategic consultancy or an acquisition.

- **Jobbing processes.** These have the flexibility to make a wide variety of products in significant quantities but with a degree of customisation. They enable an amount of volume but some adaptation. Examples would include customised furniture or a small engineering works which produce different products for customers. In service businesses, the operations of many consumer front offices rely on jobbing type processes.
- **Batch processes.** This involves making a whole batch of similar products through, say, an assembly line. Many modern products comprising, for example, plastics are made using these processes. A batch process in the service industry would be mortgage provision or the more routine work conducted by some professional service firms such as expatriate tax returns for large employers.
- **Mass processes.** This is a process for assembling huge quantities of products like cars or white goods. In this type of business, processes must be streamlined and efficient; and are heavily reliant on machines and technology. Service businesses which use similar approaches are high volume, mass services like fast food chains and some financial services such as insurance activities.
- **Continuous processes.** With these, very high volumes of a product emerge from a flow without interruption, such as bulk chemicals. Examples in the service sector include: electricity supply, 24-hour news, the police service, and accident & emergency departments at hospitals.

Some academics argue that service businesses should have different classifications, because these processes are too closely associated with manufacturing. They propose descriptions such as 'highly customised professional services' in the professions; or the 'service shop' for high volume services such as car rental; 'mass services' to describe high volume businesses like fast food; and 'service factories' where there is very little customer involvement (such as internet-based offers).

Process planning is particularly needed when a company faces major change. So, however processes are described, a company moving into the service industry must understand and implement the right processes for the right service. It must plan these processes in detail and organise itself to deliver satisfactory experiences for customers as they use the service. The operations managers involved need to set up, design and run appropriate processes and ensure that they suit the offer the company is making to buyers.

They must 'establish ownership' of processes by having managers in charge of them, with an end-to-end view, even if they cross organisational boundaries. Once decisions of ownership have been taken, operations managers then need to define those processes, making their effect visible though clear measures, establishing the best control points and, as part of their quality control, taking corrective measures to improve them. As processes are cross functional, running through the organisation, the emphasis should be on putting customer service first, whatever the organisational structure. This can yield enormous productivity gains because an activity (e.g. 'handle customer contact') can appear in a number of end-to-end processes; so that improving the activity will improve more than one process. As this emphasis is the reverse of specialisation, it avoids the myopic drawbacks that come from managers with the perspective of operating in one functional silo.

This has led some to place such emphasis on their operational processes that specialists have come to regard them as 'process-centred organisations' (see Walters, 2002) and it appears that these firms have a number of advantages in different markets. Their attitude tends to be that their services and products are transitory, because their portfolio changes with market dynamics, whereas their operational delivery processes are an enduing competitive advantage. The operations people, often working with cross-functional teams or 'matrix management' structures, concentrate on the delivery of good experiences to customers. Over the long term their productivity and quality of service tends to stand out from those companies whose people are isolated in systems which prevent them from giving excellent, integrated service.

Planning the environment in which the service will be experienced

As discussed in Chapter 3 (page 81), the environment in which a service is performed is an important part of the customers' experience and needs careful planning. The design and layout of services like restaurants, airline cabins and hotels set buyers' expectations of quality and value. They also affect the behaviour of employees and can be a source of differentiation.

Numerous books have been written for operations managers about choosing, designing and building manufacturing facilities. Operations specialists are used to designing these facilities and bring a logical, analytical approach to it. For example, when deciding on the location of a production facility, many factors will be taken into account, such as: whether they can actually design an appropriate building at the site, the availability of skilled labour, access to the right logistics capacity, cost and maintenance. They also have to consider the internal layout and the physical needs of essential processes such as: where components are delivered, how they will be received, how they get to the appropriate machinery, the work flow, and how the finished product comes out at the end. The productivity of manufacturing has been vastly improved in different industries by consistently reviewing and adjusting these issues.

The design, planning and implementation of the back office is not, however, the biggest issue when moving to a service business. The layout of the customer reception facility is just as important if not more so. If the service is, for example, to be a retail experience, it may be located on the main shopping street, just off it, in a retail park or as a franchise within another shop. If the supplier is moving into a business to business service, it needs to understand what type of office clients will visit and how it will be represented in the signage and décor, particularly if sharing a building with others. Other important elements to be considered include the 'traffic flow' of potential customers, the numbers likely to be attracted and their propensity to come in. That in turn, leads to issues of outlet design, including: the branding, the outward appearance, signage into the facility, colour, smell, furniture, queuing, interaction between people, cleanliness and internal signage. There is a skill in getting the right balance of all these elements to meet the aspiration of the leaders of the business.

Yet, designing a service reception so that customers want to enter is not as straightforward as it might seem. For example, when people visit the branch of their bank in another country and find the layout quite different, they feel at a loss when they come through the front door because everything is unfamiliar. They can be embarrassed and stressed by this simple difference because they do not know what to do (queuing, signage and behaviours can be very different); and embarrassed customers tend not to buy again. Failure to get the mix right can cause similar embarrassment in a new facility and damage the embryonic business. Customers must be taught gently and subtly, through signage, leaflets or directions from employees, what they are expected to do.

These factors are amplified even further in a complex service business like a hotel or theme park, where questions of ambience, people flow and access to service have to be dealt with thoughtfully and comprehensively. However, if the customer reception of a service is a thin veneer, as in the case of a catalogue retailer, or an internet-based service, different factors come into play. A virtual service, for instance, is dealing with customers' imaginations, which calls for an attractive design that stimulates that imagination and is also easy to navigate. This becomes even more complex when there is a combination of a physical and internet-based retail experience. Operations managers in organisations that are moving into service business for the first time should consider hiring employees or advisers with direct experience of these very different environments.

Forecasting and capacity planning

As services are intangible, manufacturers might think that demand forecasting and capacity management for a proposed service business can be vague or adjusted as demand builds. It is a common mistake for inexperienced service leaders to assume that it need not be as precise as the forecasting of physical product sales because there is no need to determine the speed and volume of manufacturing lines.

Yet all service businesses must have capacity available to meet erratic customer demand if they are to thrive. From the international technology company and the global merchant bank to the unique local restaurant or hideaway holiday resort: all must have capacity available to meet demand and processes to manage fluctuations in arrival rate. Too much capacity will inflate costs unnecessarily whereas too little will make the business unable to serve customers effectively. It is as essential to service businesses as it is to product companies to get this balance correct.

A technical repair service, for instance, will receive a range of different jobs at any time during their day. This could be an easy, routine piece of work, a more involved repair or a complex, unusual fault. Operations managers who are inexperienced in services, or who have not been given a numerical or analytical emphasis in their training, will tend to recruit to cover the arrival of the more complex work. As a result, their service will be more costly than it need be because there will be a surfeit of higher trained technicians and logistics costs will be higher than necessary. Morale of the workforce will also tend to decline because higher skilled people will fill their time with lower skilled work.

Successful operations managers in service businesses take just as precise and analytical an approach to forecasting as operations people in a manufacturing organisation. They calculate the likely volume and arrival rate of different tasks (organising logistics and staff skills accordingly) and put as much effort into forecasting as most product companies. Telecommunication companies, for example, use the same statistical tool, queuing theory, to plan the growth of their public networks as computer companies use to plan the capacity of their machines' processors (the components that actually compute commands). Similarly, consumer services such as retail and fast-food analyse demand carefully to ensure effective logistics and stock management.

Sensible forecasting and capacity management is just as important in a small service business like a local restaurant. The owners must have a clear idea of the number of 'covers' they will tackle in an evening and the number of waiting staff they will need. As they approach peak periods, customers may arrive early and leave late, causing congestion and peaks in demand. Research suggests that employees will then enter a 'coping zone' (see Johnston & Clark, 2005) managing the competing attention of different customers. The productivity and satisfaction of the employees can initially improve during these intervals because people who are natural boundary workers can enjoy the challenge of meeting the rush of customer needs. However, sustained periods of peak demand, causing prolonged periods in the coping zone, sap morale and, ultimately undermine performance, damaging business (Figure 6.2). This 'coping zone' will be different for different

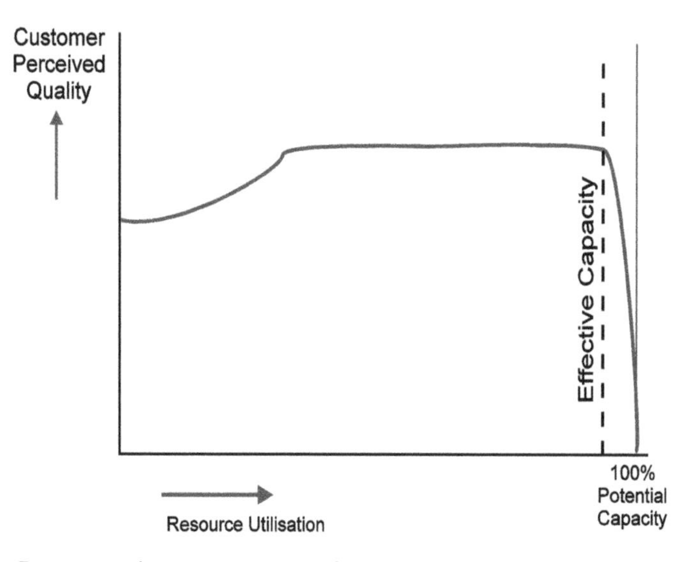

Figure 6.2 Resource utilisation in a service firm
Source: Johnston and Clark, 2005

businesses but needs to be understood and managed if quality is not to decline.

There is an important balance here between customers' requirements for service and the costs a supplier must sustain to meet those needs. Customers' perception of quality is closely related to the level of investment a company makes in forecasting and demand management. The problem for a number of companies is that their forecasts of capacity are wrongly calculated either because of ignorance or, worse, intent. There is no excuse for not forecasting the erratic arrival of customer demand and planning the deployment of resources accordingly.

Often, for example, customers become frustrated if they call a credit card company, a bank, or utility on a working day to hear a recording which says: 'we are experiencing unanticipated levels of demand at the moment', followed by a long wait. Sophisticated buyers know that these companies are lying, since they will have years' of historical tracking data and will know when to expect peaks in calls from customers. They have decided to provide sufficient employees to handle only a certain number of calls, deliberately restricting the number of people answering phones and letting their customers wait (an abuse of their customers' time). Eventually the word of mouth from irritated customers will increase, creating a negative reputation about service quality which will, in time, damage future revenue. So, an attempt to save costs through inadequate numbers of service staff will eventually generate another cost: lost customers and profits.

Even professional services firms, the ultimate intangible service businesses, can improve productivity and performance by skilled forecasting and capacity management. For instance, David Maister (Maister, 1993), in his definitive work on the subject, describes three main kinds of client work that these businesses engage in:

- 'Brains': where the firm sells its services on the basis of the highly professional and technical skills of its employees, dealing with unique and particularly complex situations. The key elements involved in work like this are experience, deep knowledge and the development of new approaches, concepts or techniques. As a result, these firms will be top-heavy with highly skilled and highly paid professionals.
- 'Grey Hair' projects, on the other hand, while needing a certain amount of customisation and intellectual flair, are addressing areas in which the firm has already had experience and can sell its knowledge, experience and judgement. Less experienced people can be employed to do some of the tasks.
- Finally, 'Procedure' projects involve well-recognised and familiar types of problems that businesses have faced many times. The client believes an outside firm will be more efficient, or that it lacks the capabilities to do the work itself, so it will bring in a professional firm with relevant experience. In these firms there will be a far higher proportion of junior staff involved in the work.

The dominance of the type of work affects the nature of the firm, the type and number of employees deployed in its work and the means by which it makes a profit. A 'Brains' dominated firm will need expensive 'gurus' and will engage in high-value, low-margin work. So a consultancy, such as McKinsey or Bain, will need to anticipate the number of these projects they will win and calculate the teams of highly-skilled people they must have available when the work comes in. A firm offering more procedural work, on the other hand, will put its focus on efficient proposal management, profit through contracting, scalable service propositions and the 'utilisation rate' of large numbers of lower level people. The 'span of control' and 'leverage' of expensive people in these firms must be forecast and managed carefully if their operations are to achieve productivity gains.

In addition, long established professional partnerships have developed methods to flex their resources according to their forecasts of the economic cycle. Many accountancy firms have, for example, independent advisory businesses which, like any project-based service firm, experience peaks and troughs in demand according to economic conditions. If not managed carefully, these can damage both cash flow and net profits. So, during any seasonal down time, they switch resource from areas associated with economic growth (such as mergers and acquisitions) to those associated with recession (such as insolvency/turnaround work). So careful forecasting and understanding of demand can ensure that even the most intangible of service businesses is highly productive.

Quality control in a service business

Quality control in manufacturing is well established and understood, having been a responsibility of operations functions for many decades. Key quality control measures (such as sampling, inspection and process control) help managers understand any deviation or variability in a manufactured product, and catch any alteration in the manufacturing process that will affect quality.

Yet quality control is just as essential to service businesses and, although altered by the different nature of these businesses, has been applied to them by their respective leaders. See, for instance, Fredrick Reichheld and Earl Sasser's article, 'Zero defections: Quality comes to services' (Reichheld & Sasser, 1990) which argues that the main quality measure in a service business is the attrition of customers. To ensure that operations are delivering as planned, service standards must be set. In environments which serve customers, these are likely to be a combination of financial targets, service delivery targets (based on technical measures such as 'average waiting time'), market performance targets (such as share of the market, rising sales levels) and customer satisfaction targets (measures of their perceptions about the quality of service, such as punctuality or politeness).

For example, in a leading professional service such as a medical or legal practice, there will often be a quality control process of peer review, whereas 'mystery shopping' is a typical quality tool in volume consumer services such as retailing, hotel management and fast food. Or, in a call centre, samples of customers will be rung back to discuss their experience of the service while it is fresh in their minds. In fact, there are a wide range of quality control techniques open to service operations which are not available to manufacturers because of the direct involvement of customers with the service.

Quality control standards and their associated targets have to be feasible so that they relate to areas that employees can control by their actions. They must also be credible to them, achievable, objectively measured and overtly contributing to the well-being of both the organisation and its customers.

The relevance and application of operations' concepts to service businesses

The productivity of operations in Western manufacturing companies has been radically improved over the past few decades, particularly in America, by the introduction and application of a number of concepts. Evidence suggests that there is opportunity to bring the same drive for productivity improvement to the operations of service businesses using the similar, if adapted, techniques. The application of these techniques to service companies seems to be just as relevant and, indeed, urgent, if, as international trends suggest, competitive success in different service industries will increasingly stem from major advances in productivity and efficiency.

'Just in time'

Just in time (JIT) is a concept which suggests that components should be delivered by suppliers precisely at the point and the moment when they are needed. It emerged in the 1970s and, although Western businesses did use it, Japanese companies embraced and refined the concept much more eagerly. JIT puts the storage and logistics costs onto the suppliers to the manufacturer, radically reducing inventory costs. It is vital for buyers and suppliers to work together to get the balance of supply and demand correct so that there are no interruptions in the manufacturing process. In addition, if a manufacturer is making any changes to products, processes or facilities, subcontractors need to be involved from an early stage so they can coordinate with any changes.

JIT has been applied to service businesses. Technology companies, for example, have applied it to the logistics of their maintenance businesses, while high volume consumer services such as fast food chains and retailers use the concept in their supply chain. In all instances there is strong evidence of productivity improvement and management.

'Outsourcing'

As Chapter 1 (pages 6–7) discussed, many firms have outsourced aspects of their business to specialist providers. The logic of the concept is that subcontractors are able to provide a service which is both better and cheaper because it is their firm's speciality. It rose to prominence at the end of the twentieth century and it took both suppliers and buyers of the service a decade to learn how to use it. A wide range of manufacturing companies have since outsourced functions that, although important, are not their prime area of business. Yet the concept, a service business itself, is used extensively in service industries.

Technology has enabled suppliers to provide international outsourcing services. For instance, call centres have famously been outsourced to countries such as India, while outsourced logistics management is now a thriving international business in its own right. Popular among large international firms and 'Anglo-Saxon' cultures, the concept is still resisted, for cultural reasons, in surprisingly large European and Asian economies. As international competition increases in service industries it is likely to be used extensively to penetrate those resistant countries or to undermine their indigenous businesses.

'Process re-engineering'

Process re-engineering came to the fore in the 1990s based on the 1993 book by Michael Hammer and James Champy: '*Reengineering the Corporation*'. They suggested that firms should first decide what future processes will be necessary for their organisation and then create an 'interception strategy' to enable a radical change in operations. That would bring a step change in efficiency rather than incremental change to existing processes.

Process re-engineering involved examining the end-to-end processes of an organisation in order to redesign it, largely with the aim of automating as much as possible and cutting out swathes of middle managers. There was a rash of, perhaps exaggerated, claims about its impact on business efficiency in both product and service businesses. However, over time, academics began to investigate the concept in depth and, as a result, process engineering is now taught as standard operations practice. So it is sensible when thinking about the evolution of their company to services, for operations managers to use some of the recognised elements of this approach.

'Total quality management (TQM)'

This philosophy and approach to quality came to prominence in the west during the 1980s, led by prominent specialists such as Edward Deming, Joseph Juran and Philip Crosby. Analytical in emphasis, it suggests that quality issues should be resolved prior to affecting operations, not checked and counted after they occur. It calculates the 'cost of quality' in the organisation and sets out to reduce failure in a systematic way, using multi-disciplined teams of people.

In fact, the prime aim of a TQM system is 'zero defects', achieved by progressively examining smaller and smaller errors in an objective and numerate way, using a range of specialist techniques. Its 'kaizen' principle of continuous improvement based on analysis, 'quality circles' (mixed discussion groups) and open suggestion boxes, is fundamental to its success and must be supported by senior management.

Where TQM is particularly powerful is in its philosophy of engaging the whole organisation in guaranteeing and improving quality. The quality activities of the organisation are not seen as a detached and specialist function. As a result, it engages the total operations function and, although, in reality, the target of 'total zero defects' might ultimately be unachievable, the approach has radically improved the performance of many companies, saving some from extinction.

Although TQM came to prominence in manufacturing companies, it was enthusiastically adopted by large, process-dominated service companies such as telecommunication operators and utilities. Many still use it today, although it is not noticeably in evidence among leading professional service firms. A product company moving into services is likely to find it a powerful way of rallying its people around a competitive standard of service and achieving productivity and cost savings.

'Six Sigma'

Six Sigma, an extension of TQM, was pioneered by Motorola and Allied Signal, although it rose to prominence when implemented by GE in the 1990s. It is a measurement-based strategy that focuses on process improvement by applying a model of: 'design, measure, analyse, improve and control'. It appears to have helped many manufacturing companies improve the quality and effectiveness of their operations.

It has been applied to service businesses. For example, in an interview in the Spring 2005 McKinsey Quarterly (Monnoyer & Spang, 2005), Claude Brunet, the management board member of insurance giant Axa, who was responsible for operations, discussed the lessons that service companies can learn from manufacturers, having embarked on a Six Sigma programme several years before. He said:

> The biggest challenge is getting service employees to understand that they use processes. After 30 years of Total Quality Management and other improvement programs, people in manufacturing already have this perspective. They know what a process is, how to analyse it and how to improve it. This is all new for people in service companies. When we started implementing Six Sigma, early in 2002, we had to get our people to understand existing operations from a process perspective. And when you look at a service company's processes in detail, they may not be as repetitive as the processes and activities at a manufacturing plant.

'Lean Service'

Pioneered by Japanese manufacturer Toyota, 'lean' operating systems have been set-up in numerous product companies.

The concept focuses on efficiency, standardisation and cost reduction. It has been applied in service industries from IT and Insurance to Healthcare.

The concept particularly encourages local employees to solve problems and initiate improvement.

Constructing a specific operations strategy for the move into service

As with any function of a business, the company's operations organisation benefits from a specific strategy because it gives direction and context to the work of the people in it. Most specialists in the field recommend that companies develop one. However, if a product company is moving into a service market, it is even more important to write a clear plan, which sets up or adjusts its operations to encompass any differences between the product and service businesses. Clearly, though, this strategy needs to relate to the overall direction of the business and to inter-relate with other functions. It needs to include:

(i) A clear understanding of the intended service market and dynamics within it

Operations people need to be told the needs of buyers, the services to be offered to meet those needs and the competitors' offers, so that they can respond accordingly. Each of these will affect the operations strategy, influencing priorities.

(ii) The proposed competitive position of the firm within that market

The market position will have a powerful influence on operations strategy. The operations of a least-cost provider will, for example, have very different objectives and imperatives from either a niche provider or the leader in the same market. Each will offer a different mixture of service features and invest different amounts into the components of the offer. Each will also have different priorities. A least-cost provider is likely to put emphasis on cost control and productivity improvement in order to pass savings on to buyers, whereas a niche provider is likely to concentrate more on ensuring that its point of difference is maintained.

(iii) The strategic focus of the new business

As discussed throughout Chapter 2, this affects the priorities and decision making of the operations function. Sometimes called the 'service concept', (see Johnston & Clark, 2005), it clarifies the prime nature of the service firm's offer, defining what it will be good at and what it will avoid. An elite professional service firm which is offering complex management consultancy will, for example, be a high margin, low volume, people-based business. Its oper-ations will concentrate on maximising the 'utilisation rate' of highly experienced (and highly expensive) people. The operations of a streamlined outsourcing business, by contrast, will be more focused on processes and automation.

(iv) Business objectives

The strategy and ambitions of the new service firm will help operations leaders create specific priorities for its function. Its business objectives will affect the level of investment and the day-to-day priorities of operations management. Objectives set to achieve cost or investment targets will, for example, affect the amount of funds available to the operations people and the pace at which they do their work.

(v) The portfolio of services offered to buyers

The operations supporting different service offers will be very different. Those in a single service firm, like a fast food chain or an airline, will be structured differently to those offering a range of different services, like many of the leading IT service companies. Clarification of the portfolio of services, as explained in Chapter 5 (pages 166 to 168), will enable the operations people to focus on effective delivery of them to customers. They will also need to plan for specific events like the launch of a new service or the withdrawal of an old one.

(vi) Planning the customer reception facility

The plan must specify the design, planning and configuration of the method by which buyers will be received and served.

(vii) Anticipated demand and related capacity planning

Operations managers need to be given (normally through an approved marketing forecast) a clear idea of the anticipated demand.

(viii) Human capital deployment plans

There must be particularly clear plans to recruit, train and motivate people who will serve customers. Their job and operational procedures must be carefully thought through.

(ix) Process design, technology deployment and automation

Operational processes must be designed and their interface with technology costed.

(x) Supplier management

Appropriate suppliers need to be chosen and the depth of their involvement in the processes of the new service business agreed.

(xi) Quality plans

Plans which clearly demonstrate any issues with quality of service need to be established and a drive for improvement in the service experience built into the fabric of the business.

Summary

It would be a mistake for leaders of product companies to assume that, just because services are intangible and high margin in a particular market, vague or poorly planned operational delivery is acceptable. In many industries, productivity is now being sought for service businesses. Many service markets have been distorted or protected, producing, as a result, fat margins. Some are now beginning to experience the rigours of market changes. As a result, the suppliers in them will be forced to find productivity improvements similar to those found in manufacturing. Service operations will be fundamental to their success in this.

7

Selling services

Introduction and overview

Whatever other functions exist in a company, it will not survive unless someone, somewhere in the world, takes an order for its products. Effective selling is obviously important for any business because, without it, there is no revenue and the company will not survive. As revenue is an obsession of leaders when they first start a business, and an important focus in recession or other troubled times, the practice of selling is one of the oldest and best understood functions of the business world. In other words, thoughtful business people know how products are sold and what exactly constitutes good salesmanship.

Selling is not an erratic, ad hoc activity, nor is it best undertaken by a loud mouth in a suit which shouts just as loud. It is not exaggeration, lies, false claims or pressurising people to buy things they do not want. That is poor salesmanship which causes bad word of mouth, terrible reputation, law suits and, eventually, business failure. Sales is a credible business function with particular skills, processes and concepts that need to be as sensibly applied as they are in other specialities. In fact, an understanding of how to apply the relevant sales principles to different sales environments is essential to revenue growth, particularly when embarking on major change or moving into new markets. This chapter looks at different sales structures, the differences and similarities between product and service selling; and the sales approaches of companies who have made the move from products to services.

How people buy

Before looking in detail at the differences between product and service selling, it is important to take a brief look at the buying process. It is difficult to sell effectively without understanding how, why and when people buy. This is not, however, as straightforward as it sounds. Human beings are erratic, unpredictable creatures driven by both their rational and emotional make up when making decisions and, particularly, when buying products for work or personal life.

Sometimes they approach decisions carefully, collecting as much data as possible; at others they return to trusted suppliers or brands and sometimes they buy, whimsically, on impulse. Although they often have fixed ideas of what they want, it is just as likely that they do not know have a clear idea on any occasion and cannot articulate their needs. As a result, considerable research and experimentation has been undertaken over decades to understand buying motivations and behaviours. Much of this is useful in giving pointers to practical sales approaches or market opportunities. Yet it is dangerously easy for a firm to institutionalise a half-baked view of buyer needs or to ignore them because it has succeeded by creating and pushing certain products in the past.

The consumer

When consumers shop (whether physically, by telephone, by catalogue, or through the internet) they may have a cluster of needs in their minds which are not necessarily refined into a fixed product purchase. They might only have an intuitive, confused mix of ideas or preferences and look for the proposition that best fits them. Their thinking process can be broadly (very broadly) represented in Figure 7.1. The intensity and duration of these

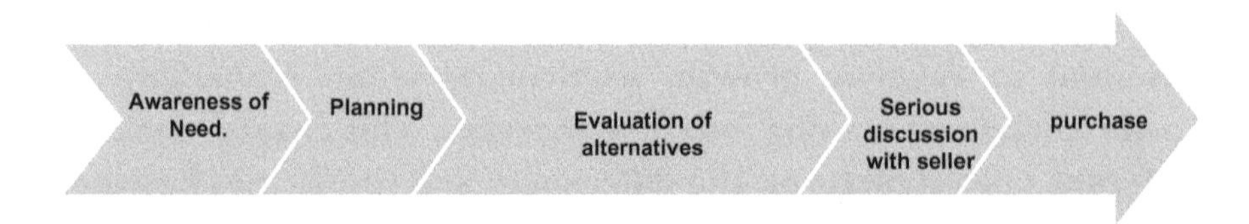

Figure 7.1 How consumers buy

different stages differs according to their experience, understanding and view of the purchase.

First they become aware of a need. This may happen quickly by the breakdown of an old domestic appliance or though growing hunger or, perhaps, by the gradual ageing of the décor in a room in their home. They will then think through what to buy, when and how to buy it. They might, for instance, research an involved purchase through the internet or by visiting showrooms. Once they have refined their search they will discuss the potential purchase with the seller before buying. Salespeople can increase their chance of success if they are able to influence their customers' thinking at the planning or evaluation stage. Really experienced sales people are able to take people who have made up their mind on a competitor product back to their evaluation and needs, matching them to their own product. Understanding, listening and matching needs to product benefits is therefore essential to the sales process.

For instance, suppose a business woman wants to buy a new pair of shoes to go with a dark-coloured dress for an important, formal dinner. She might be very familiar with the latest ranges from reading magazines or receiving other forms of publicity. She might, though, savour the experience of spending a morning in her favourite retail haunts. Or she might be too busy with her career to do either. She is also likely to have in mind a number of different attributes that her new shoes must include: style, colour, fit, brand and price (represented in Figure 7.2).

Shoes: A fictional example of graded product features

Features			
Style			
Brand			
Colour			
Fit			
Price			

Figure 7.2 Fictional features in new shoe purchase

These attributes vary in nature and importance according to individual preference, occasion and culture. Different people will describe them differently and rank them in different orders of importance, but 'price' will always be ranked after several other features. Despite what many salespeople say when they lose a deal, no-one, in any part of the world, buys products solely 'on price'. They don't go 'looking for a bit of price' but a product to meet their needs and there will always be anywhere from two to four product attributes that will be more important than price. If all of these more important attributes are exactly the same as competitor products, then price becomes the only difference. So, if suppliers do compete on price, it's because they haven't understood the cluster of needs that are in their buyers' minds, and created a distinct offer that meets those needs.

Using a research technique called 'zones of tolerance (see Ziethaml, 2003) each of these attributes can be broken down into her 'ideal', 'acceptable' and 'unacceptable' components as shown in Figure 7.3.

During the evaluation phase of the purchase, it is likely that the buyer will come across a number of different choices which meet these needs. She may, for example, see three shoes with the features shown in Figure 7.4. All three are candidates to fit her varied criteria, despite being very different. The most successful shoe salesperson is likely to be the one who has delicately elicited these needs and suggested product from stock which best meets them. Unfortunately though, they do not have Ziethaml's objective and systematic research techniques available for each shopper. They must,

Shoes: A fictional example of graded product features

Features	Ideal	Acceptable	Unacceptable
Style	High heel	Lower heel	Flats
Brand	Jimmy Choos	Kurt Geiger	Local discount store
Colour	Perfect match	Black	White
Fit	Perfect	Can only walk in	Too tight
Price	$150	$250	$500

Figure 7.3 Graduated features

Shoes: A fictional example of graded product features

Features	Ideal	Acceptable	Unacceptable
Style	Very high heel	Lower heel	Flats
Brand	Jimmy Choos	Kurt Geiger	Local discount store
Colour	Perfect match	Black	White
Fit	Perfect	Can only walk in	Too tight
Price	$ 150	$ 250	$ 500

Figure 7.4 Different choices of shoes

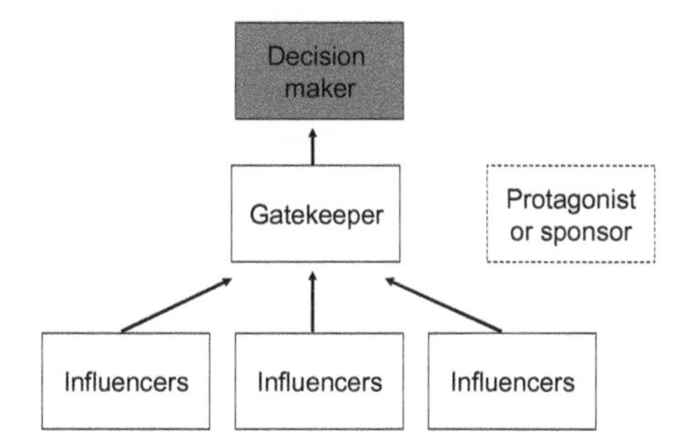

Figure 7.5 The decision-making unit

through technique, experience or intuition, learn ways to understand their customers' preferences. They have to listen, observe and diagnose before they 'sell'.

Sometimes when consumers buy there are other influences on the purchase decision. A man buying new clothes will be influenced by his partner for instance; or a mother buying food for her children will be influenced by them (and they in turn are influenced by their friends). This is called the decision-making unit (DMU) and is shown in Figure 7.5. A salesperson must understand the roles and importance of the different people in this DMU if they are to succeed. For instance, used car salespeople are taught to watch any new family coming onto the sales forecourt before approaching them. Their behaviour, and their answers to a few simple questions about what they are looking for, will reveal who is the actual decision maker and the degrees of influence of other members of the family in this particular purchase.

Business or organisational buying

One of the main differences between organisational buying and consumer buying is the more formal recognition of the role of different individuals in the business DMU. Suppliers have to become knowledgeable about the roles of these different people, the weight given to different purchase criteria and the sources of information used to come to a decision. There are influencers, who research or contribute to the evaluation of the proposed purchase, and at least one 'gatekeeper'; normally a reasonably senior person who presents the project to the decision maker. A 'sponsor' is an employee who is particularly well disposed to the supplier.

There are clear differences in the way different organisational buying groups behave in different sizes of company. For instance, the influence of the chief executive is likely to be more dominant in smaller companies and, because they have limited expertise, they are likely to filter information through trusted advisers or business networks. In large firms though the buying of some products and services (merchant banking and consultancy for instance) can still be very personal with little involvement from purchasing specialists. The situation is complicated by changing business strategy, by the network of relationships between firms, by the interactive nature of dialogue, by governance requirements and by the influence of the formal purchasing function (particularly in government or other public sector purchases).

Some academics have suggested that business buying is rational and objective because of the existence of objective evaluation processes and the buying function. Yet emotion still plays a part in business sales. People at work make emotional decisions as much as (some would argue more than) logical, objective and analysis-based decisions. A chief executive may want to buy a consultancy project from a particular firm because he fears acquisition and wants to use the brand of his supplier to reassure shareholders. A business buyer may be worried about the impact of a purchase on their budget, or their political standing after choosing a poor performing supplier. Experience suggests that suppliers who understand these emotional drivers

Figure 7.6 Steps in organisational buying

of business decisions are able to charge higher prices than those who do not.

Figure 7.6 represents the typical steps in the business buying process. The first two stages are frequently undertaken inside the firm when assessing straightforward products such as paper, chemicals or internet servers. Executives will determine the business needs and set policy. If they need information on suppliers, then the sources they refer to are: representatives of their firm, word-of-mouth, industry networks (e.g. contacts in other firms or industry associations), directories, press releases, brochures and internet searches. Each of these has different influence in different markets. For instance, research has shown that, in business-to-business markets, personal contacts with colleagues, including peers in other companies, is the most influential source of information whereas direct mail has virtually no effect. This is exacerbated with business-to-business services because they are difficult to evaluate in advance. Reputation in the market is likely to be more powerful an influence. For example, one group of researchers, (File, Mack & Prince, 1994) showed that word-of-mouth was rated as very important by chief executives of US companies buying legal, accountancy and consulting services. This is not to say that other information sources (directories, advertising, professional registers) can be neglected. Buyers often use them early in the process to build up a short list, to find alternatives suppliers or to gain a perspective on favoured suppliers.

Several companies have been prompted to move from products to services by the need to influence the first two stages of the buying process effectively. Their experience is that, if they can influence these formative stages of the purchase process, the contents of the proposal request is richer and more favourable to them. They suggest that product companies who limit themselves to responses to tenders lose out on product deals as much as potential

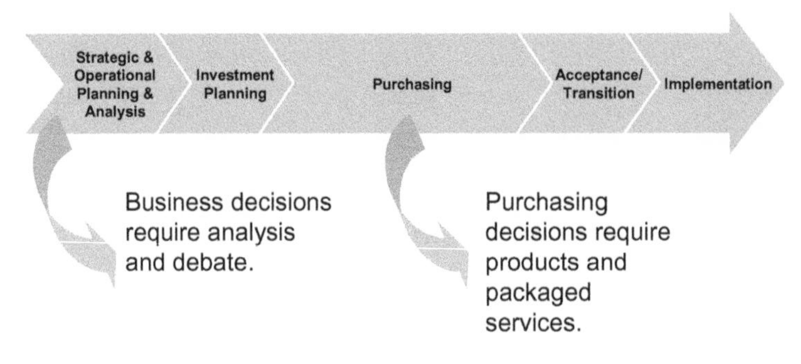

Figure 7.7 The difference in points of dialogue in the purchase process

incremental services. However, the people involved in their customers' strategy and planning processes are likely to be in different parts of the organisation to those they normally deal with and more senior. They are also more likely to weigh alternatives and seek answers to problems as they formulate policy. As a result, these first two stages can become the consultative and diagnostic stage of service projects focusing on project scoping, pricing and contractual process. In short, they can develop into consultancy purchases.

Although there has been detailed academic work, research and models developed about organisational buying behaviour, research into the organisational buying of services was a relatively neglected area until the 1990s. That decade saw the rise of outsourcing, facilities management companies, call centres and an explosion in professional services, particularly in management consultancy projects built around huge systems and change management initiatives. These firms needed to understand the buying criteria of their customers so demand for research and concepts applicable to this field grew.

How companies sell

(i) New business sales

This is the most recognisable and, in some ways, straightforward type of selling. A new business salesperson is normally briefed and trained on the details of a product in order to sell it to an intended group of customers.

They will usually have a defined 'territory' to cover, depending on the size of the total market, and sales targets to achieve each month or quarter. These salespeople have to be managed and motivated through pay, training, administrative back-up and targets; some form of payment by results being the chief of these. It is then up to them to find and gain access to potential customers who will buy; often with the help of 'leads' generated by the company's marketing programmes.

This approach has been widely used across a range of both product and service businesses (from cars and confectionery to banking and insurance) in a wide range of countries for over a hundred years. Whilst the term management did not exist before 1900, and familiar terms like 'business strategy' or 'return on investment' belong to the mid-twentieth century, sales concepts go back centuries. Not only were books being written about 'professional sales' in the nineteenth and early twentieth centuries (for instance G.K. Strong's '*The Psychology of Selling Life Insurance*' published in 1924), but firms employed a large number of people to sell their products. In 1905, for example, Singer (even then a global firm, making sewing machines in eight factories around the world) sold 2.5 million machines a year through 61 444 salespeople (see Edgerton, 2007).

Contrary to popular opinion, the best salespeople are the best listeners. The caricature of the pushy salesperson is actually bad practice and counter-productive. Even second hand cars salespeople are taught to ask questions, get an idea of the potential buyers' needs, and then begin to offer product that best suits those needs; to match the product 'benefits' to the 'prospect's requirements'. With more complex products, this approach has to become more structured and, at its most sophisticated (with, say, complex engineering networks), the listening aspect of the sale is more like consultancy. The salespeople who lead these deals, often first class scientists, are taught the sort of diagnostic and discovery approaches which are second nature to leading strategy consultants.

(ii) Account management

The concept of client account management is based on the fact that certain buyers will give a stream of business to a supplier whereas others will not. It developed when product companies found that revenue improved if they took different approaches to existing buyers than those used with 'new business prospects'. The skills of a salesperson focused exclusively on getting new customers were found to be different to those of a 'representative' dedicated to managing the orders from existing buyers. The latter is focused on creating longer term relationships and gets involved in many issues other than direct sales (such as complaints, or administrative difficulties), which might threaten the business exchanges between the two sides.

Although used in retail, consumer goods and the car industry, it was when this concept moved into the young computer industry (with its then obsession on its 'installed base of products') that there was progressive codification of 'major account management' as a discipline, particularly by the likes of global market leader IBM. It has since moved into other industries and has been adopted, to a greater or lesser extent, by many different companies. It is seen throughout the service economy and even leading professional service partnerships use 'relationship partners' to focus on the needs of one important client account.

There are several components to the approach. Firstly, the firm has to identify and define the major accounts from which business will flow. This can be as crude as listing them by volume of business and ranking accordingly. Some focus on their 'top 100', or some version of it, while others have tiered layers of prioritised accounts, each receiving different levels of attention according to the volume of business.

However, these simple approaches won't meet all of the firm's objectives in its market, and it certainly won't reveal that it may only be receiving a

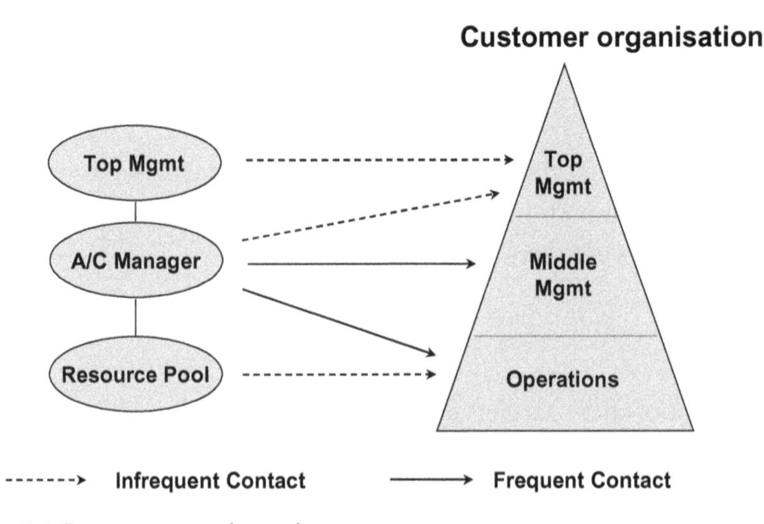

Figure 7.8 Representation of typical account management interactions

small share of these companies' spend in its product category. It may, for instance, want to identify customers with the highest potential and penetrate those further. Or it may have more generic strategies, such as wanting to penetrate a sector of the market or to take business from a competitor. Some set objectives to 'penetrate' certain types of high quality customers in order to be recognised as a high quality supplier. If these 'target customers' have low immediate spend, they may be labelled as a 'strategic account' and receive the same attention as important customers with a larger immediate business volume.

Account managers need to be capable of understanding and presenting the whole range of products, skills and services offered by their firm. At a minimum, excellent communications skills will be needed and a recognised ability to generate revenue. Successful individuals in this role are also frequently creative, able to spot opportunities and harness their own firm's abilities by forming teams to suggest ideas.

The best account management normally involves an 'account planning process' of some kind, frequently undertaken on an annual basis, which adds discipline to relationship management. It normally involves an internal meeting of employees who have an interest in the account, led by the account manager. At this meeting, the team discusses a number of issues, including:

- Objectives for the account. These might be financial, relationship building or strategic.
- Environmental awareness. A review of the customer's market and challenges, used to understand issues and identify potential opportunities.
- Creation of potential projects and sales.
- Prioritisation of marketing programmes and other events specifically for that account.
- Annual investment in the account.
- Relationship building programmes.

Sometimes, account leaders will involve members of the customer's organisation in the planning session to add perspective and depth to the debate. The output, often in the form of an account plan, is shared with relevant people in the firm (see Figure 7.9).

In addition to individual account managers (or 'account directors' for really large customers), some experienced product companies dedicate teams

A typical account plan

1. Objectives for the year. (Financial, strategic, relationship)
2. Summary of account's situation. (Strategic issues the client faces.) Also, account profile. (Decision makers, their staff changes, competitive incursion etc.)
3. Prime opportunities. (Prioritised list of what propositions are being taken to whom, when.)
4. Budgets. (Costs, revenues and billing profile.)
5. Strategic or relationship activities, designed to deepen the closeness of the two firms. (E.g. Hospitality, social events, etc.)
6. Resource plan. How many people are needed, with what skills and when? What new people need to be introduced into the account?
7. Client service plan.

Figure 7.9 Typical account or relationship plan

of people to important accounts. These can include: project managers, sales support staff, client service managers and even telephone sales staff (to handle volumes of small items). Practice in professional services firms, on the other hand, can vary. Many dedicate administrative or business development people to key accounts as well as some client service staff.

A word of caution on account management: much modern practice has been based on processes pioneered by IBM in the 1980s, when it was the global market leader in computing. It had account directors and detailed account plans with sophisticated prospecting and sales support. Yet, when the company faced its traumas due to the opening up of its market in the early 1990s it nearly collapsed because, in part, its account managers had missed changing customer needs. Similarly, after BT was privatised, it invested heavily in account managers but, within five years, its share of its prime market, the City of London, had dropped from 100% to under 20%. Yet, if account management theory (which was designed when these markets had semi-monopolistic distortions) was correct, neither should ever have got into that situation because their account managers would be so close to their customers. Account or relationship management as a discipline may therefore have flaws.

(iii) Regional sales versus industry knowledge

A product company often takes a 'field sales' approach to its sales organisation. This involves salespeople being assigned to a geographic territory and handling the approach to all potential customers within that territory. They are often managed by an 'area manager' reporting to a 'regional manager' who reports to the sales director. The ethos behind this approach is efficiency in terms of sales time. The salesperson can plan what length of time to take to visit customers within a geographic patch and management can assess this efficiency by the number of 'sales calls per day' (or its equivalent).

By complete contrast, however, the consultancy industry tends to base its sales organisation on 'industry knowledge'; familiarity with the industrial sector in which the buyer works. As problem diagnosis is at the heart of the consultative approach, clients need to be reassured that the consultants with whom they work have a deep personal knowledge of their industry. Most consultants (and in fact many professional service organisations) therefore have a sector approach to organising their practices. Very often there will be a 'practice head' who leads a group of specialists dedicated to a business sector such as telecommunications, computing or banking. This organisation is not really interested in geographic efficiency. Very often 'virtual' teams can be dedicated to an industry's specific problem from across the world. For them, the incremental revenue that can be gained from greater industry knowledge, outweighs any consideration of the number of 'sales calls' that can be achieved.

Part of the value to buyers of outside advisers is the perspective they develop from handling the problems of several companies in the same industry sector. Business customers are often curious about how they stand when compared to peers and have an open ear to issues or trends that outsiders can spot from such deep engagement. They will even attend confidential discussion sessions and briefing programmes with competitors present if facilitated by a supplier they trust and if there are clear rules for the meeting. Such a powerful position as industry expert is a very rich source of projects and fees.

There is, however, a greater reason for deep knowledge of the sector in which customers operate. Buyers rarely know the full scope of the products or services offered by a supplier and often have latent needs which, they think, cannot be resolved easily. They may not even have formulated them into potential projects or a request for proposals. An account manager who understands the priorities of firms working in a sector, is likely to spot these latent needs and identify those that their firm can meet. They can then create projects, as yet unimagined by the buyer, to solve problems. So, the primary skill needed to succeed at account management is industry and client knowledge, while the secondary skill is the knowledge of the firm's resources. This suggests that relationship managers recruited from an industry and taught a firm's products or skills will have an edge over internal recruits.

The telecommunications suppliers are a good example of this. When many of the European telecommunications companies were deregulated or privatised, some put their own staff, with the correct soft skills and characteristics, into relationship management roles. However, those who hired account managers from companies in their customers' industries (educating them in their own products) succeeded in taking market share because the account managers could envisage and create propositions from their knowledge and insight. While all of these companies have since put great emphasis on account management, those with a deep knowledge of a particular sector have tended to take the lead.

(iv) Selling professional services

There are a number of similarities between product sales and the 'consultative approach', typical in the success of many professional service firms. These are summarised in Figure 7.11 on page 228 but include:

- Needs analysis uncovers opportunities to be converted into sales by matching the benefits of a product or service to the buyer's needs.
- Both need to be able to assimilate information about their buyers and re-phrase it in ways that succinctly express the core problem, demonstrate their understanding and result in an answer to a need.
- Both require listening, 'closing' and advanced social skills, such as the ability to develop rapport with the buyer.
- Both require 'collateral' (brochures, specification sheets, case studies, testimonials, research etc.) to help the buying process.
- Branding and image are important, creating a competitive image in the buyers' imaginations.
- Payment by results is the primary motivator for both and an important factor in revenue growth.

- Understanding cash flow management and territory planning as well as being an efficient administrator are necessary requirements in both.

However, there is one very important difference: in contrast to product companies (whose sales are conducted by salespeople at middle management level), 'business generation' in leading professional service firms is led by their top practitioners who manage client relations. This is called 'partnership selling' because it is the role of partners in the firm to lead the dialogue with clients.

For professionals in any field, the moment when they make partner is a defining point in their career. They discover meetings, structures, debates and insights which they simply didn't know existed before, even though they may have been with the firm a decade or so. Client management and income generation in this context have different, often intuitive, rules which are seldom articulated in academia or the business press because most partners are either too busy with their own technical work, too focused on their own networks or, quite frankly, too rich to be bothered. The majority of product salespeople are unable to whisper in the ear of senior people and walk away with the high revenue, high margin deals, that many partners do every day. These partners are often 'unconsciously competent' at breathtaking salesmanship.

There are, in fact, several unique elements to sales (or as they prefer: 'business development') in partnerships. The first is the virtuous circle which comes from really good work. Most successful partners say that 'marketing begins with the work'; and they are right. After a good experience, clients talk, creating 'word of mouth' which turns into reputation. Industry experience demonstrates that outrageous profit can be made if that reputation can then, over time, be turned into brands like Bain, PricewaterhouseCoopers and Clifford Chance. It also shows that, if this 'demand pull' can be maintained, clients return for more and refer the firm to others. It means that work is attracted to the practitioner. This, in turn, keeps cost of sales down and prices high because the practitioner can concentrate on diagnosing and meeting the clients' needs. Closing 'sales' is quite easy in this context.

'Bedside manner' is also crucial to 'business development' in professional partnerships. Partners repeatedly say that success 'is all about relationships'.

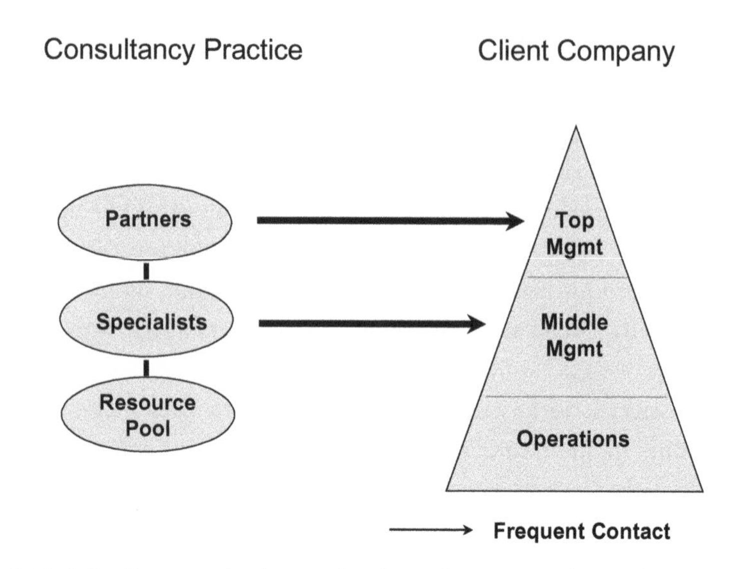

Figure 7.10 Sales ('business development') relationships in a professional partnership

This ranges from the way consumers are handled during personal projects like house conveyance or divorce, through the justification for spending on client hospitality and up to the sophisticated relationship programmes that huge global firms have with international business clients. All are designed to ensure that clients are treated well enough to engender respect and trust. Such a close, respected relationship means that work goes to tender less often and clients happily invest in a mutually profitable exchange. As a result, the ambition of most world-class professionals is to be a 'trusted adviser' to their clients.

Reputation management and client service skills are therefore two prime contributors to high margin business development in the professions. There is complexity and technique behind the application of them and it is immensely difficult to structure them into a practice. Yet, leaders of companies moving into consulting, or any other professional service, need to build these approaches into their business to ensure that techniques which are normally intuitive and unarticulated in the professions are crystallised into the day-to-day business life of their new service business.

(v) The unique phenomenon of the professional services 'rainmaker'

By far the majority of books on sales, business development or sales techniques in professional services tend to use the American term 'rainmaker' to hang their particular theory on. Yet really effective rainmakers are aberrations. They are individuals who have above average capacity to generate business but by much more than just a salesperson in a product company exceeding their targets. A true rainmaker brings in outstanding amounts of revenue. While most senior professionals generate income and revenue, these people tend to generate two or three times the industry average figures. For example, while the partners of the world's leading search consultancies happily make their fortunes by completing an average of twelve to fifteen assignments a year, one 'phenomenon' completed one hundred in their best year.

Rainmakers exist in all professional services, from architecture through engineering consultancy and marketing services to accountancy, law and management consultancy. Yet these are difficult, driven and erratic people who need the approval and comfort of huge social networks. Moreover, most of them do not understand how they succeed in such dramatic ways. It is neither possible nor sensible to build a sizeable business around their erratic behaviours.

The skills and attributes of rainmakers generally comprise:

- A driven individual. They need to achieve and put their prodigious energy, often caused by personal trauma, into business success.
- Market focus. They know the market they operate in very well and understand both developing issues and key individuals within it. They concentrate their team's skills and expertise on the market and apply their knowledge.
- Reputation management. They are ferociously proud of their own franchise, jealously guarding it through excellent execution. They create 'thought leadership' to enhance reputation and understand the use of PR. They write articles and speak at conferences to maintain a high profile.
- Client targeting. They identify high probability projects which yield high returns and seek out buyers with needs.
- Networking. They put enormous effort into building and energising networks of professional contacts. They have frequent contact with clients, building trust and relationships. They ask questions and listen to needs, identifying projects to meet those needs. They close deals and then sell other projects.
- Delivery. They become reliable by ensuring a good team works on their projects. They manage expectations and ensure that their team delivers high quality work.

- Measurement. They ask for feedback, adapt and develop. Over time, they build a track record.

The leadership of firms moving into professional service businesses (like consulting) should consider the strategies and processes by which they recruit and manage rainmakers. For instance, they are often adverse to systems, processes and administration; so may not be particularly good at management or leadership. A prospective service firm should therefore have clear human resources policies to identify and retain them outside the normal management promotion process. They should be managed appropriately and given the correct support with increasing responsibility for either markets and revenue streams or major accounts as they progress through the firm. The culture of the firm ought to be friendly to such difficult human beings. It also needs to explain their importance and their behaviour to other members of the firm who have to tolerate their erratic behaviours.

A particular area of difficulty is rainmaker development. In a large firm this is best managed with some form of apprenticeship. An experienced rainmaker should be given one or two potential revenue generators to introduce into accounts. These junior professionals, perhaps on a 'partner promotion track', need to be told that they are to work with the experienced rainmaker and adopt the successful techniques of that rainmaker in their own style. Yet as rainmakers typically do not know how they generate business and because of their dislike of administration, they will tend to be uninspiring teachers. This needs to be explained to the junior professionals so they understand the context in which they are operating

(vi) Specialist 'business developers' in the professions

Many professional service firms employ specialists who assist with relationship management or sales. Their backgrounds, role and tasks vary enormously but most provide some of the functionality of 'sales support' in product companies. They seem to have one over-riding objective: to maintain focus on client development and marketing issues while client service staff execute projects. They may assist with account planning (preparing, attending and participating in planning sessions) and they may manage the production of proposals. In some countries, they participate in account development, visiting contacts to create relationships and open doors for client service staff. Some even come from a sales background and are briefed to sell into client accounts. Many firms report success in deploying salespeople in this way, particularly in cultures that are receptive to sales calls such as the USA. However, they have to rely on partners or client service staff to finalise any deal, because they deliver the service.

The sales strategies of companies that move from products to services

Companies who have moved from products to services or set up service businesses in their organisation have approached their service sales capability in different ways. They are:

(i) Attempting to train product salespeople to sell services or to turn them into consultants

When first moving from products to services, some companies try to get salespeople to 'sell services' or 'advise on the structure of the deal'. These are two distinct approaches and some flounder because they confuse them.

The first, 'getting salespeople to sell associated services', is normally a cultural change requiring discipline and training. It may be that the firm has grown by selling products and its associated services (maintenance, finances, etc.) have been neglected. A first step is to check that all the customers who have bought products have any necessary support contracts and the administrative arrangements to pay for them. The salespeople of a surprisingly large number of first-rate companies have given service away 'free' to help the price of product sales. If so, little contractual documentation will exist for their customers' service support needs. Even those organisations that have discovered and resolved this obvious problem have to conduct regular audits to ensure that their controls continue to work. A second step is to consider rewarding salespeople on total income from a customer. For instance, if a product costs $ x, associated services can amount to at least another $ 2x over its lifetime of use. When salespeople realise this and are incentivised accordingly, they can quickly develop skills to sell associated services. This change alone can revolutionise behaviour toward services.

The second approach, 'getting people to advise on the nature of a deal', requires salespeople to engage in conversations with customers earlier in the sales process. As discussed earlier, this often involves a very different group of people; usually more senior than the salesperson's previous contacts because they are developing strategy rather than executing predetermined policy. The salespeople attempting this need to develop their listening skills more, perhaps learning advanced consultancy techniques to help the buyers to diagnose a problem and subtly propose answers to it. They also need to learn how to relate to more senior, thoughtful people. Some find this easy to do because consulting techniques merely put words and methods around listening approaches that they have learnt intuitively through years of experience; but many find they are not comfortable dealing with the vagaries of different strategic choices.

Although there are similarities between the sales techniques of traditional field sales operations and consultancy, there are very real differences (see the summaries in Figures 7.11 and 7.12). The differences must be taken into account and not ignored if a successful consultancy business is to be created. In fact a number of companies have tried this and failed. As a result, this approach appears to be the most arduous move into selling service which, over the long term, is rarely successful.

The most notable example was IBM in the 1990s. Its original move into services involved using its account managers to handle service sales. Yet it eventually had to turn around its business, laying off a large number of its then 300 000 employees and recruiting more with different skills. It found that very few of even these highly skilled and very well trained salespeople were able to make the transition to selling concepts and services. In the end,

Field sales and consultancy
Needs analysis uncovers opportunities.
Payment by results crucial to achieving sales and revenue.
Cash flow management critical.
Brand is an important issue.
Good quality collateral is important.
Characteristics of people who generate revenue.

Figure 7.11 Similarities between product sales and consultancy

	Field Sales	Consultancy
(i)	Regional sales	Industry knowledge
(ii)	Closing technique	Problem diagnosis
(iii)	Awareness building	Reputation building/demand pull
(iv)	Product knowledge	Industry knowledge
(v)	Sell benefits of products	Diagnose needs & solve problems, involving elements of strategy.
(vi)	Response to tender once needs clear	Discussion earlier in sales process.
(vii)	Contact at middle management level	Contact at senior & top management level.
(viii)	Product push	Demand pull
(ix)	Leaders manage & supervise	Leaders run projects

Figure 7.12 Differences between product sales and consultancy

IBM developed a strategy built on its knowledge of sectors and used that to penetrate the global services market. This led them, ultimately, to the massive acquisition of PricewaterhouseCoopers' consulting division.

Combining products and services with the existing salesforce can cause insurmountable problems, even after extensive training and development. Separating the two can benefit product sales as well as stimulating the growth of services.

(ii) Teaching service managers to sell

A number of companies in various sectors have handled the move into services by using maintenance technicians, engineers and service managers from their existing service division to manage the account relationship with important customers. The logic of this approach is based on the fact that purchasers of products with a long sales cycle will be visited more frequently by service people than salespeople. If a customer normally replaces their product every three years, then contact with the sales organisation will be very infrequent; whereas service people are, at least, likely to be visiting annually and could programme more frequent visits while attending to other customers in the area.

This approach has hidden costs. It will affect, for instance, the performance of the service division, increasing the time they must spend with customers, reducing their visit ratios and increasing costs. Also, it has been found that, although they have a service ethos, they are often unable to adopt a consultative approach to their customers and have limited sales ability. In addition, these service managers do not have the appropriate sales skills or motivation. As a result many companies have had to draw back from this approach over the years.

(iii) Creating a separate 'service' salesforce

A number of companies have established their service arm by recruiting new consultants or salespeople from service businesses. For example, when the computer company Unisys first moved substantially into services, it recruited one of the partners of Andersen consulting to its board who then created a specification for a 'principal' consultant, to be recruited across the worldwide firm. The company set out behavioural requirements, background experience and skills required in these people. It then recruited candidates to take over the customer relationship from account managers across the world. The logic was that clients were looking for more customised projects and that existing account managers could only sell tangible products, not intangible services. As a consultative approach was required, all account managers were to be replaced by consultants.

There are a number of advantages a specific, experienced 'service sales force' has over product salespeople trying to sell services. For instance, it can be difficult for an existing salesforce to sell new services or services that have previously been given away free. The temptation is to fall back on old habits rather than employ new techniques and approaches. Whereas service salespeople, particularly experienced consultants, are conversant with selling service concepts and adept at managing relationships with more senior people who develop strategy.

Selling products can be fairly instantaneous and can involve top-up orders or selling-in new products, line extensions etc.; whereas selling services often requires a longer sales process and the ability to generate trust. The services sales cycle is prolonged because the customer is buying the credibility of the salesperson rather than a tangible product. Time is required to stimulate the necessary trust and credibility. The danger is that the existing salespeople avoid services and concentrate on products because they deliver a quicker return. Experienced consultants, on the other hand, know how to reduce the time lag through enhanced interpersonal skills and the ability to quickly establish rapport.

Moving from a product only, to a product/service orientation, will require a major cultural shift in the sales force. They will need to change from 'free services', where service costs are carried in the overhead of the business, to a 'charged-for-services' environment. It is possible to train salespeople in new skills but attitudinal shifts of this kind are difficult for some, impossible for others. Service salespeople and consultants, on the other hand, are used to charging for their services and know how to handle specific obstacles to conceptual sales. They are not burdened by historical precedent. New consultants can easily be recruited matching an attitudinal profile, benefiting the company from the outset. They can visit existing customers and sell services to the senior people without embarrassment or fear.

The existing salesforce may have limited industry knowledge. As a result, their ability to interact at a senior level in customer accounts is questionable. Industry knowledge and experience are essential to gain credibility among principals and directors. Suitable external candidates, recruited with deep industry knowledge, will be able to understand the issues facing buyers and be better placed to recommend an approach.

Finally, adding services to an existing salesperson's portfolio may reduce the selling time devoted to products. Salespeople can be unwilling to concentrate on selling 'the unknown' even if backed by bonuses, at the expense of selling products they thoroughly understand. Dedicated consultants, on the other hand, will be able to turn service prospects into customers of the new service and may even help the sale of the company's products.

(iv) 'Solutions' selling

The need to approach customers, particularly business customers, at the moment when their requirements are ill-defined, has led to that most pervasive of sales strategies: solutions selling. This is an attempt to sell a customised package of products and services rather than a predefined product. It first entered the computer industry in the early 1990s, at a time when suppliers' main proposition to customers was to buy a new product because it would be faster and cheaper than the one they already had; but what was often missing was any analysis of changing business needs. They were not, generally, listening to their customers or taking care to understand their real needs.

The 'solutions' approach was created to encourage salespeople (who had become used to focusing on the upgrade of existing products or overhauling their 'installed base') to learn to concentrate on real customer needs. Because customers had a mish-mash of different technological products that had to be taken into account, a process evolved whereby the seller conducted a technical audit of customers' needs and proposed a 'solution', initially called a system integration project, which customised new and existing technology to meet changing business requirements.

Since then, solutions selling has been successfully used by a range of different companies to act as a catalyst for a change in the behaviours of their salesforce. It has been seen in: computing, telecommunications, copying, healthcare, and heavy engineering, to name but a few. Nokia's case study is typical of many who have set out to capture additional revenue from associated services or, perhaps more importantly, understanding the real needs of their buyers. They frequently edge competitors out of their customers' installations by offering packages that work across all technologies.

However, in the enthusiasm to adopt this approach, and use it as a catalyst of change, the difficulties it causes have been disguised, neglected or ignored. One credible study of sixty solutions providers found, for example, that three out of four companies see little gain from a solutions sales strategy (Johansson, Krishnamurthy & Schlissberg, 2006).

The first, and most important difficulty, is that solutions can cause an erosion of margin and a fall in price. When companies sell products there are established prices and controlled discounts which a sales person can apply. But when putting together a package of products and services, salespeople will often apply a discount to get the sale; and the discount is frequently applied to supplementary items outside the discount controls on products (i.e. services). Yet, when a product company moves wholeheartedly into 'solution selling', their own products can be a much smaller percentage of most orders. If it has no cost information on the other elements of the sale or, perhaps more importantly, no discount controls in place for service items or competitor equipment, the move to solutions will lose money. Yet a customised offer (such as a Saville Row suit or bespoke car) should be more expensive than the pre-packaged offer (an off-the-peg suit or mass-produced car). So a solution should be more expensive than a standard offer.

Secondly, if a supplier is seeking to run or grow a large business through volume sales, then one of its keys to success is scalability. It needs to industrialise or package its offer to customers as much as possible. Many large technology companies are based on this ethos. Their marketing, sales, distribution and delivery are all based on volume. Yet, this is in conflict with a sales approach which customises every single sale through a solutions selling philosophy. Without a profound change in process, philosophy and approach (together with the adoption of robust 'mass-customisation' technology) profit will be eroded.

The third problem is that the marketing of solutions doesn't tend to create or communicate a clear value proposition. Yet, as discussed earlier, customers often need a clear proposition if they often don't know what they are looking for or they are going to change their buying habits. Calling something a 'solution' has led to extravagant claims on the part of those who follow this route and some ridiculous product names. The satirical British magazine, *Private Eye* regularly lists some of the sillier examples, such as:

- 'Accommodation Solutions': Flats/apartments;
- 'Integrated Care Solutions': Residential, Day-care;
- 'Extra-care solutions': Nursing Homes;
- 'Chilled food solutions': Ready meals;
- 'Outsourced Vehicle Movement Solutions': Car deliveries.

Architects take an approach to their work which is similar to the 'solutions methodologies' suggested by consultants who have specialised in this field. They understand their clients' needs, often helping them to craft a 'requirements specification'. They then analyse the site and design a 'solution' to their needs; before assembling a multi-disciplinary team to build the building. Yet at the end of the project they deliver a house, a garage or an office block; not an odd sounding, meaningless package.

It is easy for new entrants or smart competitors to take the lead in markets dominated by companies who taken a customised, solutions approach to every sale. If they package their offers, perhaps going as far to offer products which capture many of the service requirements, they will be able to undercut the price of established suppliers and improve their own profit. A number of buyers will then sacrifice a degree of flexibility or customisation for price advantages.

(v) The creation or acquisition of separate service businesses

Various companies have solved the service sales capability issue by creating a separate business under the direction of an experienced consultancy leader. For example, when it first ventured into services, the French-based telecommunications company, Alcatel, created a new consultancy company to lead its venture. This was headed by a general manager, specifically recruited from one of the 'big four' accountancy firms to build the business. It had a different brand name and a separate reporting and accounting system. The management of this business was therefore able to structure it as a completely separate entity using the processes appropriate for this type of operation. Similarly, Ericsson accelerated its venture into a service emphasis in the mid-1990s by the acquisition of a strategy consultancy.

An advantage of this approach is the ability to recommend whatever actions, products or services are needed in order to meet the customer's requirements. This is very important for companies moving from a product orientation because the customers need 'best advice'. They are often suspicious that the supplier is only interested in proposing an answer which supports its products and need reassurance that advice is objective.

This approach to setting up a consultancy has been relatively successful for the companies who have adopted it. Success is dependent, however, on the unit being allowed a free hand to build its business.

Nokia Services' Business Solutions Portfolio

Nokia is a world leader in mobile communications best known for its consumer handsets. Yet its decision, in 2005, to embark on a major change programme for its business-to-business networks division and to differentiate itself from its competition (by shifting focus from selling technology to providing customer-oriented services) has transformed its prospects.

Fundamental to this change was the creation of a 'Nokia Services organisation' in the company's networks division on 1 January 2005. At that stage, several service organisations and capabilities were combined from across the company into one business unit, comprising: network planning, optimisation, network rollout and deployment, care and hardware services, consulting, integration, operations support systems software, service management software, learning solutions, managed services and hosting. This amalgamation made the existing service businesses more visible because it represented over 25% of the Nokia Networks' revenues.

The company had started to put in place 'solution selling' some years before, encouraging salespeople to work systematically with its customers, defining their needs, and combining different standalone offers into more customised and comprehensive projects. By 2005, the company had trained 1200 people in 'solution selling' methods and practices, so (in 2006), Nokia Networks was prepared for an extensive roll-out of its newly-formed 'Business Solutions Portfolio'. By June of that year, Nokia Services represented more than a third of the Nokia Networks' total revenues with very strong potential growth.

Background

The international 'mobile network infrastructure' industry had been undergoing a number of significant changes, driven by technology, consumer demand and increasing competition. In mature markets, the boom years had passed and operators were entering a phase of stability and saturation. Faced with declining revenues from traditional voice services and increasing encroachment from other communications and media industries, they were under enormous pressure to cut costs and earn revenue through new data and entertainment-based services. In developing economies, by contrast, the number of consumers continued to expand very fast, so operators needed to deliver profits from a growing number of low-revenue customers, while also updating their service portfolios to attract and retain higher-value users.

As consumer expectations rose, and as technological convergence enabled new competitors to enter the market, these pressures on operators were increasing. To meet the new challenges, they needed more than mere technology vendors. They needed (what Nokia called) 'strategic solution providers' who could help them determine which markets they should be in, which services would maximise profits and which combination of components (infrastructure, applications, content and user devices) would yield the greatest long-term competitive advantage. In short, they needed a supplier who could take a true end-to-end view of their business and work closely with them to help deliver their strategic goals.

Historically though, operators of mobile networks had seen little change in the way their suppliers had behaved and communicated with them. For example, as recently as February 2005, it was clear that most participants at an industry exhibition called 3GSM (the single most important event in the mobile telecom industry calendar) still had little to differentiate their offerings and were relying more on 'technology push' rather than 'customer pull'. Even Nokia, whose 'customer first' strategy had been launched in 2000, had not fully articulated its service-led approach, and this despite the fact that (as the world's No. 2 mobile networks infrastructure provider and No. 1 handset manufacturer) its capabilities and skills made the company better qualified than anyone to deliver true end-to-end operator 'solutions'.

Although Nokia thought there was still an opportunity in the mobile marketplace to create the innovation, excitement and growth of a few years ago; a new approach was needed This should be from a new, customer-driven, 'outside–in' perspective (rather than the traditional technology-driven 'inside–out' perspective). And the only things preventing the company from taking this approach were its own way of working and own way of thinking. The company therefore set itself the goal of transforming its thinking, processes and tools to support true cross-business synergy in a way that addressed actual customer needs, and delivered the full business value they required in the competitive environment they now faced. It was that transformation that led directly to the creation of the 'Nokia Services Business Solutions Portfolio'.

The first steps: understanding customer/market need

Understanding customers and their needs is the cornerstone of all opportunity analysis. But the radical nature of the new 'Business Solutions Portfolio' programme demanded a rethink of the process by which this information was collected. Traditionally, the company's view of markets had been gained through globally standardised tracking research into customer satisfaction, customer loyalty, market size and other metrics. However, all these processes were driven by the global organisational structures and, due to Nokia's heritage, took a predominantly product-related perspective. The challenge was, therefore, firstly, to reorient processes around business challenges (rather than simply analysing customers' purchasing behaviour) and secondly, to localise the collection of information in order to anchor it in the realities of market and customer experiences.

For the first step, market information which the company already owned (for example, research on customer efficiency and end-user behaviour) was used to understand the reality and challenges of the company's customers. This was important because that knowledge could now be drawn upon to define 'market opportunity hotspots'.

For the second step, Nokia used the 'eyes and ears' of the organisation (the customer account teams) to decentralise market understanding and gather relevant information on an operator-by-operator basis. By mid-2005, five area meetings, with around thirty participants in each, had been run, including Nokia Networks' sales directors, 'solution managers' and 'solution consultants'. On the agenda were the hottest themes and challenges the company's customers were facing in their markets.

By the end of the programme Nokia had distilled a wealth of new knowledge into approximately 50 clearly identified business challenges. This data was consolidated into five important 'customer challenge domains' which, Nokia believed, addressed the industry's toughest issues. It was these five domains that formed the platform on which the Business Solutions Portfolio was built and communicated to the market.

The results of this long and detailed process were tested in around ten workshops with customers during the second half of 2005 and the feedback was extremely positive. 'This has been a real eye-opener' and 'We would be crazy not to work with you' were typical statements from those workshops. Comments from the analyst community, with whom the new approach was also tested, were similarly positive: 'Now Nokia is using a language that makes a difference' being a typical example.

Making a pronounced shift to services

Nokia Networks' 'customer first' orientation was established in 2000. Since then, the company's evolution from technology provider to 'solution provider' had been accelerating steadily, although until 2005 the focus for services was still largely on supporting a successful equipment business. The goal of the Business Solutions Portfolio programme was to help achieve a fundamental shift in this focus, from a supporting role in equipment sales to a leading role in addressing customers' most pressing business issues.

Far more than a communication exercise, or just creating new offers, this meant turning around the portfolio development, marketing and sales approach from one based on a collection of individual services to one capable of addressing specific industry challenges (such as operational expenditure reduction or customer retention). While continuing to highlight the individual benefits of great products, software and services, Nokia Networks had to find a way of presenting them as a coherent, integrated answer to a range of questions from customers with very different business priorities.

The resulting change programme required a 180-degree organisational realignment in order to ensure that the consequent portfolio would be more than skin-deep. It involved dedicated resources, full management involvement and buy-in, organisational motivation and cross-disciplinary collaboration, as well as a completely new way of talking about skills and capabilities.

Making it happen

The first step toward the 'Solutions Portfolio' was to create a dedicated team and a few quick wins with a handful of solutions that the company knew it could rapidly bring to market. Initially a 'Solution Marketing Team' was created in the services marketing function, working with the individual business lines to create solutions that addressed customer issues of cost-efficiency and market differentiation.

These first offers were the starting point of the new portfolio and were used for illustrative purposes in customer workshops, external events and communications. They were also the basis of the first 'Solutions Portfolio' brochure and the business challenges-based Portfolio development work mentioned previously.

Changing internal perceptions

Since the primary challenges facing Nokia were within its own walls and across its many internal boundaries, it became clear that it was necessary to send out a concrete internal message and raise the innovative spirit needed to create the new approach. This in turn meant additional work with management to ensure full buy-in and support for the project.

The goal was to create a clear identity and associated behaviour to support the programme. Through a series of management workshops and with creative help of a marketing agency, the 'Solutioneer' concept was born. More than a marketer, more than an engineer, more than a salesperson, the Solutioneer identity pointed at a combination of a strong and proud engineering heritage with a commitment to solve the customers' business challenges in a holistic way and symbolically defined who the company was. The idea was launched internally throughout the Nokia Networks division (not just services) and set the scene for the solution-based thinking needed to deliver the external promise. To support the message, a range of collateral (giveaway puzzles, T-shirts, etc.) and an internal 'Inspirational Video' was developed to help explain the shift the company was taking.

Before formally adopting the term 'Solutioneer', it was also tested with customers around the world. According to their feedback, it had a number of very positive associations, including: 'creativity'; 'solution-oriented'; 'visionary'; 'expert, high level of knowledge, efficient, polite, professional'; 'The leading telecoms company which provides solutions to customers'; 'Something that works, complete, end-to-end, valuable'. The company thought this a sustainable competitive advantage.

Organisational re-tooling

As the programme moved forward, the resourcing for solutions work needed to move beyond the marketing organisation and into the individual business lines, in order to make the promise real. This phase was the most difficult, and although the Solutioneer campaign helped oil the machinery, it was nevertheless probably the single true test of whether or not the Solutions Portfolio would work. Marketing continued to lead the project, but now business lines needed to take responsibility for practical delivery to customers.

Identifying business owners for solutions which crossed several organisational boundaries was a major milestone, and through this work alone Nokia made significant progress in bringing down walls and silos within its organisation. As responsibilities were clarified and delivery work continued, a 'Solutions Portfolio Council' was created to oversee the development and approve new proposals.

The importance of credentials

Providing proof that the solutions actually worked was just as important as creating and developing the portfolio itself. As solutions were piloted, rolled out and delivered, a special campaign was launched in which sales had to generate and agree customer testimonials of business successes (with the best examples given awards by management in sales meetings). In this way, the company not only generated an important part of its external marketing tool kit, but also helped sustain internal momentum and encourage further buy-in.

Bringing the story to market

A major pillar of the external communication programme, a new sales tool (the 'Services Sales Kit') was developed to make it as easy as possible for account teams to put the new Solutions Portfolio approach into action. For the first time, they could access all the sales materials for the three Nokia Networks' business units ('Services', 'Radio' and 'Core') in a single package. Over time there would be a steady convergence towards a common approach based on the customer challenge-based portfolio and Nokia Networks-wide solutions. Using a new user interface, salespeople could access appropriate materials by defining the customer challenge, specifying the document type, or by asking questions and prompting answers from within the sales kit, using a dynamic search engine.

Conclusion

From the beginning, the project took a twin-track approach: on the one hand repositioning the services organisation within the mobile networking marketplace as a true 'solution provider', while on the other hand working internally at every level of the organisation to develop full understanding and buy-in for the changes required to deliver the external promise. By ensuring equal clarity of communication for both external and internal audiences, and by engaging all levels of management in evangelising the Business Solutions Portfolio story, the project has been instrumental in aligning real customer needs with real Nokia skills and capabilities.

General sales principles and their applicability to services

There are a number of general sales principles (a distillation of theory, research and experience) which will need to be considered and adjusted by product companies moving into services. They are:

(i) The sales cycle

Selling products (apart from the most complex and expensive) tends to be within a shorter time frame than selling services. Products can be tried, tested and returned if dissatisfied; however, services involve simultaneous consumption. So, the customer will only buy the service once they completely trust the consultant and this is likely to prolong the sales cycle.

(ii) Targeting

Like product companies, service businesses use the term 'targeting' for either the process of selecting potential customers or the act of approaching them. Methods vary enormously because they are often trying to communicate an idea or concept. Some, merchant bankers for example, tend to create ideas which they suggest to their intended clients. Others analyse their customers' businesses in anticipation of a general discussion. Still others look to develop a vague friendly relationship which, they hope, will develop into mutual work. Some create elaborate diagnostic tools or 'benchmarking data' which they use to stimulate interest. Others employ specialist telephone sales or marketing groups to 'open the door'.

Those service businesses, though, who build 'demand pull' through a strong reputation and brand will have customers coming to them. Their 'targeting' is very different from product salepeople who have to go out to get customers and tease out sales in a geography or industry sector. They are able to choose those that they wish to develop long term profitable relationships with and reject those that they don't.

(iii) Pre-sales activities

As in product sales, service companies employ a wide range of marketing techniques to create demand, stimulate leads and warm prospects for a direct discussion with a salesperson. Sometimes, pre-sales work includes getting on to approved supplier lists, from which employees in an organisation can choose. Without this no substantial work can progress. For instance, many leading Plcs maintain a list of consultants, lawyers and other service specialists which their people must use. Getting on this list may, therefore, become an objective of an account or 'targeting' plan.

At the sale itself, people who sell services have to take as much care to glean initial impressions during early stages of discussion with a potential buyer. For instance, body language, which has been the subject of many research projects and learned publications, is a powerful indication of underlying thoughts. They must also look for other non-verbal signals such as the environment for the chosen meeting. (If the approach is by telephone, it may be that the issue is not seen as very critical; if in a restaurant or bar this may be a signal that the client is open to a range of ideas.)

At this stage it is important to adopt a consultative style; to listen and diagnose. This is much more than cursory attention to words. They must listen actively, demonstrating understanding and checking back with the potential buyer. With a serious problem it may be wise to ask for time to consider the issues and book a further meeting to suggest potential approaches.

Smart suppliers try, though, at this phase in the discussion, to avoid a formal proposal. This is more common than many who have to suffer formal tenders or 'beauty parades' assume. The ability to move straight to work is an indication of the strength of relationship, the respect of the buyer and the skill of the service salesperson. In the European M&A 'mid-market', for instance, anything up to 30% of lead adviser roles are started without a competitive tender. Whilst in premium consultancy projects a common approach is to suggest different methods of solving the problem and ask which the client most favours. At a further meeting to discuss the 'draft' programme; the buyer, feeling in control of the process, adjusts the work plan to their own, unique environment. Very often the project proceeds from there.

(iv) Conducting the formal proposal or sales meeting

As in product sales, a response to a formal request for a proposal must be carefully managed. At the very least deadlines, formats and specified areas of information must be met accurately. This is particularly important in government or public sector proposals where non-compliance can mean that suppliers are automatically excluded. The proposal document, the pre-proposal process and the proposal presentation should all be treated as communications exercises. It is an opportunity to listen and respond, not to bore, pontificate or show off. If the organisation has specified meetings or people to consult before submission deadline, they should be used. In these, as much detail as possible should be asked about technical issues, the problem, budget and those involved in the decision-making process. Some clients take a lack of questioning as a sign of lack of real interest. The team formed to manage the proposal process must plan the approach to warm up those who need to be influenced.

The proposal itself must first be written as a clear communications document. Something which starts with pages of description of the supplier's resources and history is unlikely to communicate effectively. It should outline need, suggest an approach, articulate the benefits of the approach, say why the supplier is unique and give indicative pricing. The production of the document should be managed as a project, leaving enough time for proof reading and rehearsal.

However, the team presenting the proposal needs to be chosen carefully. Not only must they have the right technical skills and experience, they must also include people who will actually work on the job. Buyers are irritated if a senior person presents the proposal and is never seen again. So some suppliers make a virtue of the fact that the team presenting will deliver the work.

(v) Post-sales

This is primarily about excellent delivery of the work; but it is also about reassurance. If something goes wrong, for instance, it must be resolved quickly. It is better to admit that the supplier is not perfect and remedy problems, than to ignore them.

As discussed more fully in Chapter 8 (page 274), if the purchase of any item is emotionally challenging or if it is expensive, buyers experience 'post-purchase distress'. This is anxiety caused by the purchase and is allayed by the buyer admiring the purchased product or sales materials. Customers may be concerned about the effect on their budgets, the effort to sell the project internally, damage to their credibility or risk to their political capital. Also, anxiety is increased if the firm is operating in unfamiliar territory. The customer who buys services from a product company may be anxious due more to the risk of using a familiar supplier in unfamiliar circumstances than to normal post-purchase distress. If this anxiety is not managed, then problems occur.

Yet, as services are intangible, there is nothing to offset this anxiety. As a result, methods of summarising the emotional relief of a well executed project have evolved in some markets. They are a tangible embodiment of 'post-purchase distress'. Salespeople should think through the moments of anxiety that their buyer might experience and create physical devices to allay this discomfort. If possible, find tangible expressions of progress such as weekly progress reports and 'contact' reports, summarising each meeting. A good service manager anticipates and obviates such concern.

(vi) Pipeline management

This is a management concept and sales discipline which builds the generation of business into the day-to-day life of a sales team. It is the foundation of good sales practice and the focus of sales management in many industries. Sometimes called the 'sales funnel' and sometimes 'the book of business', it is a discipline that translates easily into the service industries, particularly in project-based businesses.

Without good pipeline management, activity can be erratic. The business experiences peaks and troughs in work flow because there is no consistent focus on the generation of future sales. Pipeline management helps overcome these difficulties. Figure 7.13 illustrates the concept, which should be approached from a hard-headed, numerically-driven perspective.

For example, starting from the right-hand side, if a consultant has a target of $2 million, and the average value of their projects is $500 000, they need to win four projects a year. The next section of the pipeline shows that, in order to win four jobs a year, they need to propose a number of projects to potential customers. If, in their marketplace, the conversion ratio is two to one, then they need to propose eight jobs to win four. In some service markets, though, there are no formal proposals and presentations. Sometimes a buyer will simply ask a supplier to start the work. Other times the project can be loosely-defined. Nevertheless, there must be some form of discussion, presentation or scoping of projects which forms the basis of the agreement to go ahead. These all count as part of this 'pitches' section of the pipeline.

The next category refers to 'leads' or 'serious expression of interest'. A salesperson will be known to a number of potential customers but, at some

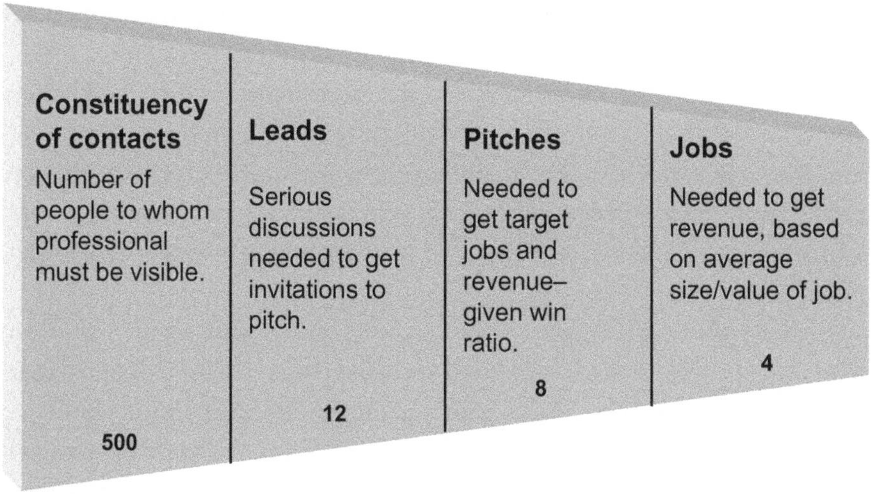

Figure 7.13 Pipeline management

stage, those buyers must express an interest in a product if there is to be a sale. This might be by telephone, in a meeting or in a social context. They discuss their needs and ask for more information. That may simply be a request invitation to examine the need, or it might be an invitation to take part in a 'beauty parade' where the firm has to respond formally to a request for a proposal or presentation of their credentials, or both. If the conversion rate in a market is two to one, there will need to be sixteen expressions of interest to get eight proposals to get four jobs. Already, then, the salesperson in this example needs to receive at least one serious expression of interest a month if workflow is to remain healthy.

The final part of the sales pipeline, the wider end of the funnel, is the 'constituency of contacts' on which the salesperson should focus. This will have several components. First, there will be those who are well known business contacts: where there is a close relationship. In some cases the professional finds it hard to distinguish between these contacts and friends. They will be seen in a social context, and there will be a close relationship of trust, built on mutual value that has been given over the years.

In service markets, the size of this constituency of contacts varies. In some professional services markets, it's quite small and focused. For example, the merchant banks focus on the community of chief executives and business development directors, which is relatively small. In others, it's very broad. Alternatively, it might be primarily in one major organisation, as when, for example, a professional is the lead relationship partner for a large client.

To use the funnel effectively, service salespeople need to build these processes into their day-to-day lives. For example, with their secretary/assistant, they can make sure they maintain regular contact with their intimate professional relationships. They can schedule personal meetings, send Christmas cards and invite them to ad hoc hospitality or professional briefing events.

In the wider constituency, they can work either with their firm's own marketing people, or a self-employed specialist, to create an individual marketing plan. This will avoid the 'feast and famine' effect of erratic marketing if managed on the professional's behalf. The plan must be based on a knowledge of whom they are targeting, where these people go for professional development, and what they read or listen to. This information will guide the media chosen and the activities undertaken. The plan will contain activities such as speaking at conferences, holding social events or publishing articles.

Pipeline management is also a powerful tool for managers. Some build the concept into IT systems so that the pipeline of the business can be seen easily by leaders. Some build in processes of performance review, to keep colleagues focused on the need to manage future business while conducting client projects. It is surprising how effective a regular meeting or conference call, focusing on actions between colleagues to follow up contacts, can be.

(vii) The trusted adviser

This concept was introduced by leading industry specialist David Maister and his colleagues (see Maister, Green & Galford, 2000). Their work seeks to put structure into the development of a professional's relationship with their client and, particularly, the need to earn trust. They argue that this relationship can develop from a basic service offer to trust based through various states (Figure 7.14).

Their work is a sophisticated development of relationship marketing theory as it is applied to, particularly, professional service businesses. They

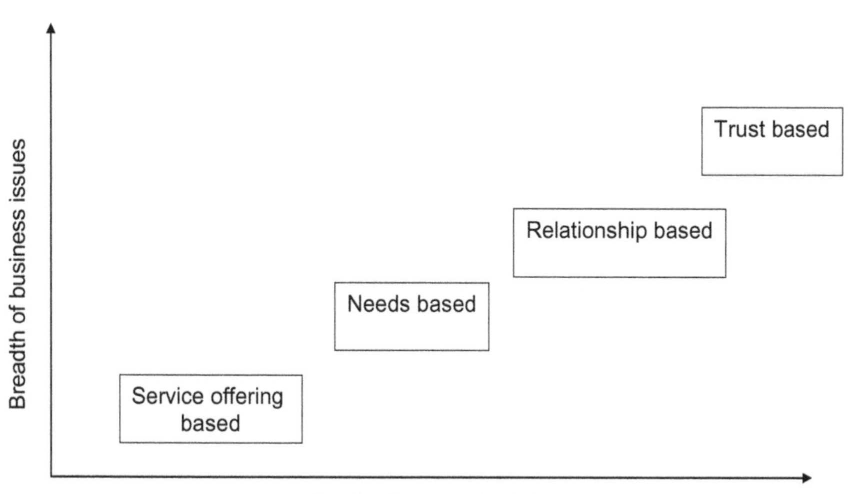

Figure 7.14 The development of trusted adviser status

illustrate the differences and benefits of a trust based engagement when compared to other forms. They also propose economic arguments to calculate the benefits arising from this approach.

(viii) Sales closing techniques

In all exchanges between sellers and buyers, there comes a moment when buyers need to make up their minds. Very often, success can be improved if that moment occurs with the seller present, so sales specialist have created tools to help focus on this moment. Called 'closing techniques', they include:

- Asking for the business. It is obvious, and therefore often forgotten, simply to ask buyers if they want to go ahead. A surprising number of sophisticated and experienced business people do not do this.
- Overcoming objections. This is based on asking buyers whether there are any reasons why they can't proceed and then handling each and every objection as they arise.
- Open-ended questions. This is an extension of 'overcoming objections'. A series of questions are asked to get further and further into the buyer's need and to match the offer closely to those needs. As consultants frequently have to start working with a client by diagnosing need, the 'consultative approach' closely resembles this technique. This is probably one of the most practised closing techniques in service industries.
- Exaggeration to the absurd. Here, the seller may take one of the objections buyers present and exaggerate it to the point of the ridiculous in order to overcome it as a barrier to purchase.
- The 'assumed close'. Here a buyer's body language signifies that they are happy with the suggestions and want to buy. The supplier moves to talking about next steps and assumes the sale is agreed. In fact, they may be concerned that, if the customer is asked for the business or asked whether they want to go ahead, barriers will be raised in their mind.
- The 'go-away'. In this context a seller is convinced that the offer matches the needs a buyer has. If the buyer tries to negotiate on price, or cut

corners, the seller can suggest that they don't go ahead. This causes the buyer to re-commit to doing the work.

Sales organisations of product companies may need to rethink their use of closing techniques as they move into services. As services are more intangible, conceptual offers than products, if the seller is too overwhelming and uses closing techniques too forcefully, once the buyer has a moment to think, he or she is likely to feel cheated and the deal might unravel. These approaches need to be handled with real care in a service context.

(ix) The loyalty ladder

The loyalty ladder seeks to classify buyers according to their disposition toward the supplier. It recognises that the lowest level is not buyers who are uninformed but antagonists. These are people who are negative about the firm. They are important because they create negative word of mouth and damage reputation.

Non-purchasers might be unaware of the offer whereas suspects are considering purchase. Repeat buyers, loyal buyers, or protagonists, are a valuable asset because they create positive word of mouth and build the reputation of the firm. Research can identify the buyers in each group so that different sales programmes can be directed toward them. Fredrich Reichheld has used this concept to propose his 'netpromoter' concept as a measurment of the

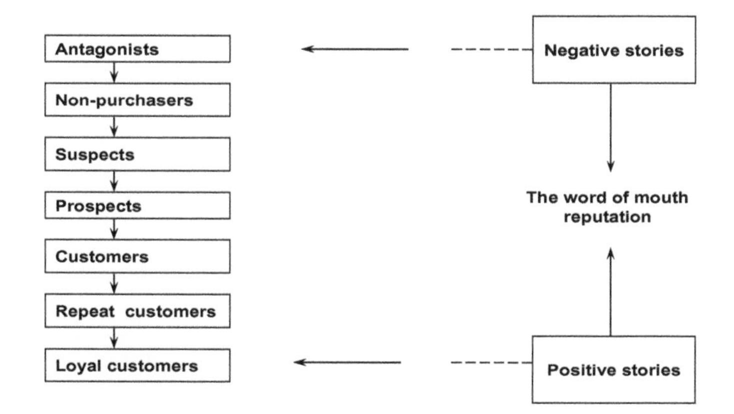

Figure 7.15 The loyalty ladder

health of service business. Essentially the difference between negative and positive stories about the service firm's operations indicates its likelihood of further healthy growth.

Channel strategy as a means to configuring the service sales capability

For companies selling products, those selling services and those moving from products to services, there is a tried and tested method of ensuring that the sales capability of their organisation is properly configured: channel strategy. A comprehensive sales strategy considers all the existing and potential routes to market open to a company. These include indirect channels (such as business partners, catalogues or the internet) and direct channels (salespeople or consultants). It then audits the effectiveness and cost of each one. If new channels need to be set up, the cost of set-up needs to be weighed against the improved revenue and, more importantly, net profits produced by the channel over an agreed period of time.

An important aspect of channel strategy is designing 'synergy' and avoiding 'channel conflict'. Synergy occurs when a new channel influences an existing channel positively to increase sales through it and conflict is the exact opposite. It is clear that many firms which have moved from products to services have failed to do this effectively. Service channels have conflicted with existing channels and not produced sufficient profit to justify the expense of creating them. As service competition increases in developed markets, leaders of firms who have new service channels should conduct an objective and numeric channel review. Those moving into service markets for the first time should do so with a clear and disciplined channel strategy.

Summary

The sales discipline is a crucial part of any firm because it ensures that the company earns revenue. This chapter has explored the differences between service and product selling. At one extreme are the hierarchical geographic structures of sales companies and, at the other, the partner led selling found in the professions. There are different types of sales structures and different sales approaches adopted by companies that move from products to services. This affects the sales principles employed at different phases of the sales cycle, plus the relevant tools and techniques. These must be understood and implemented in detail as a company moves from products to services. A clear channel strategy needs to be developed which designs new service channels effectively and, as importantly, enhances the existing sales channels.

8

Marketing services instead of products

Introduction and overview

Marketing must be one of the most misunderstood functions of modern business. Although business leaders tend to be clear about the role of IT, HR and finance in their business, marketing appears in many different shapes and sizes. It is different for: the intuitive entrepreneur, the bureaucratic plc, the conglomerate, the small firm, the professional partnership, the voluntary sector and the supply industry. Probably the most effective being that done for the intuitive business leader.

Nevertheless, all organisations undertake aspects of marketing to communicate effectively with groups of people. Although the general principles behind this marketing are broadly the same, it has to be adjusted to suit different environments if it is to be successful. This is particularly the case when marketing services. There are a number of issues which need to be taken into account when marketing services rather than, say, consumer products.

This chapter introduces the range of responsibilities, organisational structures, managerial processes and marketing activities in different settings. It then discusses how these might be different or need to be adjusted if a company moves into a service business and needs to market services instead of products. It shows why the marketing of services has to be different from that of products, and how to do so successfully.

One more time: what is marketing?

At its broadest, the term 'Marketing' is used to describe the means by which companies raise their revenue. As all companies have to draw in revenue, all undertake aspects of marketing. In fact, even charities or organisations with no business revenue, like government bodies or lobby organisations, often undertake aspects of marketing in order to communicate effectively with groups of people that they are interested in.

Presenting credentials to potential buyers, managing press relations, hosting seminars, creating new products and giving presentations at public conferences are all part of the marketing mix. So, whether they call it marketing or not, whether they have specialist marketing managers or not, firms undertake a range of marketing activities to grow their business.

In publicly-owned companies these are likely to be the responsibility of a relatively small specialist unit comprising people who are qualified and experienced in marketing. They will be responsible to the management team for creating strategy, plans, budgets and programmes to grow the business. They will also be expected to balance the skills, resources and processes of the marketing department to optimum effect and for the benefit of the business in its market. They will have delegated responsibility to manage the function effectively and will need to ensure that it has good knowledge of relevant concepts, develops appropriate competencies, uses reliable techniques and installs robust processes or systems. On top of this, they will need to engage with the whole firm to ensure that the customers' experiences are appropriate to meet the firm's objectives. In short, the marketing function needs to keep up-to-date and act as a catalyst for the business in its approach to market.

Yet, not all marketing is undertaken in the carefully organised departments of large publicly owned companies. In small firms, professional partnerships and charities, the situation tends to be more fluid and less clearly defined. Different people will initiate different marketing activities, which are frequently handled by executives who have no specialist marketing knowledge and may not be aware of other marketing initiatives in different parts of even their own company. If a marketing manager or marketing department exists, which is by no means certain, they may not have exclusive responsibility for all revenue generation tasks.

Marketing has been variously called an art (because it is creative, requiring judgement and experience), a science (because market-orientated companies use data and analysis to inform decision-making), a management discipline (one of the functions of many firms), an academic field of study (most universities have a dedicated faculty) and a profession (because it requires deep knowledge of techniques with the experience to know how and when to apply them). In reality it has all the elements of all of these but, above all else, it focuses on how a business can generate future revenue.

Opinion formers have defined it as follows:

- Marketing is the process of planning and executing the conception, pricing, promotion and distribution of ideas, goods and services to create exchanges that satisfy individual and organisational goals. American Marketing Association (AMA).
- Marketing is the management process that identifies, anticipates and satisfies customer requirements profitably. UK Chartered Institute of Marketing (CIM).
- Marketing is the social process by which individuals and groups obtain what they need and want through creating and exchanging products and value with others. Philip Kotler (Kotler, 2003).

Marketing is therefore a management process by which leaders of a firm draw in revenue and grow the business. It is not limited to the specialist function within a firm or to highly trained marketing managers. When an executive of any kind is engaging in activities or plans which affect the revenue line, they are marketing. As in all aspects of business life, these activities can be undertaken using common sense by anyone in the firm. However, they are likely to be more effective, and generate more income in a more cost-effective way, if the right techniques are used and if experienced specialists are involved in some way.

The activities of marketing, in no particular order, are:

- Competitive intelligence: understanding what competitors are doing and adjusting the firm's direction in the light of that.
- Opportunity analysis: agreeing which opportunities in the market are likely to create more revenue for the firm and how they might be addressed (whether by acquisition or natural growth).

- Managing the relationships and interfaces with buyers: the approach by which the firm gains new customers or relates to existing buyers.
- Internal communications: creating and managing messages between the employees and the leadership of a firm in order to improve performance.
- Pitch or bid processes: the process by which the firm presents its credentials or specific proposals about an offer to potential buyers.
- Press management: the way the firm handles its public appearance in the media.
- Sponsorship: any paid involvement in sporting/entertainment/arts events to improve the reputation of the firm.
- Corporate and social responsibility: engaging in the support of community projects to encourage a positive reputation for the company.
- Customer events: hosting social or issue-based events in order to attract new business.
- Direct communication: electronic or physical mailings and presentations at public conferences.
- Thought leadership: producing reports, books or other projects to demonstrate the skills of the firm and draw in new business.
- Collateral design: the production of leaflets, brochures and case studies to illustrate issues.
- Advertising: using paid advertisements in TV, radio, print and the web to spread awareness of the offer.
- Customer database management: using technology to ensure that buyer details are assets of the whole firm.
- Networking: managing relationships with a wide range of individuals in order to generate business, often supported by web based social networking sites.
- Pricing: setting charges for the firm's products and services.
- Creating new products or services: designing and launching new concepts or offers.
- Point of sale: displays on premises.
- Premises selection and design: layout of shops or other physical enviroments for customers to create the optimum traffic flow and sales.
- Sales promotion: campaigns designed to make certain products or services attractive in order to increase sales.

- Sales support (called 'business development' in the professions): administration, forecasting, bonus scheme design, incentives, bid management and short term promotions to assist people who sell directly to buyers.

Most organisations, of all sizes and ownership types, will undertake some aspect of many of these activities. All are aimed at gaining revenue in the future and are based on a combination of judgement, research and analysis. But, until quite recently, the research and proven techniques of most marketing work have been predominantly in the field of consumer products. Do they need to be adjusted in any substantial way in order to market consumer or business services effectively?

Different manifestations of marketing

The business world itself is not uniform. Companies succeed with a huge diversity of products and services with very different cultures and operating approaches in a wide range of markets. Marketing has to be adjusted to suit these very different environments if it is to be successful. Some of the main groups include:

The intuitive business leader

Rivals in the market had been conducting a competitive and high profile marketing campaign for ten years. The product had been re-cut, repackaged, re-priced and renamed. There had been advertising in railway stations, in newspapers and eye-catching outdoor sites. At one point, billboards appeared on streets, the length and breadth of Britain, which were filled with a message that could be read from 10 metres away: 'Why does a woman look old sooner than a man?'.

Messages had been projected onto leading monuments, like Nelson's column, and one over-enthusiastic foreign competitor had even daubed a message on the white cliffs of Dover; prompting *The Times* to criticise 'gratuitous exhibitions of dissolving views'. Salespeople were employed to call on retailers and to visit homes across the country. An elaborate range of competitions had captured the imagination of the population and a scientific sounding instruction booklet had been widely distributed. There had even been a long running dispute with an aggressive British tabloid, the *Daily Mail*, about a questionable price change.

A typical modern marketing campaign, using all aspects of the marketing mix, you might think. But this was conducted in the 1880s by the young soap entrepreneur William Lever (see MacQueen, 2004 and Turner, 1965). Lever was an ambitious, driven and eccentric (for much of his life he slept in a bedroom specifically designed to be open to the elements) business leader. When he took over his father's grocery business, he built it into a major, international business which still dominates its market today. Yet this highly effective and well rounded marketing campaign was designed by him before the advent of radio or TV and ninety years before Phillip Kotler wrote his seminal work on marketing management. Moreover, the main rival to his product, Pears soap, had been launched by Andrew Pears one hundred years before that (the 1770s) using catchphrases. The then leader of Pears, Thomas Barret, was just as aggressive in his marketing using for example, celebrities to gain publicity. (Lillie Langtry, an actress and the king's mistress was 'the face of Pears'.)

These creative entrepreneurs were using the principles of marketing, based on their business experience and intuition, long before they were codified. Similar individuals (from Richard Branson, Alan Sugar and Phillip Green in Britain to Donald Trump, Bill Gates and Steve Jobs in the USA) become millionaires, or even billionaires, today through similar attitudes; and many thousands of less famous business leaders do the same. They are the pre-eminent practitioners of marketing, creating enormous wealth for themselves, their investors, their employees and society as a whole. They frequently succeed by breaking rules (Harvard would not have advised young pop entrepreneur Branson to go into the airline business) and shake up or create markets. Their emphasis is on customers and markets, so they push all the elements of their business to focus on external opportunities rather than internal activities. They also tolerate both risk and failure.

As their businesses grow, the most successful learn to use specialists to round out or refine their vision and instinct. They routinely employ accountants, lawyers and merchant bankers; and most use marketing specialists (either as employees or through agencies) to great effect. Many create and run service businesses in fields such as: travel, vacations, finance, hospitality and entertainment.

The cultures of their highly successful, market orientated, businesses are focussed on understanding and executing the leader's will. Much time is taken to tease out, develop and communicate their vision and implement it throughout the organisation. Their marketing is therefore most often about connecting the leader's vision with a market opportunity. In some cases, the marketing structure is a small, fluid team, in another a trusted agency and, in yet another, the more recognisable structures of big, publicly owned firms. They use novel marketing techniques, frequently exploiting publicity opportunities and, in some cases, breaking the rules of consumer product marketing to pioneer service marketing techniques.

The large, bureaucratic business

While the bureaucratic organisation has been heavily criticised by academics and business thinkers, it is seen in most large, modern businesses representing, as it does, the need to specialise. These businesses are owned either by the public through shares, by venture capitalists or families. Authority is delegated down a professional management hierarchy by the leadership team, giving them authority to run the business on behalf of the owners. It is unfortunate that 'bureaucratic' has become a pejorative term. Specialisation of work and skill has been one of the main contributors to the evolution and success of the human race. There are, therefore, real benefits to the specialisation, progressive organisational learning, clarity of reporting, accountability and rational decision-making emphasis of this type of structure. Some of the world's leading marketing concepts have, for instance, been developed by specialists in these organisational environments.

The prime marketing activities in a bureaucracy are the responsibility of a specific specialised unit, the marketing department, depicted in Figure 8.1. It usually reports to a 'chief marketing officer' (CMO) and has the delegated authority to generate revenue and create all marketing programmes. The diagram depicts typical functions within the unit but these can vary enormously. For instance, brand management might exist within market management (because it focuses on market 'categories', a retail term) or in marketing communications. Sales and sales support might be combined with marketing under one 'sales and marketing' director or vice president. Also, there may be elements of the marketing mix in other parts of the organisation. For example, some firms place new product development and pricing under a separate director. Others have directors dedicated to corporate relations; responsible for reputation, brand, corporate social responsibility (CSR) and PR.

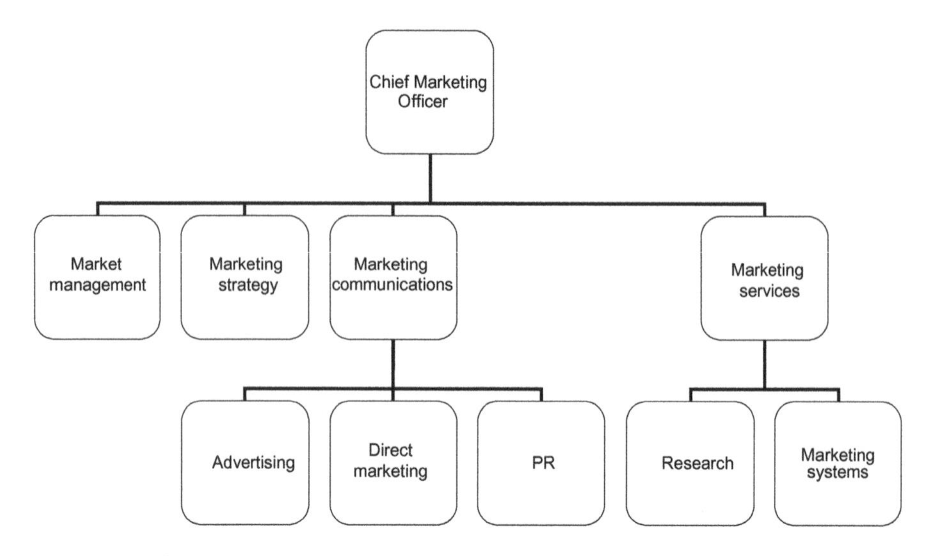

Figure 8.1 The classic functions of a marketing department

The CMO, as leader of the function, has several roles. The first is to provide marketing experience, judgement and advice to the firm's leaders about policies; to round out and inform decision-making and strategy development. The second is to lead the function, ensuring that it is properly resourced and contributes appropriately. The third is to be the voice of the market within the firm, challenging it to embrace opportunities and understand customer needs.

The ability of the marketing function to contribute effectively to income generation and the health of the business depends on the status and recognition it has in the organisation. In many long standing consumer goods businesses (Procter & Gamble, Unilever) or confectioners (Mars), it is a lead function of the business. The firm recruits the cream of the graduate crop into a professional apprenticeship scheme which provides some of the best marketing training in the world. Alumni of the programme progress through the firm from junior brand managers to marketing directors. Their role is to generate income from branded value propositions using wide ranging and proven marketing techniques.

In other industries, however, the contribution of specialist marketing people is limited to minor functional roles like sales support or brochure creation. The formal marketing function is not as valued because the income of the business is generated by other means; such as a strong and healthy natural demand for an innovative product, an aggressive sales force or systematic account management.

There is evidence that this changes as markets mature. For instance, most of the firms who have evolved first rate and leading marketing units are consumer goods companies, because they experienced market maturity in the developed economies during the 1950s and 1960s. Similarly, marketing has become more important to the car industry, the computer industry and the telecommunications industry as they, in turn, have faced market maturity.

It is only in recent decades that large bureaucratic companies in service sectors have begun to establish similar hierarchical marketing departments. Banks, utilities, travel firms and retailers have learnt to use these structures to market services as their industries have experienced greater competition or, as in the case of the newly privatised utilities, market forces for the first time.

These appear to be adapting the processes of consumer goods companies to service environments. BT, for example, had no marketing resource at all when, in 1984, it was a government owned engineering organisation. It now has several hundred marketers working on brand, communication and strategy programmes; and has several highly successful campaigns to its name. However, the marketing community in the firm are very aware that marketing campaigns alone will not grow their business. The affect of their businesses' quality of service on their customers' propensity to buy is just as important.

The conglomerate or decentralised business

Figure 8.2 depicts a decentralised organisation with devolved business units. These might be businesses specialising in different disciplines or in different geographic countries. The effectiveness and behaviour of the marketers depend on the degree of autonomy of the different units. For example, this structure is often adopted by large technology companies. In these, a 'strategic business unit' (SBU) will be expected to work within tight corporate guidelines. The marketer is likely to have a clear job description with defined competences and objectives. They are also likely to report regularly to the corporate function and participate in clear, firm-wide processes.

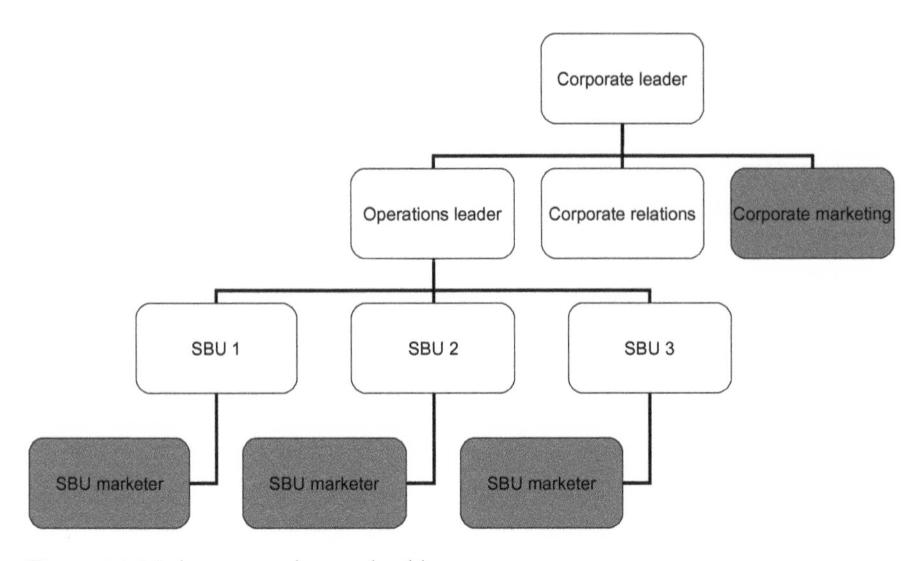

Figure 8.2 Marketing in a decentralised business

At the other extreme, there are large conglomerates which own separate firms with different profit pools (like GE or ABB). The marketers in these firms are likely to have greater autonomy within very broad corporate guidelines. Some of these businesses, like WPP, are huge service businesses and must therefore use service marketing skills.

The smaller firm

By far the majority of firms range from medium sized enterprises to tiny start ups. In these, any specialist marketing units are limited by resource constraints; often to a single, or isolated, marketer, depicted in Figure 8.3. One person is all that the business can afford and that person is likely to report to the firm's leader, gaining authority to create programmes, strategy and change from the closeness of that relationship. Constrained by lack of resources, the single marketer needs influence to get the wider organisation to take on work and the budget to rely on external contractors.

They need the capability to handle a wide variety of tasks and the humility to do much of the work themselves. In some firms they report to a functional leader who manages all specialists (HR, finance, IT, etc.). This,

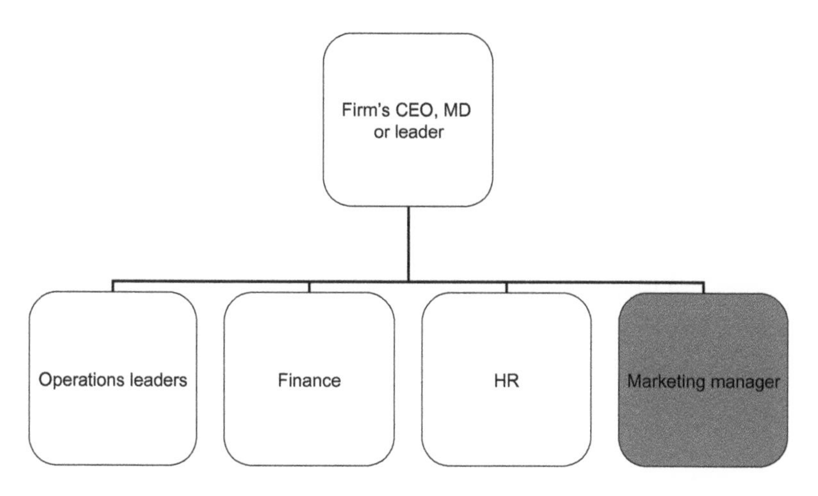

Figure 8.3 Marketing in the small firm

however, tends to be less effective because it weakens the assumed authority behind the speciality, reducing the influence of marketing. One difficulty in this environment is the marketing skills that small firms can afford. They frequently hire young professionals or marketers from middle management in other firms who have never really progressed in their career. These tend to concentrate on promotional work and are frequently unaware of service marketing techniques.

Professional partnerships

Although they are service companies, the marketing within professional service firms tends to be erratic and unstructured. Employees with specialist marketing skills are often regarded as an optional 'support' function. While the strength of partnerships lies in their autonomy and closeness to the market, a drawback is the tendency towards confusion in the skill, deployment and competence of support functions. 'Support' is an ill-defined term for non-fee earning employees and the role of the resource depends on the vision and aims of the partners in the various practices.

For instance, sole practitioners might employ a secretary who may take on marketing activities, such as arranging client hospitality events. This frees the fee earner from basic administrative tasks to carry out more client work. Larger practices might ask client service staff to take on marketing activities, some will use administrators and others will use dedicated marketing specialists.

Some surprisingly large professional networks have no central marketing department, or a very small one comprising inexperienced people. As a result, they are frequently unaware of modern service marketing techniques and make surprisingly simple errors. They also miss out on the input of high quality marketing insight into their firm's direction and, as a result, frequently have less than optimum impact on the market. There is rarely any progressive organisational learning or productivity improvement in marketing systems because new leaders tend to wipe out any former structures of the little valued marketing unit.

A number of the larger partnerships have people at partner level leading marketing in much the same role as the CMO in publicly-quoted companies. These are frequently partners of the firm, qualified in its prime discipline rather than marketing, who are undertaking a management role for personal development or political reasons. If the role is occupied by a marketing specialist, they have often come to it through a consultancy route within the firm. Few are recruited externally, as in other business sectors. Whatever their skill or background, however, the CMO is as likely to be concerned with improving the account handling skills of colleagues or the proposal management capability of business units or coping with negative press stories as the creation of a communications campaign or new service.

The voluntary sector and NGOs

Charities and their like have a variety of marketing roles. Most, though, put emphasis on their 'fundraising' specialists who, like salespeople in profit orientated businesses, generate the organisation's revenue. There are also likely to be a range of specialist marking communication people dealing with press and PR. The development and management of key messages through concerted campaigns is a key skill and a critical success factor. In many ways, campaigning organisations, like Amnesty and Greenpeace, are consummate marketers; even if they may not like to be called marketers themselves because of the implied profit motive or, from their perspective, dubious ethics.

The marketing supply industry

Much marketing occurs on behalf of clients within various specialist agencies. This is a hugely diverse range of businesses. It includes advertising, direct marketing and new product development agencies, as well as a variety of consultancies. They range from the huge conglomerates like WPP to single person businesses. Yet they frequently create revenue and profit for their clients. For instance, in his 1960s best seller, *Confessions of an Advertising Man*, David Ogilvy (Ogilvy, 1962) describes the campaign he created for Ellerton Jetté who owned Hathaway shirts. It was Hathaway's debut as a national American advertiser but, at the time, they could only spend $ 30 000 against their competitor's spend of $ 2 000 000. Ogilvy's use of clear copy and 'the magic ingredient' of an eye patch on a male model put Hathaway on the map after 116 years of relative obscurity. It launched the brand and also made Ogilvy internationally famous. Moreover, after eight years, the company was successfully sold at many millions of dollars profit. It is a classic example of the genius and creativity that the marketing supply industry can provide for their clients. Despite the fact that most of the writing and theory of marketing is developed from and for marketing specialists in large companies, much of the real added value comes from agencies.

The evolution of marketing in an organisation

Much of the academic study of marketing focuses on issues of theory, concept or practice. By and large it makes assumptions about the way the function works in a firm. It is assumed that there is a well developed organisation led by a marketing director or CMO, able to call on financial and human resources to undertake research, manage advertising or adjust product features in the light of rational, justified arguments. There is little talk of the need to convince organisations of the need for marketing, of competing for resources or of organisational politics.

The situation is rarely so clear cut. The marketing function is often underdeveloped. It has to argue for its role in the organisation and has to invest in processes, as well as running projects to generate revenue. Some companies do not understand their own need for certain marketing skills and restrict the contribution that the function makes, limiting it to, say, a minor promotional role. Professor Nigel Piercy's research (Piercy, 2001) showed that there was rarely consistency about what functions marketing leaders have responsibility for. Nor was there consistency in the shape of organisations. He observed four types of marketing departments:

- Integrated/full service: closest to the theoretical models and with a wide range of responsibilities and power in the organisation.
- Strategic/services: smaller units with less power and integration. Their influence is in the area of marketing support services or specific policies/strategies.
- Selling overhead: often large numbers and dispersed but primarily engaged in sales support activities.
- Limited staff role: small numbers with few responsibilities and engaged in specific staff support such as market research or media relations.

It appears that marketing departments evolve (from a limited staff role to fully integrated) as firms grow and marketing grows in importance within them. When a company is initially formed much of the marketing role is undertaken by the founders or specialist subcontractors (like PR agencies). Some time after that a marketing specialist will be hired to manage activities such as brochure production, new product launch and perhaps some advertising.

As the firm grows, marketing specialists are recruited into different places in the organisation, such as public relations and sales support. Later, this develops into the fully integrated marketing function, seen in many corporate firms. A large corporate entity might have several hundred marketing specialists running campaigns, integrated by both a hierarchical senior management team (culminating in a CMO) and by the use of common processes and technology.

IBM adopts service marketing

When Lou Gerstner arrived at IBM in 1993, marketing as such did not exist. As one of IBM's core strengths had long been its account management system; marketing had been limited mainly to sales support.

Making marketing happen

Gerstner, however, believed adamantly that a successful company had to have an orientation around customers and the marketplace; and consequently a strong marketing organisation. So he addressed this gap almost immediately by hiring Abby Kohnstamm, who had worked with him for years at American Express, as head of corporate marketing.

She, in turn, swiftly began to define what the marketing discipline should mean to IBM and brought in the required expertise in areas such as branding, database marketing, communications and the development of new channels.

One of the early 'wins' the team enjoyed, and which earned it a lot of credibility from some of the more sceptical employees, was the development of a new channel, the telephone, to reach the mid market. This moving of account management from a physical to a telephone relationship (using database marketing to align the right employees to the right accounts with the right levels of contacts) proved very successful. It grew to a multi-billion dollar business in a relatively short space of time and was backed by a memorable advertising campaign, 'Solutions for a small planet'.

Laying the foundation

It also helped lay the groundwork for the shift to services since mid market customers were demanding methods to integrate their products, rather than the products alone. They wanted these 'solutions' set into the context of their industries; and that helped the company begin to think in terms of marketing along industry rather than product lines. So, well before the purchase of PwC Consulting propelled IBM into a new competitive arena, it was already gaining experience in working out how to bundle products together into solutions aimed at the right market segments.

Speaking with one voice

IBM's marketing now reflects the journey the company has made into a portfolio which balances software, hardware and services; and where, crucially, their integration within a consulting and services perspective gives the company far more leverage than the individual elements would do on their own. As a result, the marketing structure, both within and across the main business streams, is complex. There are several hundred employees, covering all aspects of marketing from market intelligence, analysis, marketing communications and support.

In January 2006 the UK business, for example, moved together three departments under the leadership of the 'Strategic Brand Manager'. Reporting to the UK Marketing Director, this team oversees a range of marketing activities on behalf of all business units to ensure consistency and exploit synergies. That integrated marketing communications team is now responsible for advertising, sponsorship, the UK customer centres (known as The IBM Forum Centres), hospitality and web management: wherever, in fact, the brand touches the customer.

A special message

Even though the advertising is centralised, with almost all major campaigns originating in the USA, other countries where major campaigns are run are able to tailor them to suit their market. Also, as the advertisements are increasingly based on case studies, different markets can submit case studies for use in the advertisements to underline IBM's global reach.

These advertisements emphasised the company's strategic shift. For example, to emphasise the range and depth of its business expertise following its acquisition of PwC Consulting, it launched a campaign for the combined entity, Business Consulting Services (BCS), called 'the other IBM'. It was very successful, raising awareness in the UK market by a remarkable 11%.

A campaign launched at the end of March 2006 was built on this, bringing the services aspect back into the mainstream brand campaign. Centred around the strap line 'what makes you special?' its key message was that, in a sea of commoditisation and ordinariness, where today's product is tomorrow's commodity, companies have to do more to make their products and services unique. And what makes IBM so well-placed to transform clients' fortunes is that it is the 'innovator's innovator': it can help companies and organisations innovate and thus differentiate in front of *their* clients.

Building the brand values

By 2006 IBM had almost 330 000 employees around the world. Every day thousands of them worked at the site of client companies. So the challenge was to make sure they lived the company's brand values; values which had to be adjusted to reflect the new, innovation-based, service-oriented promises IBM was making.

The company took a democratic approach to determine the brand values and embed them internally. In 2004 chairman and chief executive, Sam Palmisano, set in place a 'values jam'. This involved inviting every single employee over a period of three days to enter an intranet site to answer a series of questions and give their views about the company values.

Following some very sophisticated data mining, a shared set of values emerged:

- Dedication to every client's success.
- Innovation that matters, for the company and for the world.
- Trust and personal responsibility in all relationships.

Living the values

These values contribute to company behaviour in a number of ways. For example, the appraisal system is now structured around them. Palmisano also came up with an imaginative way to show that the company not only talked about empowerment of employees, but did it. He set up a $ 100 million fund based on the premise that anyone could spend up to $ 5000 without prior approval to do something they considered essential, whether for a client or internally. The outcome has been to emphasise that having 'trust and personal responsibility in all relationships' works both ways.

Marketing services

Until recently, the majority of marketing theory, language and practice derived from either the experience of firms offering physical goods (particularly consumer products) or from economic theory. As a result, many marketing techniques are modelled on product examples, and most marketing teachers at leading institutes had their early career, in a product environment. It is in the past three decades that marketers have begun to move from traditional product disciplines to service environments in any significant numbers. So, coupled with the emergence of competitive service sectors in the developed economies, there has been a growing interest of marketers in this field. They are adapting marketing practice to a wider range of service businesses (whether in business-to-business or consumer, profit or non-profit, industries) and to an increasing number of activities within different service businesses.

Until the 1970s there were few well researched and objective analyses of either the role of marketing in service industries or service marketing practice. This was changed by two ground-breaking pieces of work. The first was a paper produced by G. Lynn Shostack, published in 1977 when she was a vice president of Citibank in New York and marketing director for the investment management group of America. It was a set of detailed recommendations based on the experience of a senior manager working in a service industry. Shostack clearly used the processes and procedures outlined in her article to design new services and had some success with them. She suggested a number of ideas which have formed the basis of much service marketing thinking ever since.

Her primary idea was that there are features of a service which make its creation and marketing different from the creation and marketing of products. In particular Shostack talked about the concept of 'intangibility'. She suggested that the intangibility of a service is a state which makes the offer fundamentally different from a product offer; 'it is not corporeal'. This has since become part of the fundamental philosophy of service marketing.

The next significant contribution appears to be a 1983 Symposium of the American Marketing Association which debated in detail the marketing of services. The full agenda covered the creation of new services, the management of innovation and the differences between the marketing of services and products. The meeting was clearly held as a result of growing interest in service marketing stimulated by the Shostack article and a concern that the marketing community was not addressing some of the key issues involved in the move to a service economy. The symposium stimulated various academics to contribute to this field. In particular, there appeared publications by Leonard Berry, Christian Gronroos, Donald Cowell, Roland Rust and Valerie Zeithaml. These people in turn sponsored many research projects into service phenomena and set up high quality institutes with industry.

It is not too much of an exaggeration to say that there are now three academic 'schools' following this field: the American school, the Scandinavian school and the French school. Each has a different emphasis but all co-operate in a wide body of research, much of which is conducted in tandem with people in actual service businesses in a variety of countries and economic sectors. There is, then, science behind the marketing of services. Business people wanting to adopt many of the approaches can generally rely on the applicability and relevance of much that is suggested.

How, then, does a change to a more service orientated offer affect the marketing activities and function of a firm? How should principles and practices developed from the marketing of products be adapted so that they raise revenue from service offers? Specialists in this area suggest that there are a number of ways in which the nature of services requires a change in marketing approach.

Differences between product and service marketing activities

1. The marketing implications of the intangibility of services

The lack of a physical component affects marketing in several ways, the first being pre-purchase assessment. Some people find it hard to accept or engage with a concept until it is reality, presented to them in physical form. Human beings seem to need physical clues to help them assess benefits and compare value propositions. They like to see, touch, smell and test it. In fact, the comparison of physical elements (in a new car for example) often clinches the sale. So firms that market pure services must create mechanisms to make the intangible appear tangible.

Many create sales promotion materials which represent the service. For example, a recent trend in the British retail market is the sale of 'experiences' as gifts. People can buy days at spas and on race tracks for others. These services are sold in attractive packages which can be displayed on promotion racks and easily taken, by the buyer, to tills. In business to business markets there have been similar packaging attempts. Over the past two decades, for instance, a number of the leading IT firms have offered their maintenance and project management services in attractive, packaged form. Even leading professional service providers, like lawyers or accountants, who generally detest the idea of their service being 'marketed', use 'collateral' in the form of brochures and case studies to convey the spirit and skill of their offer. Packaging and promotion are therefore one of the prime communication tactics used to market intangible services in many sectors.

More important, though, is the need to understand and emphasise the buyers' experiences of an intangible service. Just as people want to understand how a product might work in practice, they need to understand what their experience of a service might be; and this should be an important focus of service marketing. When starting a new service, for instance, many suppliers create ways to encourage potential buyers to take part in free trials or test runs. They are an essential part of the launch. Several leading hairdressers, such as Vidal Sassoon or Nicky Clark, started their business by encouraging celebrities and other opinion formers to use their services.

Once the buyer has experienced the service, they are in a good position to assess it for their own future needs but, just as importantly, for the needs of friends or relatives. So, trials overcome many of the difficulties caused by intangibility because they reduce the perceived risk of purchase. They are also a way of starting one of the most important service marketing tools: 'word of mouth'. If customers have a good experience they will talk about it to others and the reputation of the new service will begin to spread. (Although a bad experience will create negative stories that undermine any effort to grow the business.)

After launch, the most important marketing strategy is to amplify the natural reputation of the service created by accumulated service experiences. This can be captured in testimonials or printed case studies but it is most effective when gossip is amplified through a communications strategy called 'viral marketing'. This technique spreads positive recommendations of the service, and different messages, through informal customer networks, and can even create excitement, respect and demand for a service. It is a deliberate attempt to amplify word of mouth and is, at the time of writing, one of the newest areas of emphasis among marketers. Although successful leaders of service businesses have been intuitively nurturing word-of-mouth for many years, marketing specialists are, only now, beginning to properly understand and codify successful techniques to exploit it.

In a number of services, though, there are physical components which mitigate the effects of intangibility. It might be that the service itself exists to support a physical product (as in the case of a maintenance service) or has important physical components (like the seat, cabin and meal in an airline service). These can be used in the marketing of the service to help underline its benefits and overcome buyer's fears or hesitations. They are tangible manifestations of the intangible service which can be used in marketing campaigns. Airlines will therefore advertise the seat or the meal, as BA did with its new 'flat beds', and consultancies their people, as IBM has with its 'the other IBM' campaign.

In fact, despite academic assertions that intangibility fundamentally changes marketing, there is often little difference in practice between the marketing of product based services and the marketing of some products. Many products are a mix of physical, conceptual and service components. A washing machine, for example, is bought because of the physical components, the design, the brand and the service support package. (It is also bought through the service system of a retailer.)

Similarly a service might have a brand concept and a number of physical components. The white goods industry has, for example, learnt to offer extended warranty as part of product purchase, maintaining total return on the product line through service margins whilst actual product prices have fallen. Although the warranty service is intangible, it is presented as any other retail concept tied to a major product purchase.

In fact, the marketing industry already has great experience in communicating conceptual, intangible offers. Most brand managers in successful consumer goods companies, like Unilever or Procter & Gamble, would argue that they are in the business of making intangible offers; that a branded product is a concept offering valuable intangible benefits to buyers. A product such as Heinz baked beans is a combination of: haricot beans, sauce, packaging, easy distribution, image and consistency of familiar taste.

It is tangible in the sense that it contains physical components that customers can eat but enormous value is created for Heinz by careful management of the intangible, branded concept. Over years the company has invested time, money and skill in building the brand in the minds of a group of customers. As a result, there is a heritage and equity that causes customers to buy repeatedly at enhanced prices.

A wide range of brands (from clothing like Hugo Boss and Nike, through perfume like Chanel and diamonds like Harry Winston, to magazines like *The Economist* or *Vogue*) appeal to the aspirations and emotions of different groups of people. Customers associate their lifestyle with these offers and are seeking intangible, unarticulated benefits (like 'membership' or 'recognition') when they buy. The battle for profit is fought in customers' imagination and the offers are, therefore, in many ways, intangible.

So, in order to tackle intangibility, service marketing specialists should imitate many of the successful techniques of branded goods such as: positioning, packaging and progressive investment in fame. In fact, one of the prime differences between the marketing of intangible services and intangible product brands is probably the relative incompetence of many service industries in marketing processes or campaigns. They are simply not mature enough to have gone through the progressive organisational learning which puts such sophisticated and valuable offers in the market.

Intangibility also creates a role for marketing techniques after the purchase of a service. There is evidence that the intangibility of services exacerbates a phenomenon known as 'post purchase distress'. After a significant purchase, buyers can experience regret, guilt or worry and they seek mechanisms to reassure themselves that they were right to buy. They often discuss it with friends or re-examine sales literature. Some buyers of new cars, for example, return to the showroom to collect the brochure of the car they bought.

Yet, one of the greatest reassurances is the product itself. They wear the new coat, drive the new car or use the new kitchen. However, they cannot touch or examine an intangible service so their anxiety remains or, in some cases, increases. This can cause them to re-examine the deal and query value. As a result, they can cause difficulty in the time between a contract being signed and a service being delivered. Suppliers therefore need to develop techniques by which they mitigate post purchase distress. Many put emphasise on good after-care and others produce examples of previous contented buyers which are given to new buyers soon after purchase. Both provide valuable reassurance.

2. The marketing implications of the variability (or heterogeneity) of services

Manufactured products can be produced consistently, with little variation. If any aberrations in product quality get through to the buyers, customers can be understanding and tolerant of quality difficulties, subsuming irritations or complaints to get the benefit of the product. They might, for example, tolerate a shoddy retail service to get the product they have set their heart on.

Business buyers, too, will tolerate some aberrations in the behaviour of account managers, billing errors or project delays, if they have been through a tender process to identify a suitable product. The promise and reliability of established product features can outweigh minor problems. Yet, as discussed in Chapter 3 (page 75), services are rarely as homogeneous as manufactured products. In fact, it is unusual for one service experience to be identical to another. There are various marketing methods to tackle this which vary according to the nature of the service.

Firstly, service marketers seek to set their customers' expectations and their prime method is their brand. The expectations generated by consumer brands like Visa, HSBC or Harrods and business brands like EDS or Economist conferences, set different expectations. The brand positioning, for example, attracts different buyers (see Chapter 9, pages 323–325). A cut price airline will not be expected to provide high quality food or good landing access to the heart of key cities, whereas the service in leading stores like London's Harrods or New York's Bloomingdales must be as excellent as the products they offer. The brand sets expectations of a standard of quality.

Even the leading professional service firms use their brand (or as they might prefer: their reputation) to set expectations. The perception of brands like McKinsey, Deloitte, Clifford Chance and Russell Reynolds Associates attract both premium clients and high quality recruits capable of reflecting the brand's characteristics. As a result, in all firms of this nature, margins are high and the earnings of lead partners eye watering.

One particularly powerful brand strategy, which sets expectations to suit service variability, is to introduce an element of humanity or responsiveness which acknowledges that errors might occur. The Virgin empire, for example, grew through a commitment to contemporary service, which was prepared to be avant garde, while acknowledging that human errors might occur which can be remedied. Their humour and humanity, embodied by their brand icon Richard Branson, ensures that buyers are unsurprised by minor quality errors but expect them to be remedied well. Buyers are told that the supplier does all it can to eliminate errors but they should expect immediate response if any occur.

Branded volume services use advertising and signage in their premises to signal their intent to provide as consistent and as reliable a service as possible; but also to redress any errors. In many cases, these businesses show examples of the processes or systems they use to produce the service in order to set expectations of consistency. Technical documents, like a railway timetable or fast food menu, also set expectations of delivery which can satisfy or disappoint buyers. As important, though, is the appearance of the service and any physical elements in it. The design and cleanliness of premises and the uniform of employees, for instance, must be carefully managed.

A run down, scruffy service, such as the government-run British railways at the end of the twentieth century, creates an entirely different expectation of service to the clockwork neatness of the Japanese 'bullet' train. A volume service which is clean, reliable and well packaged will be more easily forgiven for unusual and minor inconsistencies. Nevertheless, many high volume consumer services emphasise in their advertising that, if errors occur, buyers should complain, so they can be quickly put right.

The prime mechanism by which professional services, at the other extreme, try to achieve consistency is through the recruitment and training of people who will deliver a certain quality and style of service. The technical delivery of the service might be highly individual and customised to a client's unique situation, but the style of service and manner of delivery must be consistent. Young professionals are schooled in both the technical skills of the firm and its approach to business. Many practices have rigorous control procedures and detailed ethical guidelines which attempt to deliver consistent standards. Yet the heart of their business is the recruitment, development and motivation of high quality 'human capital' which, without close supervision, will deliver the style of service which reflects the firm's position in the market. As a result, all of the leading firms in this industry invest in sophisticated and consistent recruitment marketing, particularly aimed at graduates in leading universities.

Other, less important attempts to handle variability include the nature of the contract and, sometimes, guarantees about quality standards, offering financial compensation if errors occur. One of the world's leading business gurus, David Maister, for example, offers a clear money back guarantee to clients. Excellent, responsive post-purchase customer care is also seen as essential to the effective marketing of variable services and, again, forces service marketers to focus on quality of service, service experience and service recovery.

3. The marketing implications of the 'simultaneous consumption' of services

As a result of simultaneous consumption, service marketing specialists have to focus on accurate demand forecasting so that resources are available when needed by buyers. They frequently use statistical modelling techniques to predict likely demand based on previous purchase patterns. Some, though, work with key buyers to share the risk of demand fluctuations. They then try to influence demand by different pricing patterns. The airline industry uses different ticket types, for example, to get commitment to purchase weeks in advance. In many cases they over-book flights, using incentives to get some passengers to change their flight if necessary.

Many seek to communicate the extent of their stored infrastructure as an asset at their customers' disposal. Others use their assets to underscore pricing and value messages. Some use downtime to create other value for their customers. For example, the audit work of the large accountancy firms tends to be seasonal. They ensure they have enough capacity to handle peak periods and, in the quiet spells, lend good staff to clients, improving the depth of client relationships, or using them to create 'thought leadership' pieces which might generate new work. Maintenance services, on the other hand, will fill troughs in demand with routine or preventative maintenance.

Again, as simultaneous consumption concentrates the executives of service companies on ensuring a quality experience, it reinforces the need for service marketers to understand and exploit quality of service issues in their work. Any marketing messages will be undermined if the actual experience is poor or the firm is slow to remedy service errors.

4. The marketing implications of the inseparability of services from the people who provide them

It is not surprising that, with the rise of the service economy, marketers have created 'internal marketing' functions. Used in some of the leading service businesses with increasing sophistication, these aim to communicate with the internal audience as professionally as the firm communicates with its external audiences. They set up internal communication media which can range from simple management briefings to sophisticated TV channels or intranet broadcasts. Many create internal communication campaigns linked to external campaigns. This involves all the usual best practices of leading marketing communication functions including: a communications strategy, the creation of messages, the segmentation of audiences and the management of responses from them; all with an emphasis on the company's own employees.

Yet, an increasing number of services are based on self-service technology, with no people involved in day to day delivery. From web services to banking and airline check in, the range of self administered services is steadily growing. For these, the personality of the company brand is used to replace the people who normally deliver service. Service marketers invest heavily in branding this type of service at all points of visibility. The emotional reassurance of a major, high quality brand, like HSBC, implies a reliable response should self-service technology fail. Clearly, with this rapidly increasing range of services the 'people' element of the service marketing mix is less prevalent.

However, there is evidence that self service technology only penetrates a market if the first buyers are shown to use it by personable people or their proxy. They need help with the initial socialisation process and to overcome any technology fear. At the time of writing, for instance, airlines are introducing self service check in technology that is very simple to use. They generally place the machines near to the 'hand luggage only' queue. Staff are trained to approach people in the queue, often frequent flyers, and show them how to use the fast, easy machines. Although many refuse the original offer they are happy to use it after the demonstration overcomes any technology fear or potential embarrassment. ATMs were first introduced to banking, in the 1970s and 80s, in a similar way. Once a sufficient number of people have leant the process, they communicate it to others and the technology penetrates the market.

5. The marketing implications of the perishability of services

Services which are perishable must be marketed in the same way as fresh food or flowers. Quality difficulties must be dealt with through an immediate, responsive recovery process and inventory must be carefully managed through forecasting and capacity management. Marketers have to cope with variations in demand and develop techniques to sell spare capacity such as those hotels use for off-season or weekend capacity. Emphasis should also be put on easy and efficient distribution and the benefit of a new, premium services.

However, the real implication of this feature is that the supplier must become expert in differential pricing. They need clear communication methods to potential buyers which demonstrate why a buyer of the immediate, 'fresh', service needs to pay a different rate to those accessing it at a later time. They need to produce special price offers, reductions to use up spare capacity and understand marginal pricing. Moreover, they need to communicate the rationale and, particularly, the fairness of these pricing practices to their customers. This is particularly important for companies with repeat customers who become increasingly sophisticated, holding off purchase to get better offers.

6. The marketing implications of the fact that ownership of a service does not pass to the buyer

This lack of clear ownership means that service sales are similar to product rentals or leases and can cause buyers to question the price they pay. Service marketing must, therefore, find ways to emphasise value and justify price. Many service firms find this hard to manage. Across a variety of industries (from computer services and telecommunications to accountancy and training) numerous valuable services have been turned into commodities because the supply industry has been incompetent at communicating value.

7. The marketing implications of the existence of the service process

Potential customers must know how to access the supplier's service system, which has to be signposted and designed to encourage use. The firm needs to use clear signage and communicate its meaning to all potential buyers. Educating them to access and use the supplier's process is, therefore, a critical component of service marketing. This ranges from the prominent visibility of McDonald's golden arches to the use of customised web sites for client intranets in business-to-business services.

Once 'in the premises', though, the buyer needs direction (even if they are virtual). If it is not immediately apparent how to use the system (the equivalent of standing helplessly in a foreign shop) the buyer becomes embarrassed and gives up. So, clear signage into the delivery process and a step-by-step guide through it are also important. On landing at Heathrow, for example, many BA flights show a video guide through the airport. This ensures that stress levels stay low and any difficulties are seen as aberrations which can be corrected by excellent service recovery.

Finally, marketing communication must concentrate on the 'outcomes' of the process rather than the benefits emphasised by product marketers.

8. The marketing implications of the phenomenon of control

As discussed earlier, new customers, using a service for the first time, become anxious and look for reassurance. In addition to a simple process, the choice of individuals performing the service alleviates this anxiety. The character, reputation and professionalism of the individuals involved can inspire confidence in the quality of the service to be received.

The corporate brand also allays stress. One example is 'Marks and Spencer's promise of no hassle service recovery. Customers know that, if there is a problem with a purchased item, they can return it without any question or difficulty. This phenomenon has given Marks and Spencer a significant competitive advantage for a number of years.

The marketing to new, inexperienced, buyers of services therefore includes:

- emphasis of the brand;
- internal communication which helps with the management of the behaviour of people;
- communication of the steps in the process.

Once the client has experienced the service process a few times the situation alters altogether. Their emotional dislike of being out of control asserts a need for change and they become frustrated with the very process that they originally found so simple and attractive. Experienced customers try to take short cuts and try to improve on the service supplier's process. They develop a desire to take back control by undertaking self-service; often without knowing why they are frustrated. If the service supplier does not anticipate this, the customer will become frustrated and will have unnecessarily bad perceptions of the quality of service.

So service marketers must ensure that mechanisms are designed whereby, as the customer becomes familiar with the service process, he or she can do more themselves or cut out steps. The design of self-service into the service system will reduce costs because some of the effort of performing the service now comes from the customer. However, it will also improve quality because the service performance is within the control of the customer and, thus closer to perceptions of timely delivery. It is therefore possible to provide better service at less cost.

Good marketing to experienced service users is therefore a combination of:

- aids to self-service;
- creating a sense of special treatment, perhaps by being part of an elite club;
- streamlined processes, with clear instructions on how to use them, how to progressively be more self reliant and easy access to help in instances of difficulty;
- use of technology as part of the service, with facilities for progressive instruction in use.

9. The importance of the service environment

The existence of a service environment must be taken into account and exploited by service marketers. After initial design and launch, the 'servicescape', the environment visible to customers, must be kept fresh and inviting. It must continue to reflect the ambitions of the service provider. Service marketers must design sales promotion campaigns and point of sale materials to stimulate sales, to increase the margin of purchases and to maintain excitement in the service. They must routinely audit the facility, ensuring that it maintains its enticing nature to customers.

10. The service performance

Marketing campaigns can be used to keep the atmosphere, motivation and experience of the service encounter fresh and exhilarating. For example, internal marketing campaigns are frequently designed in businesses with large, diversified workforces to create internal competition to achieve really good service. In professional service firms, by contrast, leaders frequently initiate new concepts, strategies or ideas to stimulate the interest of restless brains, and these often involve marketing skills.

Avaya markets the value of maintenance

Avaya Inc. designs, builds and manages communications networks for more than one million businesses worldwide. The company is a global leader in secure and reliable Internet Protocol (IP) telephony systems and communications software applications and services. Avaya goes to market through a direct sales force and indirect sales channels (a global network of distributors, dealers, value-added resellers and system integrators). The company employs more than 15 000 people worldwide and generated revenue of $4.902 billion in fiscal year 2005.

Avaya Global Services accounts for just under half Avaya's revenue. Its 8500 service professionals provide a wide array of maintenance, implementation and integration, and managed services. Global Services also has responsibility for the company's network operations centres, technical support centres and patented design and management tools. The unit focuses on six major areas: Business Communications Consulting, Applications Consulting and Integration, IP Migration, Security and Business Continuity, Product Support and Managed Services. Avaya has approximately 500 000 service maintenance contracts worldwide.

Uncover and define root causes

In 2002, Avaya management confronted a frightening financial reality: maintenance revenue was falling, threatening revenue, growth and profitability. The long-term projections put millions of dollars at stake, so there was a challenge to turn this around and identify opportunities for future success.

Executive attention focused on the need to 'reinvent the maintenance base'. However, it was initially unclear why the renewal business was eroding. Anecdotal explanations for the dramatic market change were considered. For example, the company was aware of the growing competitive inroads from independent service providers, systems resellers, and large corporate self-maintainers. But the rapid rate of decline could not be attributed solely to these forces.

Additionally, Avaya believed that a general economic downturn was affecting the renewal rate. Systems sales had begun to lag in mid 2001 in response to depressed world wide economic conditions. However, decline in maintenance contract renewal was abnormally high, particularly considering that a record number of systems were installed or upgraded in response to Y2K concerns. These installations should have been priming the renewal pipeline, but were not.

Management also recognised that its sales teams were under strong pressure to meet product quotas put in place in response to sales declines. As a result, it was possible that sales teams were spending less time on selling services renewals.

Root cause analysis

Avaya's global services marketing team was hesitant to pursue dramatic changes to either its service offerings or pricing strategies without a clear picture of the origins of the decline in contract renewal. To gain insight into the problem, they initiated extensive qualitative and quantitative market research studies with both business partners and customers. The research identified three primary issues:

- **The decision-makers had changed.** The decision-making of their customers was no longer in their customers' communications or IT department. A difficult economic climate and constrained budgets meant increased scrutiny and economic justification of all IT and communication expenditures. At the same time, analysis and decision authority had moved to higher-level decision-makers who were often unfamiliar with the operational value of maintenance services. These new decision-makers were focused on financial results such as total cost of ownership and return on investment (ROI). But because they were not the direct 'consumers' of Avaya's maintenance services, they were not aware of the types of services being provided or their value to the business.

- **Remote diagnostic technology and tools reduced on-site services visibility.** Avaya's reliance on remote diagnostics improved response times and customer 'uptime', so that system performance was outstanding. However, service technicians rarely needed to show up at the customer site. In fact, Avaya discovered that, on average, 96% of system problems were being solved remotely. This led to a misperception amongst customers of the actual need for ongoing support via an annual maintenance contract, opting instead for 'per incident' time and materials service.
- **The sales organisation struggled to communicate the value of services.** Avaya's sales channels were not prepared to respond to the changes in customer decision-making and customers' new financial concerns. Furthermore, it became evident that the salesforce lacked the training necessary to relay the financial and operational value of Avaya's contractual maintenance services.

Teamwork moves the company forward

With the main problems in the maintenance renewal business defined, Adelaide O'Brien, Director of Avaya Global Services Marketing, was asked to head a cross-functional team to turn the business around. With the support of Avaya's most senior management, O'Brien pulled together a team of experts from throughout the company, including: Avaya Labs, Technical Support Organisation, National Service Managers, Services Sales Operations, Channel Development and Services Finance.

The group was assembled to accomplish four goals:

1. Clearly define the business value associated with Avaya's maintenance service, with a focus on defining the value of the remote monitoring, diagnostic and repair capabilities.
2. Test the value proposition that was developed with customers, to ensure that it addressed the market's needs.
3. Craft and execute a plan for communicating the value of Avaya's maintenance services to customers and prospects.
4. Equip all sales channels with the knowledge and tools required to explain and sell the value of Avaya's maintenance services.

These priorities would be the key components of a new global marketing campaign called 'While You Were Sleeping'. This campaign was created as a means to communicate and deliver the full range of benefits of Avaya's maintenance capabilities (with particular emphasis on their EXPERT View remote features) to internal audiences and customers worldwide.

Defining the value: a lucky break

The team's top priority was to define the operational and business value of Avaya services. However, how exactly to quantify this value was unclear until the team discovered that Avaya's National Service Managers were already examining service records to review and summarise activities with the largest accounts. These customised reports became an important starting point for analysing the activities of Avaya's services accounts. Although the team was to face numerous obstacles, it was a highly productive beginning.

The first step was to sift through mountains of previously captured data and analyse problems as they were encountered. Ultimately, the team analysed data from more than 450 000 trouble tickets on 68 000 systems over a five-month period for its initial reporting tool. These reports were highly detailed and designed, primarily, for operational reviews by a technical audience. By uncovering patterns within the data, the marketing team was able to summarise and conceptualise the data for reports that could be used by higher-level decision-makers to generate information that was meaningful and analytical. The team also analysed data made available from the development of 'exception processes', that fell outside the norm and required additional expert analysis. IT and business transformation members then worked to capture process enhancements to automate a large portion of this analytical process.

Testing the value: early customer involvement

The process of collecting data for the tool and testing it with customers took nearly nine months. Eventually, the Avaya team designed a process to capture, analyse and convey service activity, including proactive Avaya actions, for individual customers. However, they learned that customer involvement and input was critical to the development of a meaningful tool. According to O'Brien, 'We did not involve customers until the end of the development process for the first tool, just prior to its launch. That was a mistake.'

After this initial misstep, Avaya began to incorporate detailed customer feedback into each step of the development process 'before programmers started any work'. A volunteer customer panel was emailed all the reports and presentations and feedback was gathered via a 15-minute survey. This testing was also done with Avaya's business partners who would be offering the tool to their customers. Further customer testing was conducted at the company's annual user group meeting in 2002. A mock-up of the tool was presented to attendees who provided critical feedback on the reports.

Communicating the value

The centrepiece of the campaign

After incorporating this feedback, Avaya was ready to introduce this data to a larger customer audience in the format of the new Avaya EXPERT View reports. These reports gave each customer personalised data on remote problem resolution, the value of improved system availability and uptime to their business. Avaya mined existing trouble reporting systems to generate the data for the reports and reformulated this into meaningful summaries of maintenance activities relevant to both their customers' senior executives and to people in Avaya sales channels.

Critical to the success of the initiative was expanding the communications about its capabilities to the larger market. The marketing team developed and executed a comprehensive marketing communications plan; the first phase of which focused on general market awareness of its service capabilities. The campaign included advertising, new web pages, case studies, trade shows and direct mail. A customer awareness programme was launched that included 'webinars', online forums, customer events, road shows, user groups and CIO advisory panels. Overall, these programmes were very successful.

Equipping the sales channels

A parallel effort was underway to work with the sales channels to prepare them to use the new reports and to help them communicate the value of Avaya services. Early on, the sales leadership recognised the importance of the new tool and committed their teams to 'mandatory' training. Sales management also required its teams to test the tools and reports with customers. Once armed, the services sales teams covered nearly 80 % of their accounts within three months.

The results were impressive. The vast majority (89 %) of customers surveyed found the initial reports 'valuable to extremely valuable' in understanding the value of their maintenance agreement. At the same time, 90 % of salespeople rated the report 'useful to extremely useful' in communicating the value of Avaya's services.

The reports became the centrepiece of the 'While You Were Sleeping' campaign. They were an innovative means for the sales channels to illustrate the value of Avaya's maintenance services and became integral to the services sales process. Avaya then delivered live presentations to its largest customers involving both a sales and a service representative who had strong knowledge of the account. This ensured that questions could be answered and any data anomalies could be explained. These positive results confirmed that the 'While You Were Sleeping' campaign was off to a very positive start.

Incorporating empirical data: customers define Avaya's next steps

Customer feedback led to two substantial improvements in the EXPERT View reports:

- Empirical financial data to support the value of Avaya's proactive service capabilities compared with 'time and materials' services, third-party service or self service.
- 'Monetisation tools' to reveal the return for the maintenance agreements.

Results

Avaya's efforts to analyse and address carefully and thoroughly a very serious revenue situation quickly delivered the results the company was looking for. Its maintenance contract renewal rates stabilised during the 3rd and 4th quarters of 2003. By Q1 2004, the company achieved growth in renewal rates and services revenue. There was a significant boost to customer satisfaction with Avaya's maintenance service and its reporting; nearly 90% of customers expressed increased satisfaction with the information received in the EXPERT View reports. The sales organisation also successfully incorporated the tools and knowledge into their sales processes, improving sales effectiveness in closing maintenance renewals, as well as positioning maintenance as part of initial systems sales.

Additionally, the success of the EXPERT View reports has led the company to expand the concept to its small and medium size business customers. Avaya developed 'EXPERT View Lite' as an online tool to be used by Avaya's call centres and telesales groups working with these customers. Telesales groups have been using this reporting tool to increase renewal rates among small and medium size customers.

This case study is published with the permission of ITSMA.

Specific marketing techniques emphasised in service businesses

A wide range of marketing techniques are used by service businesses in different industries throughout the world. They have been successful with mass advertising (McDonald's, BT, Accenture and IBM global services), branding (Amazon and HSBC), price management (Wal-Mart and Tesco) and publicity (Virgin and Body Shop). However, there do seem to be a range of techniques which are unique to, or more heavily emphasised by, service businesses. Manufacturers should assess them and consider using them if they are to move into service businesses. They are:

(i) Reputation enhancement

As service firms depend on the quality of their customers' experience to succeed, their reputation is especially important to them and an important focus of their marketing. This is particularly emphasised by professional service firms because their growth in revenues relies on the creation of 'demand pull' based on a reputation for excellent work. Any marketing approach in these businesses should begin with mechanisms to enhance the natural reputation caused by customers talking about their experiences. This will increase both repeat business and referrals.

The first step, as shown in Figure 2.2 (on page 52), is to undertake objective research into the quality of the firm's competitive reputation. The issue here, though, is the competitive reputation in the minds of customers when they buy. How does the firm rate in their buying criteria? Every professional takes pride in the quality of their work and none sets out to do a bad job. However, customers may use different criteria to assess a firm's performance, based on more than technical expertise. So, any marketer beginning marketing communications for a service firm ought to start with an audit of competitive reputation. Having understood that, the second step is to put in place mechanisms to amplify that natural reputation. The sort of mechanisms likely to do this are PR-based initiatives that make visible the expertise and accomplishments of both the firm and individuals.

(ii) Thought leadership

Thought leadership is a term used commonly within the service industries for the publication and dissemination of ideas for commercial advantage. In practice, it can range from an article in a magazine to a major, sponsored programme or a complete book. The technique has been used very effectively by technology firms, accountants and consultants for many years.

It is one of the most successful marketing strategies that the world has seen and encompasses a vast, influential and diverse range of activities. At its best, thought leadership programmes produce systematic, iconic work like the McKinsey Quarterly. The worst, though, has been mocked by *The Economist* as 'Thought Followship' because it is frequently just the erratic, whimsical jottings of specialists from different disciplines trying to 'market' themselves between projects; some of it is not leadership and some of it isn't even clear thought. Yet the power of this approach to amplify an excellent reputation and draw in buyers is undeniable.

It works because ideas which resonate have powerful influence on business leaders. In certain circumstances, it generates the business equivalent of 'urban myths'. For instance, most management audiences will recognise the following ideas developed by charismatic individuals:

- '*50% of my advertising budget is wasted, I don't know which 50%*'; attributed to Lord Lever but made famous by David Ogilvy, in his 1962 book, *Confessions of an Advertising Man*,which sold a million copies.
- '*it costs more to recruit a new customer than retain an existing one*'; came from Frederick Reichheld's book *The Loyalty Effect* much of which he has now reconsidered.
- '*the average dissatisfied customer tells 13 other people if they experience bad service*'; made famous by ex-McKinsey partner, Tom Peters in presentations about his book *In Search of Excellence*. He was quoting 1980s research into American supermarket shoppers, unlikely to be relevant to modern businesses.

Leading companies tend to create dedicated groups of specialists to handle their thought leadership activities. Often comprising academics or specialists in different fields, these teams can be large and international with considerable resources at their disposal. They can be headed by ex-professors or business editors recruited for their skill in handling concepts. Their job is to '*look across the work in the firm and create new concepts that will help clients create value in their business*'. In other words, they fashion ideas to sell to customers.

Yet really effective thought leadership is not only the province of massive businesses. Interbrand, for example, is a relatively small brand consultancy, founded in 1974. It secured its place as an authority in its field with an annual survey of the world's 100 most valuable global brands, a survey it has been carrying out since 1997. For the first two years it was conducted with the *Financial Times* but, in 1999, it formed an association with *Business Week* to get wider exposure. In the survey, Interbrand uses its brand valuation process to determine, as closely as possible, the true economic value of what it describes as the 'complex array of forces' that make up a brand. Now, when people think about brands, they will often think about the company's league table. For instance, in 2003, Interbrand's 'Top 100 brands' came third in a USA survey of tables which chief executive officers value.

Thought leadership can be enormously expensive in terms of both cash and time costs. It is sensible, therefore, to create a discipline to manage this type of investment across the firm. This might include:

- Proper cost management. Cash costs include: research, printing, promotion and publication. Time costs include the opportunity cost of staff taken away from chargeable work and the salaries of dedicated staff.
- Criteria for approval. These might involve: payback, commercial opportunity, quality, reputation enhancement.
- Anticipated revenue or leads stimulated.
- A timetable of all projects.
- Management: a leadership team should be responsible for the firm's thought leadership programme. It should manage, using peer review, proposals for thought leadership investment.

So, Thought Leadership is a proven tool to grow the revenues of service businesses ranging from single individuals up to massive international networks. There is substance behind this technique which warrants investigation if a business is seriously moving into service work.

(iii) Events and hospitality

The service industries (particularly business services) invest heavily in hospitality for customers and sponsorship. This ranges from large customised events, through packages bought at large public occasions (such as the Ryder Cup or Wimbledon) to individual meals with clients. The philosophy behind it is that the informal situation will help to create a relationship with customers which will encourage further work. A well-managed and targeted event can contribute to closer relations, especially if part of a wider communications programme.

Sponsorship also plays a useful part in building the awareness of a brand. It might comprise a range of activities from 'brand awareness advertising', through product placement in feature films to high profile event sponsorship; a cost effective means of helping an intended group of people become familiar with a brand. It makes sense because it is based on a clear business case and has defined objectives. The sponsorship has context. It works best, though, when the firm is prepared to invest properly in a well articulated, long term brand strategy.

Another valid use of sponsorship is in areas where there are restrictions on other forms of marketing. Cigarette companies, for instance, now have very few opportunities to promote their wares, so they use sponsorship extensively. Some professions are similarly restricted due to the nature of their work. Few clients want to let it be known that they have been helped by an insolvency practitioner or that a forensic accountant has uncovered a fraud. Marketing in these cases needs to be subtle, restrained and appealing. Sponsorship is a useful tool for these practices if targeted properly.

Sponsorship specialists and proponents of hospitality events argue that the relative cost of getting a name seen at, say, a sporting event is much less than advertising on a cost per view basis. This is obviously relevant to large consumer services whose customers are likely to attend sports events. Yet most of the people that attend football or rugby matches have no idea what some business suppliers stand for and don't need to because they are not in the target market. Those that do know what these firms are about are more likely to wonder why they pay high fees if their suppliers can be so lavish. Moreover, the comparison with advertising is fallacious. When advertising is properly planned, it conveys an engaging message which no board at a stadium can get near to matching and, with modern narrow casting techniques, can be very closely targeted.

Hospitality events and sponsorship need to be well-planned, with the objectives, suitability and target audience carefully thought through. If not, it can be ineffective and based on no clear marketing principle. The sponsorship of public conferences, with the attendant presentation spot, for instance, gives very little return. The box at the concert hall actually allows little time to talk with guests and is probably used mostly by employees. Even more dubious is the sponsorship of annual award ceremonies which most people have difficulty remembering later.

A more significant problem with sponsorship is the attendees at any related event. Real decision-makers are normally very busy and focused on their work with little time to spare for optional, pleasant events. Sensible senior people allow themselves just one or two a year. Other than that, they normally prefer to spend their scarce free time with their family and friends. As a result attendees can be 'stand ins', perhaps using a reward from their boss, or persistent hospitality takers with no real authority.

Nevertheless, for a wide range of service industries, this is their largest and most visible marketing tool. The sums spent by banks, accountants, lawyers and consultants are large and routinely renewed.

(iv) Marketing to and through employee networks

One of the main communication channels to customers is the employees of the firm. Service marketers should therefore take into account the views of employees when preparing any external communications. At the very least, people should be told about any campaign before it is released to the public. However, effectiveness is dramatically improved if employees are drawn into the campaign and enthused to talk to customers about it.

There are several components to first class internal communication. For instance, there should be a specific internal communications strategy. What is it communicating, to whom, and why? What are the objectives of the leadership in communicating with its own people? What are the core messages and what are the outputs and behavioural changes that they want to achieve through the investment in communication? And, most important of all, what other internal briefings will be stopped or held back; what will the leadership say 'no' to?

Probably the most neglected area of internal communication is message planning and management. This involves crafting the message to employees and prioritising it against the many other routine business communications. As with external communication, messages need to be sustained, simple and relevant. Just as important (since putting out multiple messages can give rise to conflicting communication) is to make sure that they do not conflict with other internal messages.

Yet, with internal communications, one of the prime considerations of any message is credibility. Employees must be able to give some credence to the thrust of senior management claims. The ideas and actions of leaders need to be properly aligned so that, either overtly or subtly, they don't undermine the professed direction of the firm. If they do that, there is a danger of lowering morale which, in turn, can have a detrimental effect on service to buyers. As with external messaging, it takes time for internal audiences to accept and internalise messages. Core messages about the firm's values and priorities should be unchanging or, at least, slow to evolve.

It is also important to manage the media through which employees receive the message. The best media is their line management and the second best is gossip. Both need to be valued and influenced by communications planners. Employees rely on their internal network to receive information so their leaders and their immediate group of contacts with whom they work daily are much more relevant to them than other messages. Gossip, the informal exchange of messages through those networks, becomes more effective than the deluge of emails, magazines and other publications. This is an internal form of 'viral marketing', where 'word of mouth' is used to influence the behaviour and motivation of the people. It makes sense to dedicate a member of the internal communications team to understanding viral marketing techniques. They need to be familiar with the different internal networks, how those networks communicate, what the gossip is and how to influence it. (Other typical internal media include: 'town hall' meetings, internal email, the web and staff magazines.)

Some service firms go so far as to design their external advertising with an eye to motivating their own people. This was a consideration, for example, in Accenture's choice of advertising in airline departure halls. Many of their staff fly regularly and gain encouragement from being part of a large firm, able to communicate on this scale.

Internal marketing is improved by the use of communications campaigns. A campaign is a group of activities co-ordinated together through the available media over a period of time in order to reinforce one message with a target audience. The communications manager needs to have a clear idea of who the target audience is, what the communication objectives are and the available budget. They need to refine and agree the message and concentrate on the media to be used over whatever period of time. A firm adopting a campaign approach to internal marketing will ensure that all its campaigns are known to the communications manager and there is no conflict when received by the internal audiences.

Experienced service firms develop response mechanisms from their employees to understand their reaction to internal communications. These need to be open and reliable methods through which the response to messages can be measured. Many carry out internal staff surveys to get objective measures of their reaction to messages and direction. These frequently have to be anonymous, in order to encourage honest feedback.

The aim is to do more than merely inform employees. Service leaders are out to motivate their people. In addition to giving them messages about company direction, they aim to excite them about working for their customers in a particular way and delivering an appropriate style of service. Some even try to discover the behaviours that different customer groups like and then elicit those behaviours in the employees who serve them. Many are struggling with issues such as how to continue to motivate people to perform good service over a long period of time and what to do after the first few years of 'smile training' programmes. Others are experimenting with programmes to improve the behaviours of people who are part of their service but not directly employed by them (such as dealers, subcontractors or self employed people). Some have demonstrated that it is even possible to maintain good motivation in a climate of recession, decreasing job numbers and declining job skills as the effect of new market forces and new technology undermines old job patterns.

Good service leaders understand that the correct management of people in line with changing customer needs is a critical success factor of service firms. The skills to understand, communicate with and motivate them are part of service marketing.

Once assured of their own people, though, many service companies then use them in their marketing campaigns. In industries as different as consumer banking, airlines, car hire, fast food, IT consulting and merchant banking, employees have been used as the human face of the service. Some use actors whereas others use their actual employees, often in uniform. The aim is to convey the essence of the service by showing the people that buyers will encounter.

(v) Collateral

Collateral is a term which covers the manifestation of marketing messages in brochures, case studies and other physical handouts. It also includes 'virtual collateral' such as web sites. These need to be carefully designed and crafted to communicate benefits clearly. It is normal to create a 'collateral strategy' for the whole firm covering: intended use, design structure, renewal and reprinting methods, plus the types favoured for particular clients.

In retail services (like opticians, dentists or hairdressers), collateral is generally 'point of sale' which, properly devised and presented, helps customers to choose and reassure themselves about the purchase. It is frequently provided by manufacturers, but in large chains is self-generated. It needs to reflect the brand of the firm and the objectives of the campaign. It should also be easy to assemble, durable and have high impact. The chain needs to control the number of point-of-sale (POS) campaigns and their effect on shop space, to ensure there are no adverse consequences.

Collateral is also important in the business-to-business context, particularly for those buying for the first time. It may be that a client is in emotionally distressing circumstances, such as a significant medical or an important business problem, or it may be that the service seems expensive. Collateral plays an important role in these circumstances.

For example, if the firm is presenting its credentials to a business customer during a 'beauty parade', those involved should leave behind a bound copy of the presentation in a format acceptable to the client, so that they can leaf through it and consider it after the meeting. Also, at the point where the client is about to make a decision but hasn't yet signed a contract, it makes sense to send a case study of a company which has purchased a similar service from the firm, so the client has something physical to refer to. Finally, after signing the contract, it is sensible to leave behind a directory of the key people involved in the project, their experience and contact numbers in a format the client can use internally to show others. At the very least send a thank you note to the client for their business.

Collateral is not just printed material. The internet, for example, can be used as very effective collateral. Currently, the most common online behaviour is for people to research products, services and suppliers before purchase, so the web site can act as the 'Welcome' mat of the firm. Also, when buyers meet a service provider for the first time, it is very likely that they will look them up on the internet, when back at the office. So some put an individual micro-site on their employees' business cards which contain the biographies, articles and examples of expertise.

All of these communications, from the written material through to the web micro site on the business card, are techniques to make the intangible tangible and to manage the emotional discomfort of potential customers.

(vi) Viral marketing

As discussed earlier, 'word of mouth' plays an important role in building service revenue. Marketing managers and agencies alike are currently exploring the potential of word of mouth marketing to grow a wide range of offers in different industries. Customers can, for instance, be offered incentives to recommend the service to others. This testimonial from respected colleagues, friends or family overcomes some of the hesitation caused by intangibility among potential buyers.

Techniques to enhance word of mouth have been particularly used in internet marketing and have come to be called 'viral marketing' (viral because the aim is to spread an idea among a target community in much the same way as a virus spreads in a body). Internet users have demonstrated the propensity of human beings to chat and gossip. They copy emails and jokes to each other. For example, there have been several famous instances of sexual indiscretions being discussed in emails with friends and then being copied to so many people that, within days, they are reported in national newspapers. Some companies have exploited this by creating short, humorous video clips that are for the internet alone. Probably the most powerful manifestation of it, though, are the many, fast growing social networking sites like Myspace, Facebook and Beebo; based entirely on social interaction in virtual space. As viral marketing involves the transportation of an idea from person to person, it is a powerful way of judging popularity.

However, the internet version of viral marketing has distracted attention from an effective use of the technique exploited by consultants and IT companies for several decades: the marketing of business ideas and thought leadership concepts. A new idea will emerge from a business thinker or a consultancy in the form of a 'white paper' or book. It will be presented at a few leading conferences. (It is most powerful if it gets a hearing at a chief executive-level conference such as the World Economic Forum held each year at Davos.)

Product managers in conference companies then spot the idea, allowing time on agendas for it to be presented. Soon whole conferences are dedicated to it, articles published and books authored. Leading consultancies then dedicate partners and staff to practice in the area. They adjust case studies from past projects and present briefs to their clients. At this stage, academics get funding for reputable research into the idea and add to its visibility. The new idea is 'viral', carried and reinforced by debate in the business community.

Many management concepts, both credible and not-so-credible (such as process re-engineering, CRM, Total Quality Management, globalisation, shareholder value, customer experience management and innovation management), have grown in this way. After a while, however, the ideas are challenged ('Has process re-engineering damaged corporate America', 'Does TQM pay back?'). Some are then exposed as short term management fashions and then fail. Others become established concepts, validated by academic research. (The 'Boston matrix' as a strategic planning tool, process management and quality management are but a few.)

Service firms exploit this phenomenon to gain revenue and competitive advantage. They pioneer ideas (the most costly approach), validate new ideas (an approach open to leading brands), join the wave as a sales tool (most powerful when professional services, IT and City firms all join in) or play the sceptic. Each is a viral marketing strategy which can enhance the reputation and position of the firm if properly resourced and managed.

(vii) Creating stars and gurus

This technique is most powerfully used in celebrity marketing. When specialists like Simon Cowell or Max Clifford take on a client, they set out to groom, manage and build a high profile, celebrity reputation. Although high risk, it creates enormous value for all involved as audiences become fascinated and familiar with these individuals. High profile service leaders (like Richard Branson), well known business gurus (like Peter Drucker or Tom Peters) and senior professionals (like lawyers and accountants) seek to enhance their reputation for excellent work using very similar techniques.

Star creation is often at the heart of private professional practices, from the single practitioner firms and small boutiques right up to the huge international boutiques. It is the main plank of the single practitioner 'guru' strategy which has been so successful in management consulting and architecture. In large firms with strong brands it redresses the balance toward strong individualistic practitioners. (Individuals who join these firms can get lost in the size and reputation of the firm.)

It is the one way that professional service firms can stand out or differentiate themselves. They set out to create a 'star' in practice areas which the firm wants to emphasise. Partners with expertise may speak at conferences, write books and publish articles to gain attention in that field of expertise. These people must, though, be genuinely outstanding practitioners or, once tried by clients, they will not develop a reputation, no matter how much publicity they attract.

(viii) Relationship marketing

Since the early 1980s, businesses in many different industries and interested academics have been exploring, researching and testing the concept of relationship marketing. This focuses on the buyer as a human being, their preferences and behaviour. It also gives attention to the interaction between human beings (the customer and salesperson) in transactions. It suggests that organisations seek to understand their buyers' purchasing habits through, among other things, research and analysis of buying data. Businesses are then able to create communications programmes directed at these buyers which are more targeted, personalised and relevant. As buyers respond to these, so the supplier can adjust their plans further, creating a virtuous circle of improved profitable engagement.

This concept is based on the assumption that long term mutual value is created for both sides if the buyer, and the interactive relationship with the buyer, become a focus of the supplier's policies, processes and people. The marketing of the firm then stresses enduring profitable relationships with buyers, rather than individual random transactions. It changes the entire context in which salespeople operate and many of the criteria by which they work. For some companies, this has caused a profound change from a short term transactional sales environment to a longer term, enduring 'relationship' in which the way the customer is served is critically important; which is why it has been embraced so positively by service firms.

Many successful business leaders have taken this approach to the value of long term service. Some even before it was codified into modern business theory. For instance, Lord Sieff, who once ran the famous British retailer, Marks & Spencer, was asked why (in the mid twentieth century) he put such emphasis on service and offered no-argument refunds on defective goods. He is reported to have said that, if a young couple marry and move into an area, there is the likelihood of many years of profitable purchases from their growing family. Why damage that over an argument about one defective sweater? This early example of, what later became known as the 'lifetime value of buyers', epitomises relationship marketing. The lifecycle of the buyer's engagement with the firm is the priority, rather than one transaction.

This concept, which started largely in the consumer products industry, led to the creation of tools such as Customer Relationship Management (CRM) systems and data warehousing. For many it fills a large gap in marketing theory by recognising the role of human relationships and communications in the buying and selling process. It has proved particularly relevant in business-to-business markets.

The basis of relationship marketing in business-to-business purchases is often the interaction between two people. However, as these people have interaction with other professionals, there are really two interconnecting networks of relationships through which information flows. These networks flow in and out of the supplier firm, embracing competitors, industry commentators and professional associations. In Figure 8.4, for instance, a partner in a professional service firm has a business relationship with a representative in a client firm, who also has links to both a competitor and the trade association. The supplier can strengthen the messages and input to the contact by developing a link through the trade association. However, they need to be aware that any innovative ideas and proposals are likely to be communicated to a competitor.

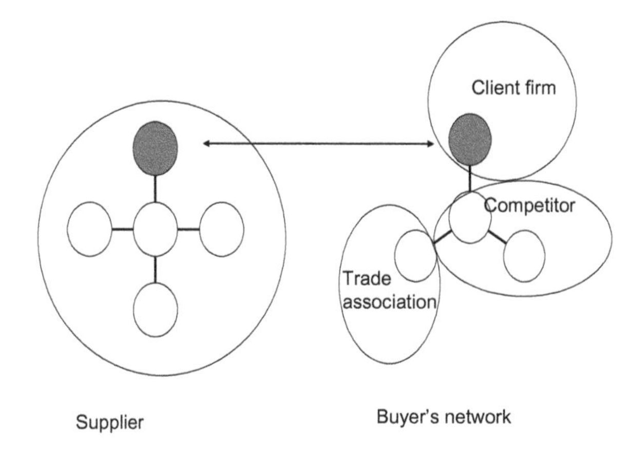

Figure 8.4 Relationship networks

As with technical networks, these relationship networks have 'nodes' where suppliers can bring great influence to bear. The web sites of industry commentators, influential conferences and industry specific research groups are examples of these. These can be identified and influenced by service marketers.

Mapping these relationship networks is fundamental to the success of the approach. Academics have proposed three levels of categorisation of business relationships: 'activity links', normal business transactions; 'resource ties', exchanging and sharing resources and 'actor bonds' which are created between people who influence each other. These concepts can be used to map and categorise communities and networks which are valuable to the service firm. For example, non-executive directors are very influential in the purchase of some professional services. Suppliers therefore buy databases of board representatives and then map those who influence their key clients. Proactive marketing programmes are then created to reach and influence these people.

Drawing it together: the 'marketing mix' for services

Marketing authors and academics recommend a four-step shorthand to remember the successful ingredients of a product marketing programme. They are the 'four Ps' of marketing:

- The 'product'; or the offer to buyers.
- The 'price' at which the product is offered.
- The 'promotion' of the product to the target buyers.
- The 'placing' of the product in the market through sales and distribution channels.

Classic marketing training emphasises that all these elements need to planned in detail to achieve success. However, there are two other vital ingredients. The first is a clear knowledge of the target market. Suppliers need to know, in detail, the attributes and benefits that the buyers will value. The second is the 'mix' of components that will most appeal to the buyers. These need to be planned and balanced carefully.

In reality, though, few marketers have direct line responsibility for all the components of the mix. They therefore need to influence these other areas in order to achieve their objectives and to create value for their employers. Experience suggests that they will fail to have impact and, in some cases, their work may as well not be attempted, if they are restricted to just short term tactical aspects of one or two components of the mix.

However, based on the differences between product and service marketing, the marketing mix for a service business is different. It is generally accepted that there are three extra 'Ps'. They are:

- The 'people' who deliver the service because the buyer often cannot separate them from the value they buy.
- The 'physical evidence' or tangible aspects of the offer designed to help deliver perceived value to the buyer of intangible service.
- The 'process' through which the buyer moves while using or buying the service.

Also, as there is limited physical 'product', that is better changed to 'proposition'. Again, all aspects of the mix need to be designed to match the aspirations of the intended buyers. This is represented in Figure 8.5.

There is, of course, complexity behind the marketing mix concept. Each 'P' has, in practice, subtleties and many detailed components to handle. The word 'promotion', for example, is an inadequate representation of modern responsive, marketing communication techniques and 'place' has been complicated by CRM advances. Nonetheless, the marketing mix for services is

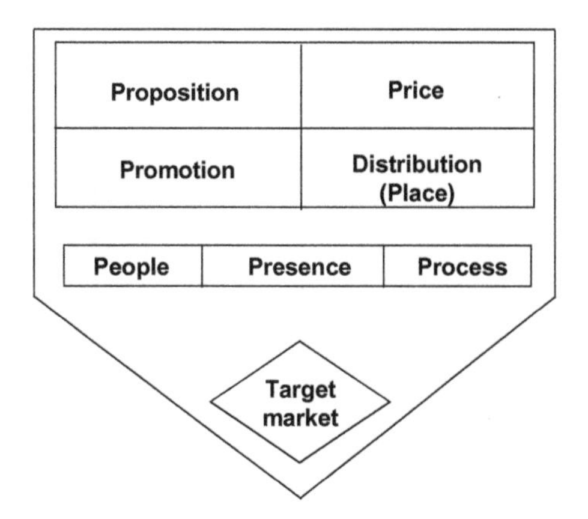

Figure 8.5 The marketing mix for services

a mnemonic for marketers in businesses moving from products to services. It is also a useful tool in management dialogue or communication with colleagues involved in the change. It helps explain the issues that service marketing must address and can act as an informal checklist to ensure that all aspects of a service marketing programme have been properly considered. However, it can also be used in detailed marketing planning. Once strategy has been decided, a full campaign which comprises all elements of the mix should be created for each intended service market.

Organisational differences in service marketing

The differences in approach to service marketing imply that there should be different functions set up in the company's marketing organisation as it moves into services. These include:

- internal marketing;
- corporate brand management;
- new service design;
- collateral production;
- thought leadership;
- viral marketing.

It is also sensible, to avoid confusion, to change the name of the company's 'marketing services' function to, say, 'marketing support'. This is represented in Figure 8.6.

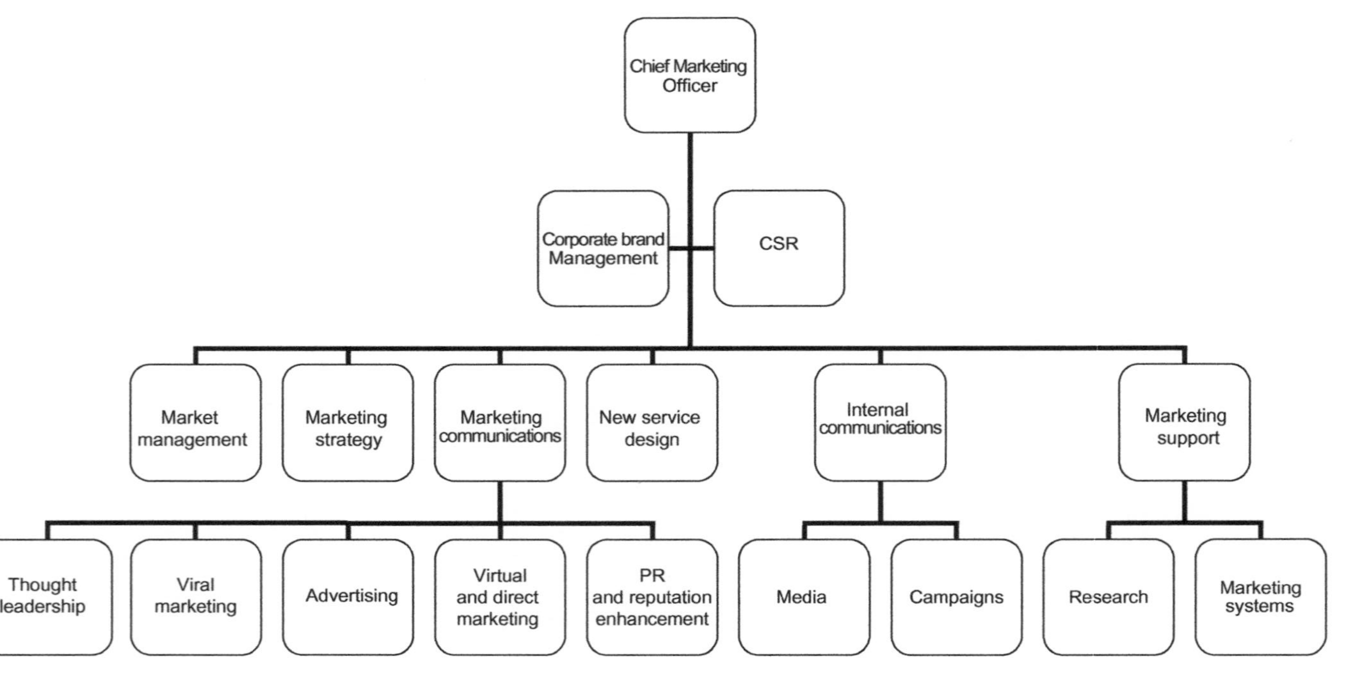

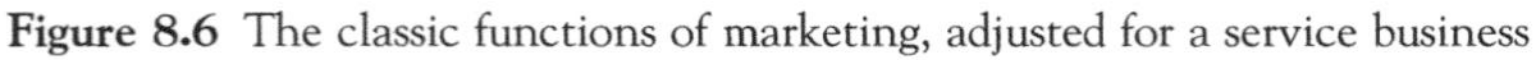

Figure 8.6 The classic functions of marketing, adjusted for a service business

Planning the marketing of a company moving into services

Most businesses produce specific marketing plans as part of their annual strategy, planning and budgeting process. These specify the new products to be launched, the markets to be entered, the sales volumes to be achieved and the campaigns to be commissioned. They allow the business to allocate resources at the appropriate time to stimulate sales and revenues. Any strategic intention to move into services will require a marketing plan (or perhaps a number of marketing plans over years of progressive change) to support it.

- Corporate objectives.
- Consequent marketing objectives (e.g. revenue).
- Brief summary of analysis.
- Key markets and aspirations in them (positioning).
- Growth targets.
- Brand development goals, including collateral development.
- Internal communication programmes.
- External communication programmes.
- New service development (including pricing and withdrawal).
- Sales & marketing programmes.
- General organisational development to meet market demands.

Figure 8.7 Contents of a well rounded service marketing plan

Yet a market plan for a service business is likely to cover different items than that for a product company and to emphasise different techniques. These are likely to be the items covered in Figure 8.7. Product companies attempting to market services for the first time should plan each of these items in detail.

Summary

Whether conducted by line managers, leaders, specialists or agencies, marketing comprises activities and management processes which generate an organisation's revenue. It evolves in organisations over time. When a firm is small, it is often undertaken by the founders or is sub-contracted to specialists. As the company grows, though, the way the leadership approach marketing should become more sophisticated; to the point where marketing is developed into a fully integrated function with well-defined roles and responsibilities, processes and proper measurement techniques.

Various aspects of marketing (strategy, research, NPD and communication), must change in the light of the different conditions created by service offers. It affects pre-purchase, purchase and post purchase reactions. It also introduces new techniques like: viral marketing, to influence 'word of mouth', thought leadership and internal marketing to motivate employees. Companies moving into service businesses need to understand these in depth and plan the use of those most relevant to their new business as part of their transition strategy.

9

Positioning a product brand in a service market

Introduction and overview

Brands, whether they represent the products a company offers, the service it provides or the organisation itself, are amongst the most valuable, yet least tangible, assets it possesses. Managed carefully, they can be the basis of sustainable competitive advantage by building strong, profitable bonds with loyal buyers. Yet, this can only be achieved by creating a branded proposition that stands out from the crowd and consistently delivers what it promises.

Those companies moving from products to services need to claim their space in the most important market of all: the minds of their buyers. They need to 'reposition' themselves in the service market, convincing their buyers that they are as good at creating relevant services as they were at creating appealing products. With the right visionary leadership and political will, firms can create and manage a branded proposition in such a way that it gives a clear direction to everyone involved, whether customers or employees. This chapter explores how to develop a successful service brand (from understanding strategic issues through to design, communications and measurement) and how to reposition the brand in a service market.

What brands are and the effect they have

A brand is an entity that engenders an emotional response from a group of human beings so that they pay more than they probably should for the purely rational components on offer. It is a changing, multi-faceted entity which creates a variety of impressions in the minds of different human beings through many different stimuli. It causes people to buy again and again, often at an inflated price, creating valuable equity.

As the respected advertiser, Jeremy Bullmore, a director of marketing services group WPP, said in the annual lecture of the British Brands group:

> Brands are fiendishly complicated, elusive, slippery, half-real/half-virtual things. When chief executives try to think about them, their brains hurt.

A brand is also a very valuable intangible asset comprising the goodwill of buyers and nurturing their future buying intent. Or, as Tim Ambler of London Business School has said, it is 'the future cash flow of the business' (Ambler, 2003).

Brands are among the most valuable and powerful propositions ever created by businesses. They differentiate an offer from competitors, create a price premium, enhance margins and encourage customer loyalty. Moreover, their effect is enduring. There are several brands in existence today that were created over a hundred years ago.

Effective brands are most common in the consumer goods industries but are also found in both mass services (e.g. Virgin, McDonald's and Thomas Cook) and in professional services (e.g. Deloitte, McKinsey and Clifford Chance). They affect the price of every product or service these firms offer in every part of the world. They set expectations of quality and communicate subliminal messages of the firm's *raison d'etre*. They are one of their owner's major intangible assets and should therefore be one of the prime strategic issues for leaders to address.

It is surprising, therefore, that brand management is not more generally recognised to be the powerful tool that it is. It has certainly had more impact on profit than many things attempted over the past years by different management teams. During that time companies have reached for changing management fashions (such as 'total quality management', 'process re-engineering', 'CRM' or 'globalisation') as a means to create profit. It is astonishing that more have not invested resources and attention in this proven and enduring approach.

One reason for this is that brand work involves such a wide spectrum of activities. At one end, creative agencies and consultancies help to design new images or new names. These projects attract public attention and, sometimes, criticism or even ridicule. At the other end, journalists like Naomi Klein (Klein, 2000), have challenged the ethics and integrity behind brand building. They have suggested that brands exploit workers and trick buyers, generating outrageous profits for unscrupulous owners. Moreover, the range of experts operating in the field of brand management proliferates by the day. In addition to professional brand managers in large corporations, there are strategists, design consultants and valuation specialists.

Despite the disparity of work, it is beyond dispute that a carefully designed image rests in the memory of buyers and helps them to choose products and services. Numerous firms have proved that, by managing that image carefully, a product or a service will appeal time and time again to a group of interested buyers. It becomes a familiar part of their life, giving them consistent benefits in their day-to-day activities.

As a result, they will pay a premium for the offer and develop a loyalty towards it. Over time, they become fond of these entities and, if they think about it, regard them as part of the landscape of their life. What starts as simple reassurance about quality or consistency becomes, on a deeper but hard to measure level, an emotional bond in a hectic modern lifestyle. Consequently, there are people who feel warmth towards a tin of paint, a sugar-filled drink and sports shoes. In fact, these items mean so much to them that they can be as upset and unforgiving if they think a favourite brand has been damaged, as when a favourite soap character is killed off.

This simple, yet hard to manage, strategy has created enormous wealth over the past century for both product and service companies with either a consumer or business emphasis. Yet it is hard for inexperienced firms to identify and manage all the components of an effective brand programme. As a result, many companies have ignored, to their detriment, the precious role that brands can play in the life of both companies and buyers. It is therefore possible that they might miss a very powerful, proven source of enhanced profit.

Aspects of successful brand strategy

Many companies that attempt the move from products to services do not have product brands and do not have a company name which commands a brand premium. They are therefore at a major disadvantage when trying to enter a service market because they do not have reputation, fame or allegiance that they might use to help convince people to buy their new offers. Nor do they have the competence to create and manage branded propositions or, usually, the political support from their leadership.

Yet, convincing their buyers that they have moved to a service offer and positioning themselves effectively in the service market is crucial to the success of the whole venture. Without it they are unlikely to sell many services. They need to learn and apply the concepts of brand management as part of their service entry strategy if they are to be successful. These include:

Brand integrity

The concept of brand integrity is the basis of the success of all brands. It means that the promise and expectations created for buyers by the brand name are always delivered when they use that product or service. Consistent delivery of an offer is the fundamental principle from which brands originated. In pre-consumer times, at the start of the industrial revolution, most buyers could not rely on purchases of any kind to be consistent, reliable or safe. As in the undeveloped world today, a brand gave a much-needed promise of quality and delivery.

An advertisement from the 1880 *London Illustrated News* for Pears soap refers to the fact that the company had then been offering that product to the London market for over one hundred years. The main emphasis of the advertisement is not based on differentiation, nor is it focused on identification with aspirations or health issues. It is about consistency. It has been an 'honest' product.

Consumer brands have to deliver the promised function of the product, time after time to be successful. Today's enduring brands became market leaders through consistent delivery to the expectations of buyers. Admittedly, expectations change over time and there is a need to keep pace. For instance, some food products reduced their sugar content dramatically in the last half of the twentieth century. However, this happened step by step as consumers' tastes changed, moving in line with expectations so as not to lose the precious brand franchise.

Consistency of delivery is also important for service brands. It is essential that the promises of the advertising and the expectations raised by promotion are properly reflected in the service experience. This means that the cocktail of service components (the way people behave, the process through which the clients move, the environment in which the service is experienced, and the technology deployed) must embody the brand promise. Moreover, this must happen every single time that people experience the service process. This is probably the most challenging and difficult aspect of service management experienced by any specialist in the field, for two main reasons.

First, the delivery of all services is unpredictable and variable. It is hard enough to translate research insights into product propositions. It can also be difficult to communicate the essence of a brief to design agencies and production people in order to create or change a physical product. Once done, however, the factory can normally continue to produce it without difficulty.

It is much harder to ensure that a service delivers the promise time and time again. Many mass services (in the airline, fast food and car hire industries, for example) set out to achieve this by sophisticated process design and the use of technology. They seek to industrialise their service. However, this is more complex for business services, especially professional services, because they comprise sophisticated employees who do not wear uniforms or adopt any of the behaviours of mass services. The firm has to understand the common values that its professionals employ in their work and embed them in the design of their brand. Reverse engineering the brand in this way, around the client's experience, is the only way they can ensure that its promise is consistently delivered.

The second reason is scope and responsibility. Service delivery is normally the responsibility of the operations of the business but there are important components (HR, marketing and IT, for example) that are not usually under the direct management of a common unit. Brand specialists are unlikely to be given the power to affect all operations directly. They must work through influence to achieve the desired experience for customers. In short, specifying, designing and managing consistent service to meet a brand position is both very important and very difficult.

For service businesses, then, brand integrity rests in the service experience. The people who deliver the service and the environment in which the service is experienced must match the communications to the market. It is much more than designing a corporate logo, adjusting a strap-line or choosing a snappy name. When dealing with services, brand specialists have to focus on attitudes, principles and values that run through the organisation and which buyers actually experience.

In fact, it is normally best to start by understanding what they experience and engineer that back into the communication to the market about the brand proposition. The emphasis of the firm should be on how the brand is experienced on a day-to-day basis and all of the components of the service must be integrated in one programme in order to reinforce the brand claim. This is, of course, doubly difficult for a manufacturing company moving into a service market because it has no customer experience to build on. It must make its claim by creating a brand image and then ensure that the service is engineered to meet the expectations raised by that claim from the very first moment of launch.

Fame

A phenomenon of modern society is the cult of fame. Actors, musicians, singers, politicians and even criminals are admired and followed for their recognition as much as for their particular skill. Some are even famous for little more than continual appearance in the media; famous for being famous. Alongside favourite TV shows and magazines, these celebrities become a familiar part of day to day life. They are intriguing, beguiling and incredibly valuable as a result. People feel a sense of warmth toward them and tend to follow their own package of celebrity, magazine, style and soap opera.

Brands also occupy this arena. Their fame and their familiarity to different groups of buyers is part of their success. In the same way that a consumer might buy Burberry and be a fan of Tom Cruise, a business buyer might buy Pink's shirts, read *The Economist* and choose McKinsey. The wide knowledge in the general population of what these brands stand for enhances their appeal to those that buy them.

Often called (rather meekly) 'brand awareness', fame is a major ingredient in the success of brands. Firms that have been successful in exploiting this phenomenon have invested, over years, in marketing programmes aimed at improving awareness, or 'recall', in the minds of a wide range of people. These might comprise a range of activities from 'brand awareness advertising', through product placement in feature films to high profile sponsorship. All are aimed at the very simple objective of helping both the potential buyers, and the larger population, to remember the brand and to aspire to have its benefits. In other words, they set out to make their brand famous. In fact, research suggests that sales and revenue decline over time, as memory fades, when these programmes are stopped or paused in difficult times.

Aspiration is an important aspect of the fame phenomenon. People mimic their favourite film stars or sports heroes because they want to be associated with the success represented by their lifestyles. This is often subliminal, but nevertheless very powerful. A young woman styling her hair like Jennifer Aniston or teenage boys dressing like British soccer star David Beckham are all associating with perceived success, and buy associated merchandise as a result.

Association with fame and success is also evident in business-to-business markets. The leader of a modestly sized business who wants a big four firm as their accountant, the director who stands on an awards platform with a well known academic guru and the chief executive who basks in the glory of the latest acquisition led by one of the big merchant banks, are all reflecting this phenomenon to a certain extent. Even at the very highest levels of business fame, or brand awareness, plays its part. A chief executive might choose a consultancy because they trust an individual in it as a result of a long and healthy business relationship. However, they may regard the quality of the firm's brand as a mechanism to legitimise their decision, communicating to their staff that their enterprise will receive quality work.

The creation, maintenance and exploitation of brand awareness are, therefore, key components of brand strategy. To succeed a brand has to become famous. Yet companies that are inexperienced with brands are reluctant to spend sufficient funds on marketing and associated work in order to make their brand famous. This attitude has to be changed if successful repositioning is to be achieved. They must be prepared to invest.

Brand essence or personality

Each brand has a simple truth or 'essence' which it leaves in the mind of its intended buyers and its wider, admiring, audience. This is a promise that creates expectation and demand. For example, the essence of the Disney brand might be 'childhood magic', whereas the essence of an accountancy brand might be 'financial rigour'. In clarifying this brand essence, the firm seeks to understand the fundamental truth about its promise to its buyers and to build its presence in the market around this truth. This is sometimes called the brand message, the main idea communicated to the market about the offer, creating a reason to buy. Over time, this brand essence develops depth and different aspects as buyers use it. It creates a brand 'personality', to which buyers relate.

A famous product firm (like IBM, Ericsson or GE) that wants to move into services might, at first, be hampered by its heritage. Both the public image and the views of its direct customers will be linked to its manufacturing and product development skills. In fact these are likely to be major considerations in both purchase behaviour and share rating. If it is to move effectively into services it needs to convince these audiences that it has similar competence in service production and delivery. A key ingredient, then, is to understand its brand essence and use that as a basis of its claims to the new services market. It must distil its brand heritage into fundamental messages that can then be translated into positive service messages.

The brand in employee behaviour

As explained in Chapter 3 (page 77), the employees of a service business are a very important aspect of its approach to market because their appearance, language and behaviour affect buyers' views of the firm and their willingness to buy again. If they disappoint or under-perform, part of the value proposition of the service is destroyed. The living representation of a service brand is therefore the behaviour of employees towards customers. Their day-to-day activities are, in fact, probably the most influential aspect of the activities which build brands.

Leaders need to ensure that the promise of the firm's reputation and brand is delivered through its people every time the buyers experience its service. For instance, if the brand promises technical excellence, elite heritage, 'guru' style insight, or humour, then the people that buyers interact with must demonstrate these characteristics in their dress, language and behaviour. If not, the brand will be devalued over time, affecting earnings and margins. So, the people of the firm need to be chosen and trained to reinforce its brand characteristics. Recruiters should be briefed to find certain behavioural and attitudinal characteristics (in addition to technical skills) which clearly reflect the organisation's brand values. These values also need to be reinforced through training, communication and example.

In established service businesses this is not too difficult. The language and behaviours of people employed by firms as different as Virgin, McKinsey, Goldman Sachs and Disney are established and people are only recruited if they will embrace them. The personality, dress and work style of the people reflects the aims and objectives of these different leading brands. The front line employees of Virgin's businesses reflect the individualistic, modern wackiness of the Virgin brand as much as the consultants of McKinsey demonstrate its haughty, cerebral, first-class business problem solving.

Employees who understand and identify with the culture and objectives of their employer are more likely to give appropriate service and satisfaction to buyers. A mass service such as an airline, a fast-food chain or a hotel group, will therefore make enormous efforts to make sure that staff are presentable, properly trained and able to take initiative within the scope of their jobs. This is more complex in a professional service practice or a business supplier, however, because the service is being carried out by people who are highly trained and also highly individualistic in their approach to life. They are self-motivated and committed to the technical areas of their work. They are extremely unlikely to wear uniforms or respond well to either over-engineered processes or unrealistic company propaganda. So, internal communications programmes to motivate such sophisticated employees to give appropriate service must be carefully crafted.

Specifying and influencing the human behaviour needed to reflect the brand is the hardest part of most brand programmes but it is particularly challenging if the firm needs to find a new position such as moving into services for the first time. Executives who are handling this change need to understand the attitude of any existing service people to their work and to the firm itself. They also need to understand how customers view these employees' behaviours. The brand position and values should then be crystallised into specific human behaviours by the firms marketing function. If for instance, one of the values is 'integrity', what does that mean in terms of day-to-day behaviours? A gap analysis will then show the degree of change needed to achieve the desired position from current attitudes.

So, employees of the firm need to be the first focus of the brand manager or planner and need to be considered carefully in the design stage. When creating the brand position and brand values, designers should derive their work from the attitudes of employees and customers' perceptions of them. Unfortunately, brand designers often start with a blank sheet of paper and build brand concepts around the leadership's perceptions or aspirations. If, however, these are not dominant attitudes and behaviours at the customer interface, the brand will seem remote and irrelevant. It is better to start with a hard-headed audit of what is experienced by customers and make that the foundation of the strategy. Aspiration can be built on that.

Once a brand concept which is relevant to the service market is created, it should be tested on groups of employees to check that it is credible. Designed properly, this is an opportunity to unite the firm in a clear direction and motivate all the employees. Done badly, it will demotivate and undermine the credibility of the leadership. The design and strategy should be adjusted in response to employee discussion groups as much as with customers.

Once the concept is finalised, a detailed launch and communications plan to employees should be constructed. This should be executed before it is launched to customers. If the firm has a thousand employees, there are more than one thousand opportunities every day for the brand to be communicated and, more importantly, demonstrated, to customers. This will affect their perception, causing them to buy again, develop relationships and recommend the firm to others. In short, it will increase revenue. An investment should therefore be made in a carefully crafted internal communications programme which is credible and sustained.

This is immensely difficult for a newcomer to achieve. Leading service companies who want to change their brand perception find it a major task to motivate employees to adopt new brand values. Product companies moving into a service market find it nearly impossible. Not only must they reposition their brand in a new, unfamiliar market, they must also embody the new brand values in people's behaviour as much as in any design or packaging. For most that have succeeded, it has been a decade long journey of trial and error using world class branding and HR techniques.

Brand attributes or brand values

It is possible to identify a number of 'attributes' or 'brand values' which resonate with potential buyers. These will be either functional attributes which describe what the brand does (such as 'diagnose', 'solves problems', 'advises') or characteristics which are judgements of value (such as 'integrity', 'quality', 'innovation' or 'excellence'). By making these values explicit and communicating them effectively to the intended customer groups the brand can be more effective.

Some of these characteristics, called hygiene factors, are essential if the firm is to compete in the market. They are likely to be strong in all competitors and discounted by customers. 'Motivators', on the other hand, are brand values which are meaningful to customers. They might include soft factors such as 'generosity'; describing the tendency of a supplier to give insight and help which is not always charged but is part of a professional approach. On the other hand, they might be matters of style, such as the way relationships are conducted. Emphasis on these will, over time, differentiate the brand from competitors.

If this technique is to be successful, it is essential that the values are really experienced by the customers who use the firm's products and services. If not, it will be merely a theoretical and meaningless corporate statement which is unconvincing to them or staff. The firm should use properly-conducted diagnostic research techniques with each of these audiences to understand how the service can be crystallised into a few realistic brand values. This is sophisticated and carefully engineered work, which must endure over years and not turn into a meaningless, changing wish list.

Corporate branding: the brand strategy for service companies

There is a major difference between the way product and service brands are created and managed (see Figure 9.1). A product company can create a brand entity which has its own presence in the market and is independent of its owners. When it is properly managed, buyers respond to the proposition itself, incorporating it into their purchase habits and returning again and again. The corporate entity behind the product proposition can be irrelevant to them (e.g. British chemical giant, ICI's ownership of Dulux). In some cases, the owner's name does become associated with the product brand (e.g. the Mars bar, Heinz ketchup and Kellogg's cornflakes) but the owner is often unseen and irrelevant to the consumer's interaction with the brand.

The dynamic with service brands is completely different, however, because the emotions engendered by the buying process are different. Every service

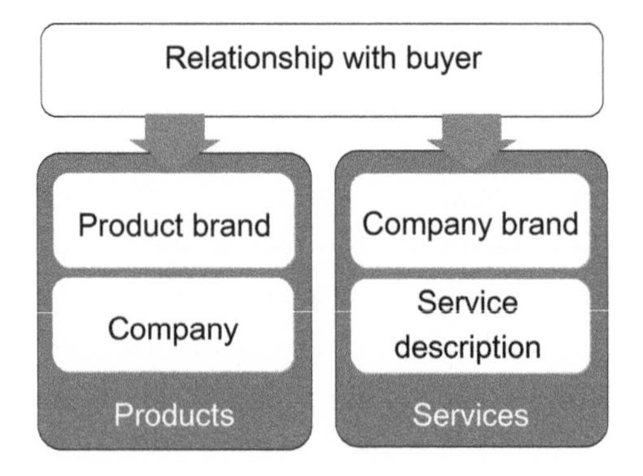

Figure 9.1 The difference between product and service branding

(from a mass consumer service to customised or sophisticated professional services) has a process through which the buyer must move. They must surrender themselves to the service provider and this yielding of control creates anxiety (which increases with the importance of, or unfamiliarity with, the service). As a result of this anxiety, service buyers reach around the service proposition itself to seek emotional reassurance from the entity in charge (without being aware that they are doing so). As a result, the great service brands tend to be corporate brands (e.g. Virgin, Wal-Mart, Tesco and BA).

This has implications to many aspects of brand development and naming strategy. For instance, a product company can organise itself so that brand management is handled by a division of specialists, sometimes under a director of brands. While being integral to the health of the company, the brand group can be managed as one function within it. However, brand management for a service company is about dealing with the corporate brand, the name of the company itself. It therefore involves a different set of stakeholders, including the firm's leadership, and a mix of responsibility. The corporate name might, for example, be the responsibility of a corporate relations director while the move into service might be led by the service director or marketing director. Competitive positioning and brand essence for a service company involve the whole firm and are therefore very difficult to handle; especially if the firm is inexperienced in, or unsupportive of, brand approaches.

Naming strategy is also different because the names of individual services have to be simple functional descriptors. Examples might include: business class from Virgin versus business class from American Airlines; or audit from KPMG versus audit from Grant Thornton. It is the corporate brand that gives a promise of style and difference to the service category. Branded service propositions or made up names are unlikely to be successful.

One company which found this out to their cost was a UK retail bank called 'Midland' (now part of HSBC) in the 1980s. Its research showed that the population's attitude to banking was changing. It hired an experienced marketing director from the consumer goods sector who created a range of new bank accounts for young professionals and other customer groups. Called 'Vector' and 'Orchard', they were extensively researched and launched with millions of pounds worth of advertising. They were impeccably designed using state-of-the-art consumer product techniques and were intended to be stand alone offers in the market. However, they failed to draw in new customers and, after an embarrassing waste of funds, the bank 'returned to traditional banking'. Similar attempts to 'productise' services or create an independent range of named services have failed in the computer and consulting industries. Service brands tend to be corporate brands.

Creating a brand where none exists

It is possible for firms of any size to create a brand which customers prefer, and pay a premium for, over many years. There are a number of steps which, although they sound straightforward, are profound and difficult to achieve if a company has no brand experience. They are:

Step one: decide which buyer groups to focus on and concentrate on them to the exclusion of others (as described in Chapter 4, page 109–115)

Step two: invest in understanding the rational and emotional needs of the group of buyers

If there is one difference between brand literate companies and others it is their concentration on customer knowledge and their willingness to invest in research to get it. The leadership of their companies know, through bitter experience, that their sales success hangs upon the intimacy of the customers' response to their brand. They invest in regular, deep research to understand this dynamic and to adjust to it. Moreover, they invest in recruiting and training brand experts whose job it is to understand this relationship.

Step three: develop a brand strategy

The company needs to create a specific strategy by which it will develop and handle its brand. They might adopt, for example, a 'monolithic' brand strategy. This means that the company will have only one brand which will be reflected in all the company's 'public face' (from building livery to the behaviour of its people). This is normally appropriate for service businesses for the reasons explained earlier in this chapter. It also allows the firm to invest in one intangible asset and to communicate that one entity through all points of contact with buyers. To succeed, all identity and communication pieces must reinforce the values and image of the master brand.

'Sub-branding', by contrast, is the creation of many different brands. These might be offers in their own right or linked to either the company brand or a generic brand. While completely stand alone brands are unlikely to be successful for service companies, a form of sub-branding that is open to them is to apply the brand to organisational groupings. By applying the corporate name to different business units, the firm signals that the sub group is operating its business with a similar style and approach as the corporate entity.

For example, a group of businesses competing in business strategy could be branded as follows: 'KPMG Advice' or 'McKinsey Strategy' or 'IBM Business Insights' (all fictitious). Each signals a different approach to consultancy subliminally communicating a different 'flavour' of service, based on the main brand's essence. This form of brand architecture can support different organisational groups and their position in different markets.

Step four: design the brand

The success of a brand rests on the shorthand it creates in the minds of the buyers. So a clear, unique proposition needs to be designed to represent it. A professionally managed design process needs to be used for this and is not as straightforward as it sounds. First, a designer needs to be employed to create a colour scheme which reflects the mood and style that the firm's leaders want to achieve. For instance, a two hundred year old law firm may want a 'classic' style, whereas a high tech service management firm may want a modern image, or a management consultancy may want an open-minded, fresh approach.

Colour gives this subliminal message. A designer should first produce a palette of colours representative of a 'mood and style' which reflects the firm's objective. There is added complexity if the firm is international, because colour gives different subliminal messages to different cultures. For example, to British eyes pure white means freshness and cleanliness. To a Japanese eye, on the other hand, it is the colour of mourning. The firm must therefore take on board the subliminal message of the intended colour scheme and not just the aesthetic appeal to its leaders.

The design scheme must cover all of the 'public face' of the firm in every physical manifestation of the firm's presence. This encompasses such things as: signs on buildings, design of reception halls, letterheads, fax headers, business cards, invoice formats, email, presentation slide format, the web site, proposal documents, report covers, conference appearances and so on. Some organisations even apply it to staff briefcases, PCs, vehicles, tool boxes and other items regularly seen by customers. Large firms often have to undertake an extensive audit of all of the points of contact with their public and are frequently surprised by the extent of the project. A useful technique here is a 'contact audit' which ensures that all points of interface with the public are identified.

A designer needs to apply the colour scheme to representations ('mock ups') of all these items. These must be tested in discussion with customers and employees to gauge their reactions to the design before being finalised. Some companies are hesitant to put unformed propositions about their own business to customers. However, experience suggests that customers are often willing to help a worthy supplier to find their way and the risk of launching an unpopular or negative design is worth the much lesser risk of imposing on a customer's time a little.

Very often a firm uses a strap-line, which is a short statement intended to communicate the essence of the brand, to reinforce the thrust of its approach. For example, at the time of writing, PricewaterhouseCoopers (PwC) uses 'connected thinking', Goldman Sachs uses 'every catalyst elicits a reaction' and Morgan Stanley 'one client at a time'. A strap-line should reflect the brand essence. If its claim isn't truly reflective of the firm's approach, then neither staff nor clients will see it as having any relevance and it will have no effect on the brand's asset value.

It is absolutely essential that any words associated with the brand or names are checked before implementation. This might seem to be common sense but some firms fail to do it. There are many chances of mistakes in this area and they can be very costly. Choosing a name, for instance, where the web address (URL) is already owned by someone else, or means something obscene in a foreign language, is more common than is usually admitted publicly. Choosing a strap-line that will not translate into other cultures is also very common. Before the project is finalised all names should be trademarked, URLs tested, and translation into key cultures of the world undertaken.

It is a huge task to ensure that all contact points with customers in all parts of the firm are subject to the redesign. Once implemented, however, it is essential that someone is responsible for controlling the integrity of the design. There will always be a reason why employees feel they need to adapt a colour, a piece of design or a strap-line. This should be resisted at all costs as it undermines the subliminal message of the brand and damages the financial value of the asset. Even a slight change in colour will create an impression of confusion and diversity in a client's mind once a number of pieces of material are produced differently in different parts of the world.

Current practice is to develop an internal web site where all standards and materials, together with an explanation of the importance of compliance, are set out in full. Managers across the firm can access and download materials from the site. This helps ensure that all aspects of brand design are produced in accordance with the overall design scheme. It is absolutely essential, however, that leaders at all levels of the firm reinforce this necessity. If they do not, they are damaging a valuable intangible asset of the firm and are being negligent.

Step five: test, launch and communicate it

One of the inhibitions that inexperienced firms often have about brand building and brand management is a wrong perception that success is based on expensive advertising alone. Yet several well known, successful brands have been built without advertising. See, for example, an article by the academics, Joachimsthaler and Aaker (Joachimsthaler & Aaker, 1997), which demonstrates that there are several ways to communicate a brand promise to a market.

The first is through the experience of the service. If a firm has a particular style and approach in its work, it will cause a reputation to evolve through word of mouth which will, in turn, create its brand position. The second is by investing in and managing internal communication so that employees are clear of the firm's position in the market and speak with a common voice to customers.

Another tool is PR. There are good examples of brands built through PR and publicity because they have gained fame or a strong reputation through sustained public profile. Several companies which started with a modest budget have, through targeted reputation management, turned their brand into a substantial intangible asset. Their techniques include media relations (pro-active work with journalists and editors), sponsorship and publicity. Yet this must be realistically based on the actual reputation that the company or its leaders has. The firm must first identify and measure its reputation and only then use sustained PR to amplify it.

The main tool, though, is broadcast marketing communications: advertising consistent marketing messages in radio, terrestrial TV, newspapers, presentations at conferences and specialist TV or radio channels. The latter, called 'narrow casting', can sometimes be more effective than the former expensive broadcasting. A buyer listening to a jazz station in the car on the way home or viewing a favourite TV channel on a specialised station, may be more influenced by this cheaper media than by a nationwide advertisement. This needs to be sophisticated and carefully planned communication run by specialists who manage spend judiciously and target precisely the intended audience.

Whatever the chosen method, the firm should ensure that regular funds are set aside to enhance its brand through building fame by direct communication to the chosen market.

Repositioning and brand extension strategies as a means of entering service markets

So, how should a manufacturing company that already has a strong brand or reputation reposition itself in a service market? How can it convince its existing customers, or any potential new buyers, that it has a viable service to offer? A main plank in this transition strategy is to understand the aspects of the existing brand that can be translated into the intended service market. To use marketing jargon: it has to 'reposition' itself.

The start of this risky process is a clear understanding that the brand exists in the most important place of all: the imagination of its customers and potential buyers. Years of successful product business and rewarding transactions for both the business and its buyers have created a valuable heritage; a 'brand equity'. The goodwill towards the company might have slightly different meaning to each buyer but each nuance is encapsulated in the brand. It is this which the firm needs to move progressively into the service market.

This manoeuvre needs to be undertaken carefully, taking customers with the strategy and picking up others *en route*. Moreover, under no circumstances must it endanger the existing business or brand franchise. A poorly executed programme is likely to cast doubts on the competence of the firm. It will cause customers to wonder if the company can still run its existing business effectively.

The leadership needs to demonstrate that it is applying its established business approach, resources and skills to the new business opportunity. It might have been innovative or respectful or fun or thoughtful in its product manufacturing. It needs to be the same in services. For example, the Finnish mobile manufacturer, Nokia, is currently moving into services. As its established reputation is for excellent design and fashionable products, it needs to approach services in the same way.

Consumer product companies have been very successful at repositioning product brands. Cosmetics companies extend one brand into ranges of products and confectioners into different types of chocolate bars and ice cream. Buyers seek a familiar taste or style in the new category of product. An example of this is the Mars bar launch into ice cream and the extension of the Dove range of personal hygiene products from one soap.

Some service companies have also succeeded at penetrating markets through similar brand repositioning. A famous example is the Virgin Group, run by British entrepreneur Sir Richard Branson. It moved from entertainment to airlines to trains and many other retail services. Each move had a sound business reason (normally based on shaking up a stodgy, cosy market) but each time the brand took existing buyers into that market and picked up others *en route*. For instance, the early Virgin flyers were young business people who had learnt the group's style by experiencing its entertainment before they started their career. They also moved with it when they were ready to invest in financial services. Yet, with each move, the brand picked up new customers too. It is a classic example of successful repositioning.

Repositioning also occurs in sophisticated business services. For example, at the end of the last century the large accountancy partnerships in both the US and the UK decided to enter the mergers and acquisitions market. Their entry was based on the 'due diligence' work they undertook for many deals on behalf of leading merchant banks. This required painstaking accuracy, speed and, sometimes, the willingness to challenge a course of action or advise on alternatives. They used this as a basis to advise on 'mid market' deals. Their brands suggested that their analytical, thorough, systematic and financial approach to work would be applied to this field of business; that there would be a contrast to some of the established lead advisers. Their reputation and brands were an integral part of their success. In short they 'repositioned' themselves.

There are several steps to successful brand repositioning in a service market:

Step one: undertake a brand audit and identify transferable brand values

The firm needs to understand the strengths of its brand and the franchise it holds with four distinct audiences: its existing customers, its employees, city investors and the general public. A 'brand audit' is a research process which determines this. It identifies the image that each audience has and reduces these to identifiable values. It also highlights any areas where there may be inconsistencies. These range from items where the design conflicts with perception to operational issues such as flaws in customer service.

The leadership must use this data to identify brand values which might be a basis for a position in the service market. For instance, the firm might be seen as 'responsive', after years of listening to customers and responding to them. Or it may be perceived to be 'high integrity' or 'high quality'. All of these are values which meet service needs. Any negatives that are identified by the brand audit should be confronted honestly. If they are major perceptions or impediments, they must be confronted by the future strategy and by clear, effective communication plans.

Step two: identify the intended brand position

The 'perceptual map' was introduced in Chapter 4 (pages 115–118) and the firm must use this, or a similar tool, to choose its intended market stance.

For instance, if the firm intends to become the leader of its industry, it must adopt the behaviour of a market leader, taking a stance on price, quality and leading industry issues. Alternatively, it might find that it can maximise its margins by remaining a niche provider. In this case it needs to determine exactly how it is different from the market leader, communicating that to employees and customers.

The map can be used to determine the likely number of customers, the most relevant value proposition and to anticipate the likely reaction of other competitors. It can also be used to work out the service style which is appropriate for the firm's intended strategic position. The service strategy must match the competitive position or strategic intent of the firm. Perceptual maps can also help with internal communications. It can encapsulate any gaps between what the firm believes and what the buyers actually experience. This enables the firm to create internal communications and education programmes to bridge the gap.

The UK accountancy market for insolvency services illustrates how useful these maps can be in determining position (Figure 9.2). In the early 1990s the market was divided between the big firms and boutique practices at the higher end and individual practitioners who dealt with the lower end of the market (about 40%). They had become accustomed to being given insolvency business from leading banks, which dealt with problems in companies to which they had lent money. These banks tended to use a virtual rotation system, choosing from an approved list of firms to lead assignments. Larger insolvencies went to the bigger firms (either because of perceived complexity or international reach), whereas boutiques tended to be awarded smaller, more price-sensitive jobs. But the market was changing.

Firstly, many of the banks had changed their strategy and had a 'cleaner' lending portfolio than previously. Secondly, there was a growing emphasis

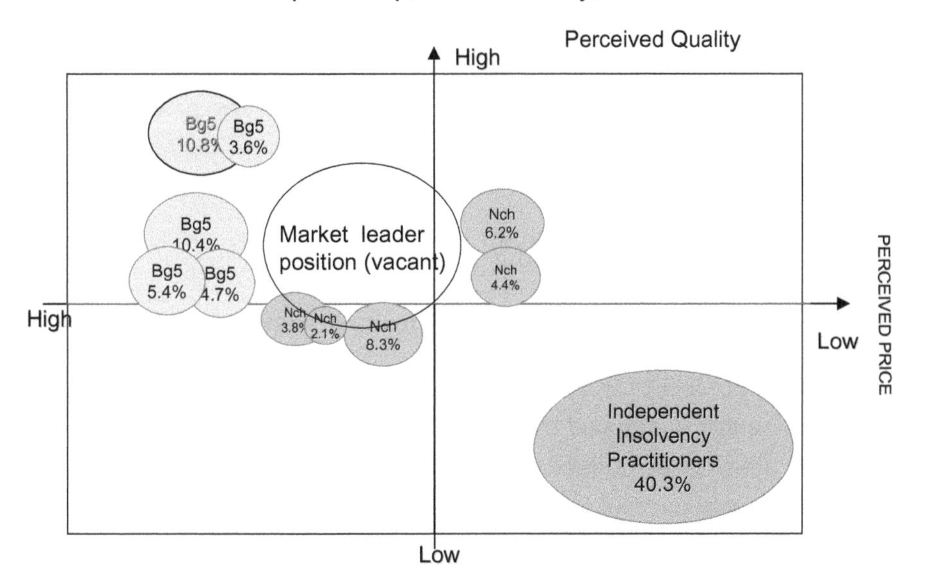

Figure 9.2 Perceptual map

on turnaround, requiring different management skills. Thirdly, there were new lenders entering the market, both foreign banks and asset-based lenders who were not so tied to traditional suppliers. In addition, a new insolvency law was mooted which would change the responsibility for choosing an insolvency firm, swinging the influence on the buying decision away from the banks towards their smaller, often regionally-based clients.

All these factors would disrupt this tidy market and change behaviour. The barrier between the big firms and the individual practitioners would begin to disappear. This, in turn, would mean that they could no longer be complacent about business and would have to find ways to market to this new audience.

The perceptual map, if constructed using client data, would give insight into market conditions and help to chart a course through the changes. For instance, at least two of the then 'Big Five' firms claimed to be market leader, but analysis showed they were not. Based on the perceptual map, once the semi-monopolistic distortion was removed from the market, a new market leader would emerge, threatening the position of the bigger firms. This could come from two sources: a big firm could move into this position by increasing its volume through finding a new value proposition. Alternatively, one of the niche providers could take a more dominant position because they were nearer to market pricing expectations and more in tune with the new buyers emerging in the market.

Step three: create a transition strategy

There are a number of ways in which a brand can be moved into a service market. The first is a phased transition. If the firm has a strong brand, it can create its new service business by association with that brand. For instance, a product company could create a separate division which specialises in services. This might be labelled as 'XXXX services' or 'XXX, a service division of YYY Company'. Long term the association can be dropped as the customers get used to the new name.

IBM used this strategy as it moved substantially into services. 'IBM Global services' is now one of the world's largest services businesses and has a healthy brand reputation. The juxtaposition of the company name with services signalled to buyers that the approach and values of the firm were to be applied to the service market. The heritage, quality and expertise of the world market leader could be experienced in the service market. At the time of writing, however, the firm has just begun to adopt a new advertising approach: 'the other IBM'. It is signalling that the firm itself is now a service company and that the transition is over.

A second transition strategy is the dramatic move. This is best achieved through acquisition or joint venture. A product firm is unlikely to have the competences to successfully set up and run a new service business very quickly. A less risky investment is through purchase or mutual partnership. Acquisition is an immediate commitment. It gives the firm the ability to create its own direction with the new service business from day one and, as importantly, signals its intention firmly to its customers. It can change the brand name immediately or it can phase the change. When, for example, IBM bought PricewaterhouseCooper's vast consultancy business it changed the name immediately, signalling the intent to integrate this organisation into its core service business.

A third transition strategy is to build on gradual organic growth. A manufacturing firm is likely to have some service business based on, for example, maintenance work. This can be used as a basis to build the service business. However, it is usually difficult to finally convince the market that the business has become a service company, even when it is the dominant nature of the business.

Step four: launch and communicate the brand

Whatever transition strategy is chosen the firm must communicate the new brand. As explored earlier in this chapter, this involves serious investment in convincing the market that the firm is now a service brand. The communication strategy must match the transition strategy though. The communications plan to match a dramatic move, like an acquisition, must be shaped very differently to that supporting a phased transition.

Step five: measure the brand change

As the brand is such an important asset, it is sensible to set up measures of its health in the marketplace. It is normal, therefore, to establish some form of brand tracking survey. This can either be by buying into one of the many generic surveys run by large marketing firms, or by creating a proprietary survey.

The firm needs to know the view of both customers and non-customers of its brand, relative to competitor brands. The best surveys use some form of conjoint or trade-off technique to break down the elements of the brand and the way it resonates with customers relative to competitors. Such surveys allow the firm to adjust the strategy in light of changing customer views and competitor actions.

UNISYS builds a service brand

Unisys is a worldwide technology company, formed in 1986 from a merger with Sperry Rand and Burroughs. Its history is awash with 'firsts', including the first commercially viable typewriter in 1873 and the first large-scale, general purpose digital computer in 1946. The company's core activities include consulting, systems integration, outsourcing, infrastructure and server technology. For instance, Unisys processes and clears 60% of cheques around the world, while it also runs the Callminder service for UK telecoms provider BT.

What the company defines as services now accounts for about 80% of its revenues (which at the end of 2005 were $5.76 billion); whereas ten years previously services accounted for only 20% of revenues and 20 years previously it was minimal. This has changed dramatically because Unisys, like many of its counterparts in the industry, has been focusing on transforming itself into a services-oriented company to find new, profitable revenue streams. Services are seen as one of the few sources of differentiation in the light of the rapid commoditisation of hardware markets.

That strategy was consolidated in 1997 with the arrival of Lawrence Weinbach as chairman, president and CEO. His previous position had been as managing partner–chief executive of worldwide consultancy firm, Andersen. His ambition was to build up the services portfolio and, critically, the services mentality consistent with this positioning.

The beginning of branding

By 2000, the company had begun to get to grips with the concept of branding, and the role it should play in altering perceptions of its changing profile. For example, in Europe, the company hired Ian Ryder as its first-ever vice-president, brand & communications for Europe. (Previously, he had been director of global brand management for HP.)

His remit was to get a technology-oriented company to appreciate the importance of branding and, in particular, to help employees understand that their ability to deliver what the company was promising would be pivotal to success in this new service environment.

One of his first major initiatives in the UK was a successful programme called 'Vision On'. This was a purely internal programme, which included every office being 'brand dressed' with appropriate posters and other elements which were intended as both information delivery and humour-based facts to inspire both employees and visitors. These were changed every month to keep them fresh.

There were many teams (VOLTS: Vision On Location Teams) around the company to keep the programme alive and moving along with many local activities. There were also monthly employee recognition programmes, message boxes all over the company and a very active web site.

Another part of his strategy was to visit the management teams throughout Europe to explain how a strong brand could be instrumental in underpinning the company's strategy, rather than be dismissed as a cosmetic add-on. In addition, Ryder was working toward getting a segment on the Unisys brand and its importance into every induction course and every training course.

A major ingredient in the organisational shift was the development of a vision and set of principles, including the strap line, 'Imagine It. Done.' The vision was:

> Deliver precision thinking and relentless execution to drive clients' business transformation.

It was rooted in brand values like:

- external obsession;
- absolute integrity;
- best or nothing;
- invent the future;
- be bold;
- team for speed;
- deliver or die.

Signalling the new direction

Reputation was now one of the key elements in the company's thinking. And, by 2005, under the new president and CEO, Joseph McGrath, the company was gearing up to a corporate level brand programme to coincide with a major portfolio rationalisation to emphasise the strategic shift Unisys had made in becoming a services-oriented organisation. The objective was to give Unisys its own profitable niche in the services marketplace using the new positioning of 'secure business operations'. This was seen as one which builds on its expertise and competencies in secure, 'business-critical' operations.

It was designed to give more focus to the company's portfolio, service delivery model and operational management by targeting five high-growth areas. ('Enterprise security, Microsoft enterprise software, open source and Linux support and solutions, outsourcing and real-time infrastructure'.) Of these five areas, only one was product oriented.

The global branding programme which accompanied this reorganisation began in June of 2005. Research was conducted among customers around the world to examine current perceptions of Unisys. Both a strategic brand consulting group and a design execution group were used to develop concepts and run focus groups. The result was the development not only of a completely new 'story' for Unisys, but also a completely new 'go-to-market' model. The rebranding was launched in New York in October 2005 to the industry analyst community and customers, and then subsequently in London and around the rest of the world.

A note on political will and leadership vision

So why hasn't brand strategy been more fully adopted by different companies? Unfortunately, all the famous branding exercises look good in retrospect. Before Nike emerged as a leading sports brand, people bought gym shoes or sneakers. Teenagers (and their parents) would have been astounded to be told that they would pay for expensive 'running shoes' and would wear them in a social context. Similarly, before Intel, microprocessors were just 'chips'. It took visionary leaders to invest in the development of those brands, to invest in brand strategies which turned a near commodity into a value proposition. The leaders of firms as diverse as Nike, Intel, Body Shop and Virgin had to put their personal political capital behind the risk of a commitment to brand.

Truly adopting brand management involves both visionary leadership and a change of organisational emphasis. The brand, once created, should give direction to everyone in the business. However, large firms do not typically have the political commitment to alter the balance of power radically in their internal operations in order to achieve this longer term benefit.

They have to be driven there by relentless market forces, often going through traumatic management change en route.

Smaller companies, on the other hand, can be daunted by the power of better known consumer brands like Coca-Cola or Nike. They forget that many successful brands (like Virgin or Body Shop) were built from scratch by business leaders with very modest initial resources. However, whether brand success has resulted initially from vision (Mars) or luck (Virgin) or the ravages of the market (the car industry), the steps needed to succeed are well known.

If the firm's leadership is committed to the change from product to services, radical change plans need to be put in place. Brand strategy ought to be part of those plans.

Summary

Effective brand management is, then, a powerful tool and an important aspect of the move into service. It communicates the firm's approach to customers, engenders loyalty, distinguishes the firm from the competition and contributes to the firm's success in the service market. It can only succeed, however, if forcibly backed by the personal political capital of the firm's leaders.

10

In conclusion

This book has used a wide range of different sources to examine the phenomenon of manufacturing companies taking on service businesses. Leading companies that have been involved in these transitions have been consulted and some have generously agreed to be case studies, sharing their perspectives on their experience.

Published articles and books by leading business people, all cited in the text, have also been examined. Apart from recognised business journals, the work of academics specialising in: business strategy, operations management, consumer psychology, service marketing, branding, technology, history and economic history have also been consulted. The latter have been particularly helpful in understanding context and mega trends.

The perspective of these non-business disciplines is fascinating. Their very different professional expertise suggests that the business world tends (through books, conferences and gossip) to reinforce its own ideas and prejudices, creating in some circles a 'closed world view'. It was startling to find, for instance, that some respected economic historians (Eric Hobsbawm and Niall Ferguson; see, for instance, the latter's book *The War of the World* Penguin, 2007) think that the great age of globalisation, with freedom of trade, movement and investment, was in the decades immediately prior to 1910.

The insights of technology specialists (like Professor David Edgerton in his *The Shock of the Old*) are equally refreshing. He suggests that modern technologists present a biased, 'innovation centric' view of the world which is grossly exaggerated. He also traces back a hundred years the belief that technology is fast changing, difficult for societies to cope with and forcing political integration. He makes many of today's claims sound as ridiculous as H.G. Wells' suggestion that the then new aeroplane networks, following fast on the telegraphy and steam ship routes, would bring about a global government by the mid twentieth century.

This is important because (if the world is not getting quite so global, if markets aren't changing quite as fast, if technology is not moving at the rapid pace of change that innovation centric technologists claim and if the move into services is not inevitable) business strategies and operational decisions may be different. In fact, it would seem that the misinterpretation and misrepresentation of some of these mega trends, however well intended, causes real damage to businesses and reduces shareholder return.

In the light of all this, there seem to be a number of interesting conclusions:

The rise of the service economy

It does seem that a number of sociological and economic forces have given rise to an explosion in service businesses throughout the world, starting in the developed economies. As countries have become richer, rising middle classes have looked for a range of services to enhance life.

They have paid for better education, health for their family, holidays and financial security in pensions. On top of that, they have enjoyed a wide range of new entertainment and leisure services with the free time resulting from easier working lives in their richer societies. Also, as they have invested in consumer products, they have bought services to support them. A wide range of products, from cars and washing machines to beauty products and alcohol, have spawned an equally varied range of services.

Similarly, in business markets, there has been an increasing appetite for service and services. Companies have developed demand for professional services, financial products and services to support their infrastructure. The changes in American governance requirements after the Enron debacle have prompted, for example, a step change in demand for professional services like accountancy and law; while stunning creativity in the financial markets has created demand for new products and services associated with corporate mergers and acquisition.

The consultants, the academics and the professions have also, through the innovation of new concepts, created demand for a wide range of new skills and policies. For instance, as modern executives have changed their business practices, concentrating on their own skills and outsourcing other functions to specialists, whole new industries have emerged.

It would appear, though, that it is not necessarily true that the service economy is replacing production or manufacturing. There is certainly a rise in service sector employment but it is simply not the case that manufacturing is being outsourced *en masse* to cheaper, third world countries, while American or British youngsters are condemned to employment in fast food chains. There have been astounding advances in production techniques affecting productivity, such as the new flexible manufacturing lines at German car producer BMW. It seems that manufacturing is, like agriculture before it, set on a trend of producing more while employing fewer people. While it is indeed true that there has been an explosion of service jobs, successful economies seem to thrive on both the emergence of a successful service sector and the innovation or management of production.

In fact, it seems that some service demand is exaggerated or false; and that product companies could penetrate service markets with the right investment and marketing strategies. Across the world, for instance, there is a rise in the use of self service technology. From ATMs and airline check in to supermarket bar coding and internet shopping, consumers are developing a taste for technology based services. In sophisticated business markets too, buyers are actively exploring the 'co-production' of services with trusted suppliers. From commoditising legal services to IT infrastructure, technology and 'end user engagement' is replacing expensive service employees.

This needs to be balanced though. If customers feel that suppliers are pushing them into frustrating automation (such as complex levels of automated call answering) simply to save their own costs, negative word of mouth will grow, creating a back lash against remote, unhelpful service. In some markets there will therefore be a tussle between 'performed service' and 'self service technologies' which will keep marketing people busy for years to come.

There is, nonetheless, opportunity for product companies to penetrate service markets. Although many consumer businesses, like McDonald's and Wal-Mart are, for example, highly complex, they keep that complexity inside their business and make it simple for their customers to use them. By complete contrast, many IT companies have let their complexity fall straight through to their customers who have had to pay extra to manage their 'platforms' or 'infrastructures'. The integrators and outsourcers have, as a result, built up multimillion dollar businesses by managing this complexity. Yet it remains open to manufactures to set product and investment strategies which could take away this market.

The marketing of some software companies says that, for every dollar of their software, they create additional dollars of value for their 'partners' (who are focused businesses adjusting or adding to the basic software product). At various times, technology companies have made similar propositions about services. Yet, in other sectors, business leaders would be ashamed to say that their products were so poorly designed and so unfit for purpose that their customers had to pay up to a thousand per cent more to integrate it with existing purchases or for advice and customisation expertise to make it work properly. With the personal PC, the Ipod and the Blackberry, the technology industries have shown that they can, at last, marshal design, investment and marketing to create real value propositions. If the same can be done in some business infrastructure markets, service businesses and revenues will wither.

An increase in international competition in service business

The statistics of reliable organisations, like the United Nations, show that there has been a steady increase in international trade and export of services. Although there have been healthy international exports of services for several centuries, they have risen at dramatic rates in the last two decades.

Europe and America take the lion's share of this trade but a number of developing countries have set policies to encourage their business leaders to grow into service export. India and China, for instance are developing skills in this field.

Interestingly, these countries seem to be undergoing a similar evolution of export standards to that experienced by Japanese product companies in the 1970s. In the 1950s and 1960s Japanese manufacturing was cheap and not necessarily high quality, but it allowed them to steadily grow their economy and to progressively penetrate Western markets with more reliable and more complex offers. It is the stuff of business legends and case studies that they then ravaged the car, motorbike, and consumer electronics industries of the West by using reliable techniques to offer high quality product at reasonable prices. At the time, stodgy Western manufactures were left gasping and had to move fast just to survive.

Apart from banking giants, like Nomura, it seems, though, that Japan's international export drive did not apply to services. This appears to have been due to cultural issues and the collapse of their economy at the end of the last century. Some of the newer service exporters have no hesitations though. Whereas the original international service exports of, say, India (in 'off-shoring' of IT support or call centres), were originally based on price; they are now becoming much more proficient. International services are becoming progressively more complex, better quality and sophisticated.

A number of leading professional service firms have, for example, outsourced the preparation of their client proposals to Indian suppliers. The content, case studies and credentials can be prepared cheaply and remotely overnight. Yet to set this up, the supplier needs sophisticated IT systems that interface with the client, refusing some whose systems are not up to scratch. (This leads to the hilarious phenomenon of a small Indian start up declining the work of some of the West's leading law and accountancy firms because they are of insufficient quality.) It also needs highly accomplished sales and service management to handle the complex cultures of these partnerships. Such a service would have been unimaginable only a decade ago.

It seems, then, that a number of countries are intent on succeeding at the international export of services. If they can copy in service businesses, what the Japanese succeeded at in product categories, a number of the West's leading businesses will again be left running to catch up.

The change from products to services is profound, affecting a wide range of functions and, as a result, it has taken newcomers time to make real money there

This book has explored in depth the changes necessary to become or adopt a service business, and the methods used to initiate or manage the change.

These are not uniform and it does not seem easy to deduce generic principles from such a vast and diverse experience.

The method of change can be initiated at the top of a company or, surreptitiously, at lower levels. At some stage, however, it needs to be endorsed by senior management and resourced properly. In fact, it seems that those companies that have moved extensively into service needed a senior champion to handle the cultural resistance and channel conflict it causes. They seem to start this next phase of momentum by drawing together all the service units across the organisation into one business unit; in order to give the service initiative more weight. Having structured these disparate groups into a sensible embryonic organisation, they then seem to build their business by a combination of organic growth and significant acquisition.

A major component in the change process seems to be the appointment of a respected senior leader, who had a successful career outside services, to lead the initiative. This was, at various times, a significant signal to colleagues in companies like IBM, Unisys, GE, Ericsson and Nokia. It gains respect for the service businesses and gives them a voice in the organisation.

There are a number of differences between a product business and a service business, explored in depth in the book. The degree of change and the resultant level of risk depend on the nature of the existing business and its similarity to the intended service operation. A business-to-business supplier with technology expertise will find it easier to move into, say, outsourcing or remote support than sophisticated professional advice.

For many, their ambition requires changes to many of the functions of their company including: sales, marketing operations, financial controls and new product development. This leads to a reduction in margin as the new organisation starts a new 'experience curve' in a new market. In other words, net profits are low as the management team learns the dynamics of the new business.

One of the hidden stories of the move into service by product companies is that it has taken time, sometimes a decade, to learn the new business and net margins have reduced while they have done so. A large business with high earnings in, say, technology based maintenance or tied professional advice on its own products has lost money while it has moved into new service businesses, even though revenues from services look high.

A number of service businesses have not made good money from services because they are unclear about their strategic imperatives

A number of research projects examined for this book tell a story of lower earnings or suppressed margins while management teams have learnt new service businesses. This is a particular problem if the company is new to services or if the embedded service business has been initiated at lower levels in the organisation.

New service businesses continue to suffer, it seems, because they are unclear about their strategic intent and can be in conflict with other parts of the organisation. It is not uncommon, for instance, for senior management in a technology company to run the operations of a service business from, say, America and have management teams across the world which are restricted to low level tactical work; whereas the locals know that a certain amount of adaptation is needed.

These businesses need to create a clear, achievable strategy. What is their *raison d'être?* Are they essentially about competitive defence, working to satisfy customers of their own products in order to ensure they buy again? Or are they primarily about growth and margins from service skills? And what is the basis of their competitive capability? Is it volume based processes, requiring them to thrive by 'industrialising' all the services they offer? Or is it the insight, skills and capability of their people, requiring them to compete in the professional service industry as, say, high margin consultants?

Fat margins in existing businesses or relatively sheltered markets have allowed many newcomers, with inadequate skills and muddleheaded management, to survive in service businesses. However, if, as described above, more efficient and effective service competition is to come, say from overseas, these businesses will be vulnerable. It would be sensible to clarify their strategic intent now and tighten the capabilities of these newish businesses around a clear *raison d'être* before any potential crisis occurs from these potential competitive in-roads.

There is a need to use service operations to secure the competitive future of many businesses that have moved into service

Manufacturing operations are a tightly controlled and well understood function of many firms with well developed concepts and techniques, taught at leading universities. Economists, city analysts and business writers track investment in this field as a sign of competitive health. True to form, it is revolution and investment in manufacturing techniques, with associated R&D, which has contributed to remarkable productivity gains in, particularly American, industry over the last few decades.

Service operations in a range of industries (from the great accountancy and consulting partnerships to volume based businesses like fast food and airlines) are equally sophisticated. They invest in process, technology and concept to improve effectiveness and efficiency. They also have to invest in the management and motivation of their people; who are a critical part of their service (even though a number then set out to improve productivity by the replacement of performed service by technology to enable self service).

The theoretical concepts and academic depth behind service operations seem less well developed though; and there is even less of a recognised framework to help businesses adjust operations when moving from products to services. Also, as the offer of service assistance is less tangible than the need to construct millions of physical products through a manufacturing line, the service operations of some of these newer entities can be less clearly designed and less sophisticated; and, as a result, lower quality. It is likely to be in this field that competitive success, margin improvement and, even, survival will be found for a number of these businesses.

A move 'from products to services to solutions' is not inevitable

In numerous business presentations, books and articles it has been suggested that 'the move from products to services to solutions is an inevitable business model'; that service businesses must be reconfigured to offer these new, highly customised, service entities to meet the needs of demanding new customers in markets which are fast changing and merging. This, however, does not seem to be the case.

Product companies in several markets have taken the decision that they will not move into service markets or they will resist the temptation of reputedly high margins as a false chimera that is not open for their particular team to exploit. Admittedly, in some instances, this has been the result of bull-headed senior management who, used to service as a low level tactical operation in the 'after market', are unable to see the potential of a service business.

Some companies, though, have withdrawn from service businesses, as the Unilever case study shows, after a carefully planned and properly resourced test of investment in potential service opportunities. Others have conducted careful strategic reviews by properly resourced senior teams with expert and experienced advisers. In a number of unpublicised cases, these businesses have decided not to invest in new competitive service businesses.

In one example, for instance, they simply concluded that they could make a better return on an alternative investment. In another, that their management, used to running manufacturing businesses, would not be able to change sufficiently quickly and would find specific issues (like, for instance, the need for new financial measures and systems) difficult to adjust to. They have simply decided that they are a product company and can make decent return by continuing to increase the efficiency and productivity of that business; that service would be a distraction and a hindrance. Their results suggest that this was not an unwise decision.

If the move into services is not 'inevitable', the change to a 'solutions world' is certainly not. As explored in the book, a range of leading companies in a plethora of different markets have used this as a catalyst of change to their sales strategies. Sales teams which were used to selling the benefits of, primarily, product upgrades to technical buyers have been sent back to school *en masse*.

They have learnt to suggest projects which diagnose the relevance of changes in technical infrastructures to business operations. This has involved them in discussion with different buyers in different functions and at different levels in the organisation. It has led to them earning revenues from highly customised 'solutions'.

However, as discussed in the book, a company that is based on industrialisation and volume is not best suited to offer unique, customised projects to every customer. The instinct of these firms is to try to replicate and to gain volume; their culture is against the grain of customisation. Some have tried to cope with this by adopting 'mass customisation' investments and others by experimenting with 'lean' principles in service businesses.

Just as important, some firms have not had tight discount controls on their service portfolio or the prices of competitor products, often bought to fit into some of these solutions. So sales people have tended to reduce prices on these items to win deals. This has meant that the 'move into solutions' has, in fact, reduced the earnings of a number of service businesses, increasing revenue and being presented internally as a competitive success, but decreasing margins.

Some markets are now dominated by sales and marketing programmes that offer solutions; producing many daft sounding, meaningless propositions. ('*Klaxon evacuation solutions*' for fire alarms; '*neat feet medical foot solutions*' for chiropody; '*doggie solutions*' for leads and collars and '*stainless steel solutions*' for scrap metal – are just a few spotted by satirical magazine *Private Eye*.) It may be that suppliers in these markets will improve profit through sophisticated 'mass customisation'. However, a clear eyed competitor could easily take share in these markets by offering cheap, consistent, packaged services or even products. Eventually buyers inundated by ridiculously vague names and time hungry analysis processes are likely to compromise a degree of flexibility for straightforward, cheaper offers.

A number of readers and business people will disagree with some or even all of these conclusions. I trust, though, that the subjects covered in the body of the book, the sources cited and the case studies will help busy executives to thrive and to develop more effective policies in any service based initiative.

References

Alexander, J.A. and Hordes, M.W. (2003) *S-business: reinventing the organisation*. Select Books.

Ambler, T. (2003) *Marketing and the bottom line*. FT Prentice Hall, 2nd edition.

Ansoff, I. (1957) 'Strategies for diversification', *Harvard Business Review*, Sept–Oct.

Auguste, B.G., Harmon, E.P. and Pandit, V. (2006) 'The right service strategies for product companies', *The McKinsey Quarterly*, Number 1.

Bateson, J.E.G. (1985) 'Perceived control and the service encounter', in *The Service Encounter*. Heath.

Bateson, J.E.G. and Hoffman, D.K. (1999) *Managing Services Marketing*. Thomson Learning.

Berry, L. (1995) *On Great Service*. The Free Press.

Berry, L. and Parasuraman, A. (1991) *Marketing services: competing through quality*. Free Press.

Boston Consulting Group (1968) Perspectives on Experience.

Bundschuh, R.G. and Dezvane, T.M. (2003) 'How to make after sales services pay off', *The McKinsey Quarterly*, Number 4.

Cerasale, M. & Stone, M. (2005) *Business solutions on demand. How to transform from a product-led to a service-led company*. Kogan Page.

Cowell, D. (1984) *The Marketing of Services*. Heinemann.

Davidow, W.H. and Uttal, B. (1989) 'Service companies: focus or falter', *Harvard Business Review*, July–August.

De Bretani, U. (1991) 'Success factors in developing new business services', *European Journal of Marketing*, **25**(2).

Edgerton, D. (2007) *The Shock of the Old*. Profile Books.

Fifield, P. (1998) *Marketing Strategy: How to Prepare it – How to Implement it*. Butterworth-Heinemann.

File, F.K., Mack, J.L. and Prince R.A. (1995) 'The effect of interactive marketing on commercial satisfaction in international finance markets', *Journal of Business and Industrial Marketing*, **10**(2).

Gerstner, L.V. (2002) *Who Says Elephants Can't Dance? Inside IBM's Historic Turnaround*. Harper Business.

Grönroos, C. (2003) *Service Management and Marketing*. John Wiley & Sons Ltd.

Hakanssson, H. and Snehota, I. (1995) Developing Relationships in Business networks, International Thompson Business Press.

Hamel, G. and Prahalad, C.K. (1989) 'Strategic intent', *Harvard Business Review*, May–June.

Haley, R.I. (1968) Benefit Segmentation: A Decision-orientated Tool, *Journal of Marketing*, July, 30–35.
Hammer, M. and Champy, J. (1993) *Reengineering the Corporation*, HarperCollins.
Heskett, J.L., Sasser, W.E. and Schlesinger, L. (1997) *The Service Profit Chain*. Free Press.
Joachimsthaler, E. and Aaker, D.A. (1997) 'Building brands without mass media', *Harvard Business Review*, Jan–Feb.
Javalgi, R.G., Martin, L.M. and Todd, P.R. (2004) 'The export of e-services in the age of technology transformations.' *Journal of Services Marketing*. **18**, 560–573.
Johansson, J.E., Krishnamurthy, C. and Schlissberg, D.E. (2006) 'Solving the solutions problem', McKinsey Quarterly, Spring.
Johnson, G. and Scholes, K. (2004) *Exploring Corporate Strategy: Text and Cases*. FT Prentice Hall.
Johnston, R. and Clark, G. (2001) *Service Operations Management*. Prentice Hall.
Johnston, R. and Clark, G. (2005) *Service Operations Management*; 2nd edn. Prentice Hall.
Klein, N. (2001) *No logo*. Flamingo.
Kotler, P. and Armstrong, G. (2003) *Principles of Marketing Management*. Prentice Hall, 10th edition.
Levitt, T. (1960) 'Market Myopia', *Harvard Business Review*.
Levitt, T. (1972) 'Production line approach to service', *Harvard Business Review*, Sept–Oct.
Levitt, T. (1976) 'The industrialization of service', *Harvard Business Review*, Sept–Oct.
MacQueen, A. (2004) *The King of Sunlight*. Bantam Press.
McDonald, M. (2002) *Marketing Plans*. Buttterworth-Heinemann.
Maister, D. (1993) *Managing the Professional Service Firm*. Free Press.
Maister, D.H., Green, C.H. and Galford, R.M. (2000) *The Trusted Advisor*. The Free Press.
Monnoyer, E. and Brunet, C. (2005) 'Manufacturing lessons for service industries' McKinsey Quarterly, Spring.
Ogilvy D. (1962) *Confessions of an Advertising Man*. Southbank Press.
Palmer, A. (2005) *Principles of Services Marketing*. McGraw-Hill.
Peters, T.J. and Waterman, R.H. (1982) *In Search of Excellence: Lessons from America's Best Run Companies*. Harper & Row.
Piercy, N. (2001) *Market Led Strategic Change: Transforming the Process of Going to Market*. Butterworth-Heinemann.
Reicheld, F.F. and Sasser, W.E. (1990) 'Zero defections: Quality comes to services', *Harvard Business Review*, Sept–Oct.
Reicheld, F.F. (2006) 'The Loyalty effect' *Harvard Business School Press*.
Ringland, G. (1997) *Scenario Planning: Managing for the Future*. John Wiley & Sons, Ltd.
Ruskin Brown, I. (2005) *Marketing your Service Business*. Thorogood.
Shamir, B. (1980) 'Service and servility: role conflict in subordinate service roles', *Human Resources*, **33**(10).
Shostack, G.L. (1977) 'Breaking free from product marketing', *Journal of Marketing*, April.
Shostack, G.L. (1982) 'How to Design a Service', *European Journal of Marketing*, **16**(1).
Turner, E.S. (1965) *The Shocking History of Advertising*; Penguin.
UN; United Nations conference on trade and development (2007) *UNCTAD Handbook of Statistics*.
Vandermerwe, S. (1993) *From Tin Soldiers to Russian Dolls: Creating Added Value Through Services*. Butterworth-Heinemann.
Walters, D. (2002) *Operations Management*. Prentice Hall.
Welch, J. (2001) *Jack, Straight from the Gut*. Headline Book Publishing.
Ziethaml, V. and Bitner, M.J. (2003) *Services Marketing*. McGraw-Hill.

Index

Lightning Source UK Ltd.
Milton Keynes UK
UKHW011826030320
359710UK00001B/9/J

9 780470 026687